THE PRESIDENT'S WAR

*The Story of the
Tonkin Gulf Resolution
and How the Nation
was Trapped in Vietnam*

THE PRESIDENT'S WAR

ANTHONY AUSTIN

A NEW YORK TIMES BOOK

J. B. LIPPINCOTT COMPANY
Philadelphia and New York

For Bett

Author's Note

A definitive history of the circumstances under which the United States, in effect, went to war with North Vietnam over the Gulf of Tonkin incidents of August, 1964, cannot be written until all the secret documents involved are made public or the key decision-makers of the time, both in Washington and Hanoi, reveal all they know. This book, the product of three years of research, is an attempt to put together what can be obtained in the meantime from available materials and interviews with knowledgeable persons, including present and former officials of the government.

I am aware that my inability to provide sources for much of my information, given me on a confidential basis, can be regarded as a shortcoming—albeit an unavoidable one in any current work of this nature on a subject that is still charged with controversy and emotion. I hope, nevertheless, that my book may contribute to the placing of the evidence before the public, and I am confident that when the full record is disclosed it will confirm the narrative presented here.

To those who made this book possible by permitting me to draw on their knowledge, counsel and time, my deepest gratitude.

Contents

A Constitutional Crisis

1

There are moments in the lives of nations when the ground on which their assumptions are built seems to shift and there is a queasy sense of the basis of things slipping away. Such a moment made itself felt on the morning of August 17, 1967, in the wood-paneled hearing room of the Committee on Foreign Relations of the Senate of the United States. At the long raised table behind which twelve committee members sat listening to their State Department witness, the kleig lights of the television crews caught a tableau of surprise, offense, disbelief. Senator J. William Fulbright, their chairman, let the seconds tick by in silence as he sought to adjust to what the witness had said.

The outer forms of a public hearing of an important Senate committee were all there—the tone of full and frank consultation between the two coequal branches of government, the hierarchical division of Democrats on the chairman's left, Republicans on his right, the witness's table fifteen feet in front of them, the huddle of press representatives attuned to the inner meaning of query and riposte, the rows of spectators sheepish under the weight of a state occasion; not much different, any of it, from the days when Henry Clay was the committee chairman, allowing for the grander scale of the New Senate Office Building and the blessings of air conditioning in the humid Washington summer. The Senate's power of "advice and consent," the first system in modern times for democratic control over foreign policy, was still at work. The institution that had functioned for nearly two centuries was, on the surface, still in good order.

But there was a rot at the center of it, and the hearing that day was not of the usual kind. The committee had not been called to pass on a foreign treaty or an ambassadorial appointment or a bill or other measure affecting the country's foreign affairs, or to deal with one of a jumble of minor matters involving Americans serving, trading and traveling abroad, or to exercise its responsibility for overseeing foreign relations in general. "Not since I entered the Congress twenty-five years ago," Fulbright said, "have we ever attempted any . . . examination [like this]." The purpose of the hearing was to find out what decay in the system had permitted President Lyndon B. Johnson to send half a million Americans off to war in Vietnam, the longest war by now in American history, a war he could neither win nor end, without giving Congress any sense of having been consulted about the commitment, let alone of having authorized it.

The Senators had heard the previous day from an academic authority. Professor Ruhl Bartlett of the Fletcher School of Law and Diplomacy at Tufts University had taken the committee back to the year 1787, when a remarkable group of men drawing on their study of history and their experience in colonial self-government wrote a charter for an independent United States.[1] The framers of the Constitution knew the power of the British Crown to declare war and drag the British people into foreign adventures that exacted their sacrifices and stole their liberties, and they did not propose to give the same power to an American President. Hence the draft submitted to the Constitutional Convention gave the power "to make war" to

2

Congress. When the debate brought out that Congress might not always be able to move expeditiously in responding to an attack—its sessions were planned for not more than one month a year and would be difficult to convene for an emergency in a country of great distances and primitive roads—James Madison and Elbridge Gerry moved that the clause be amended to give Congress the power to *"declare"* rather than "make" war. The purpose of the change was clear: It would leave to the President, Madison wrote in his notes, "the power to repel sudden attacks." [2]

"The important consideration here," Professor Bartlett emphasized, "is that the authority to *initiate* war was not divided between the Executive and the Congress; it was vested in the Congress and the Congress alone." Article II of the Constitution said, "The President shall be Commander in Chief of the Army and Navy," but the sole purpose of this article was to provide for civilian control over the military. As Commander in Chief, Bartlett testified, the President would "have not only the right but the duty to use the armed forces at his disposal to 'repel' sudden attacks on the United States, and . . . he would direct the armed forces for any purpose specified by the Congress, but these authorities and duties did not extend to the *initiation* of hostilities. This is not a matter of interpretation or controversy, it is simple fact." In Jefferson's words, the Constitution applied "effectual check to the Dog of war by transferring the power of letting him loose from the Executive to the Legislative body, from those who are to spend to those who are to pay." [3]

The first Presidents complied scrupulously with this provision. No offensive military action was taken in the undeclared naval war with France or the brushes with the Barbary pirates or the friction with Spain over Florida without direct authorization by Congress. During the nineteenth century the edges of this canon frayed. It was considered permissible for the President to use the armed forces on his own authority for such purposes as suppressing piracy, "hot pursuit" of criminals across frontiers, and protecting American lives and property in primitive areas or where government had broken down—so long as no military action was taken against a sovereign state. Some might say that Presidents Polk, Grant and McKinley stretched this rule beyond reason when they sent the army into disputed territory on the Mexican border, attempted to annex the Dominican Republic, and landed 5,000 troops in China at the time of the Boxer Rebellion; but it was in the twentieth century, under Presidents Theodore Roosevelt, Taft and Wilson, that Congressional control over the use of armed forces abroad was seriously weakened for the first time by a series of military actions and occupations in the Caribbean, Central America and Mexico. There was less Congressional control after that. Franklin Roosevelt placed the United States in a state of naval war with Germany before the country's formal entry into World War II. Truman intervened in Korea without asking Congress for authority. Eisenhower intervened in Lebanon. And now there was Johnson's intervention in Vietnam.

In short, Professor Bartlett testified, "the positions of the Executive and Legislative branches of the Federal government in the area of foreign affairs have come very close to reversal since 1789. . . . The President virtually determines foreign policy and decides on war and peace, and the Congress has acquiesced in or ignored or approved and encouraged this development." It was good, he said, that Presidential usurpations sanctioned by time and usage were at last being challenged by the Senate. (The purpose of the hearing was to hear the views of constitutional authorities and the Administration on Fulbright's proposed corrective —a Congressional resolution defining a foreign commitment as one specifically provided for by a "treaty, convention or other *legislative* instrumentality".) Some such move, Bartlett said, was badly needed. For unless "the Senate will . . .

4

say to the President . . . 'We will not stand for this any longer,'" the outlook was for "a gradual assumption of Executive authority which leads in the direction of an authoritarian state."

Thus the Professor from Tufts. But now the committee had another witness before it, the distinguished former Attorney General of the United States and current Under Secretary of State, Nicholas deBelleville Katzenbach, and his view of the situation was quite different.

"The framers of the Constitution," Katzenbach testified, "recognized the impossibility of compressing the idea of the separation of powers into a simple formula. . . . The Constitution left to the judgment and wisdom of the Executive and the Congress the task of working out the details of their relationships. . . . As a result, controversies over the line of demarcation in foreign affairs have been settled in the end by the instinct of the nation and its leaders for political responsibility. . . . Despite occasional differences and debates, history has surely vindicated the wisdom of this flexibility. . . ."

And today, though the world has become still more complicated, "the constitutional allocation of powers continues to work well. . . . Congress has been a full partner . . . . In fact, I believe the relationship between the Congress and the President have never been better than they have been in this remarkable period in the postwar world. Throughout that period the Congress has given magnificent support to the proposals of the President."

But does the State Department, Fulbright asked, support or oppose enactment of the proposed Senate resolution?

Katzenbach's enthusiasm drained away. "I could not support the resolution, Mr. Chairman. . . . It seems to me that it could be interpreted to seek to join the Congress with the President on those matters which I think the President, in his capacity of conducting foreign relations of the United States, has the constitutional authority to do."

5

"That is a good starting point," Fulbright said dryly. "It joins the issue, in any case." But the witness did agree, did he not, that it was to Congress that the Constitution gave the power to initiate war?

No, Katzenbach replied, not to initiate, simply to declare; "our history has been that the wars we have declared have been declared at the initiative and instance of the Executive."

The Senators were perplexed; Katzenbach hastened to elucidate.

"The point is this. The use of the phrase 'to declare war' as it was used in the Constitution of the United States had particular meaning." War in those days was regarded as a valid instrument of national advancement. But with the establishment of the United Nations, "the idea of aggression . . . of conquest" has been rejected. What remains is the danger of the Communists' seeking to advance their position through limited wars, such as in Korea and Vietnam. Of course, Congress should *participate* in decisions to use force in such emergencies, for the President "acts most effectively when he acts with the support and authority of the Congress." The question is: What *form* should that participation take? "A declaration of war would not correctly reflect the very limited objectives of the United States with respect to Vietnam. It would not correctly reflect our efforts there . . . to use an outmoded phraseology, to declare war."

Fulbright was frowning. There was incredulity in his voice. "You think it is outmoded to declare war?"

"In this kind of a context I think the expression of declaring war is one that has become outmoded in the international arena."

Nick Katzenbach, who usually reminded people of a rumpled, ruminative bear, was appearing as a witness in an extraordinary situation of deadlock in which the Foreign Relations Committee and the White House were barely speaking to each other, so far had the acrimony over Vietnam gone. Fulbright had wanted Secretary of State Dean Rusk to testify, and the President had said no. They had compromised on Rusk's number two, who actually would be even more authoritative on constitutional issues as former Attorney General. A former law teacher at Yale and the University of Chicago, Katzenbach had been recruited for the Justice Department by President Kennedy, and his balding head had gleamed from the nation's television screens the day he had gone down to Tuscaloosa to integrate the University of Alabama and been "barred at the schoolhouse door" in a brief grandstanding play by Governor George Wallace. On the New Frontier he had been a natural ally of liberals in Congress like Fulbright (except, of course, on integration, a special problem for the Senator from Arkansas). But he was a Johnson man now, and here was an issue to turn liberal against liberal and bring the liberals and conservatives in Congress closer together. The Senators on the committee had had plenty of evidence since 1964 that "instinct" and "flexibility" and the "wisdom of the Executive" were not enough to keep the powers of Congress and the President in proper balance.

There was ice in Fulbright's last question; Katzenbach's voice roughened. After all, he said, Congress *was* given an opportunity "to express its views . . . in the instance, if you will, of Vietnam." In 1964 Congress passed the Gulf of Tonkin Resolution. "That resolution," he said, was the "functional equivalent" of a declaration of war.

The Senators stiffened; the reference to the Gulf of Tonkin Resolution had touched a nerve. They had voted on that resolution three summers earlier, on a day of anger and apprehension, after the President had informed the country of deliberate and unprovoked North Vietnamese naval attacks on American destroyers on routine patrol in the international waters of the gulf, the first clash between American and Communist armed forces since Korea, an outrage in which some discerned the hand of Peking; and the resolution they had recommended to the Senate had been passed overwhelmingly by both houses. And now, thinking back on it, they were prey, most of them, to doubt, resentment and remorse.

Katzenbach sensed their resistance to what he was saying, and his voice came in just under a shout.

"Didn't that resolution authorize the President to use the armed forces of the United States in whatever way was necessary? Didn't it? What could a declaration of war have done that would have given the President more authority and a clearer voice of the Congress of the United States than that did?"

✿
✿ ✿

A *New York Times* reporter, E. W. Kenworthy, had ducked out of the room to telephone his bureau. He advised them to order a copy of the official transcript. "All hell's gonna break loose," he said, and excerpts from the transcript would make interesting reading. On his way back he saw Senator Eugene J. McCarthy leaving the hearing, which was still in progress. The Minnesotan seemed shaken out of his customary aplomb. Kenworthy asked him what he thought of the testimony.

McCarthy exploded. "This is the wildest testimony I ever heard! There is no limit to what he says the President could do. There is only one thing to do—take it to the country."

Appeal to the country against Nick Katzenbach? That was not what McCarthy meant—or what he proceeded shortly to do by running for President, privately citing Katzenbach's testimony as the trigger for his decision. It was the overbearing, sentimental, crude, sensitive, wily, idealistic, proud, insecure, driven man in the White House whose power and purpose oppressed the committee hearing.

8

It was as a reflection of *his* concepts that Katzenbach's testimony acquired its stunning force. When Lyndon Johnson had said in Omaha a year before, "There are many, many who can recommend, advise, and sometimes a few of them consent, but there is only one that has been chosen by the American people to decide,"[4] his words could be discounted as Texan hyperbole incited by the rise of popular dissent against the Vietnam war. But when the top-echelon aide he sent before a Congressional inquiry into the legalities of the issue said essentially the same thing, clothing it in constitutional doctrine, it was a claim to arbitrary power that had to be taken more seriously.

What Katzenbach had said in his opening statement and defended in almost two hours of questioning was that the President *should* consult Congress before making use of the armed forces overseas, since it was much better if Congress gave its consent to such action—as it had, in the case of Vietnam, by passing the Gulf of Tonkin Resolution —but that if Congress withheld its consent, he *could* still act under his inherent power as President and Commander in Chief of the armed forces. If that was so, Johnson had, for all practical purposes, repealed a clause of the Constitution without going through the amendment process.

❋

❋   ❋

Resolved by the Senate and House of Representatives of the United States of America in Congress assembled, That the Congress approves and supports the determination of the President, as Commander in Chief, to take all necessary measures to repel any armed attack against the forces of the United States and to prevent further aggression. . . . The United States regards as vital to its national interest and to world peace the maintenance of international peace and security in southeast Asia. . . . [T]he United States is, therefore, prepared, as the President determines, to take all necessary steps, including the use of armed force, to assist any member or protocol state of the Southeast Asia Collective Defense Treaty requesting assistance in defense of its freedom. . . .[5]

The Gulf of Tonkin Resolution—written within the Executive branch—was a cleverly worded document. It authorized the President to engage in war without conceding that he could not do so without Congressional authority. The resolution achieved this effect by using such words as "approves . . . supports . . . as the President determines" and avoiding words like "authorizes," "empowers" or "directs." It thereby implied that the President might already have authority as Commander in Chief to do what the resolution, in substance, authorized him to do. This, of course, was a beclouding of the war-powers issue. In that respect, the resolution was a refinement of the formula employed by the Middle East Resolution of 1957 ("if the President determines the necessity thereof, the United States is prepared to use armed forces") and the Cuba Resolution of 1962 ("the United States is determined . . . to prevent by whatever means may be necessary, including the use of arms, the Marxist-Leninist regime in Cuba from extending, by force or the threat of force, its aggressive or subversive activities to any part of this hemisphere"). It was, by the same token, a shift away from the straightforward language of the Formosa Resolution of 1955 ("the President of the United States . . . hereby is authorized to employ the Armed Forces of the United States as he deems necessary for the specific purpose of securing and protecting Formosa and the Pescadores against armed attack")—language that seemed to some at the time to reflect the spirit of President Eisenhower's pronouncement at a news conference the previous year: "There is going to be no involvement of America in war unless it is a result of the constitutional process that is placed upon Congress to declare it. Now let us have that clear. . . ."[6] Yet Eisenhower's subsequent action denied his rhetoric, for when he intervened militarily in the civil strife in Lebanon in 1958 he did so without any reference. to the Middle East Resolution of 1957 but, seemingly, on the strength of his own alleged powers as Commander in Chief—"to protect American lives and . . . to encourage the Lebanese Government in defense of Lebanese sovereignty and integrity."

At any rate, considered on the basis of what it actually said, the Gulf of Tonkin Resolution was indeed, in a sense, a "functional equivalent" of a declaration of war, as Katzenbach described it, in that it authorized the President to take military action at his discretion in Southeast Asia, and in that it functioned as the President's legal underpinning for the war in the years to come. Which is precisely why the committee found Katzenbach's phrase so objectionable. Authorizing war was not what the Senators or the Representatives thought they were doing when they voted for the resolution. What they thought they were voting for on the day of August 7, 1964, was a statement of national unity and resolve requested by the President for its cautionary effect on the Communist adversary in one particular emergency, the attack on the American destroyers in the Gulf of Tonkin.

Few of them had given much concern in those days to the broader conflict in that distant corner of the world. There were, in that August of 1964, some 16,000 uniformed Americans serving as "advisers" in South Vietnam, seeded through the Saigon's bureaucracy and army, and some 200 of them had been killed in action. But there were no American combat troops in South Vietnam, or any North Vietnamese troops of any kind, and no American or North Vietnamese army, navy or air force unit had breached the border between the two halves of the divided country; the fighting was between the Saigon government and the Vietcong insurgents and, so far as Congress and the American people were told, the United States had no intention of entering the war. Yet that is precisely what it did after the clash in the Gulf of Tonkin and the resolution that was passed three days later.

That was why Katzenbach's testimony inflamed the issue. For if resolutions of this type were to be the "functional equivalents" of declarations of war in the twentieth century, then Congress and the people were without the power to stop the President for a solemn moment of genuine deliberation before deciding whether to take upon themselves the dislocations, sacrifices and hazards of war. How could members of Congress, men who seldom owed their election to sophistication in foreign affairs, be expected to produce a majority against an urgent Presidential request for an expression of resolve in a foreign crisis? As Professor Bartlett testified, it would have been "enormously difficult" for Congress not to have passed the Gulf of Tonkin Resolution, "because the [advisory] troops were there, people were being killed, and the country was excited, and the President had made a retaliatory attack already, and so then to come to Congress and for the Congress to say, 'We think this war is wrong and we will not give you this authority,' is almost an impossible thing to do." And once a resolution of this kind was passed, what could Congress say if its words of determination were later thrown back in its teeth as authorizing the action the President had taken in the interim?

Johnson had said in 1964 that he wasn't about to send American boys to fight in an Asian land war, and now 20,000 of them had been killed in Vietnam; he had said he didn't want to risk war with Communist China, and now American planes were bombing within ten seconds' flying time of the Chinese border. If this was "limited war" that should not formally—in the old-fashioned, "outmoded" sense—be declared by Congress, Congress was effectively bypassed. For it was the possibility of American involvement in more of precisely this kind of "limited war" in the politically volatile regions of Asia, Africa and Latin America that was now the central issue. Anything less "limited" in the present-day context would mean war or threat of war with Russia, and in a dire national emergency precluding consultation with Congress the President's authority to respond to sudden attack was unchallenged.

How could the plain meaning of the Constitution on an issue governing the nation's very life have been so muddied? Was this the cumulative outcome of the disposition of successive Presidents or their advisers to find convenient rationales for what they had done or the military had done in their name—ex post facto tampering with the Constitution, begun in a minor way in the nineteenth century—and the failure of Congress to challenge this expedient philosophy because it didn't seem to matter when measured against the satisfactions and benefits that came with the use of the republic's new-found strength? It didn't matter much when an American contingent joined the European powers in a military expedition against the Dragon Throne in Peking, or when General Pershing pursued Pancho Villa across the Mexican border, or when, to skip across the years, the United States Seventh Fleet took on the defense of Taiwan or the marines landed in Lebanon. It mattered some when public opinion began to be alienated from "Truman's War" in Korea, but Eisenhower came along to put an end to that bloodletting and the issue was forgotten. It took the ordeal of Vietnam to make the issue of the limits of Presidential war powers really matter. Only now, under the impact of Katzenbach's bluntness, did the Senators of the Foreign Relations Committee seem to realize that what they were examining was nothing less than a constitutional crisis.

It would be hard to tell how many Senators shared the certainty of their former colleague, Arthur V. Watkins of Utah, that "the Constitution was drafted under Divine inspiration," but most of them would subscribe to the opinion of Senator Sam J. Ervin, Jr., of North Carolina that "apart from the faithful observance of the Constitution by the Congress and the President and the courts, neither our country nor any human being within its borders has any security against anarchy, on the one hand, or tyranny on the other." And most of them would agree with Justice Hugo L. Black that "The United States is entirely a creature of the Constitution. Its power and authority have no other source." [7] Their love of America encompassed the belief inculcated in every American schoolboy that theirs was a government of checks and balances, of a division of powers, a free people's best defense against oppression. Was this genius of the American system now on its deathbed?

The situation was doubly ironic for the liberals on the committee, for it was the liberals in Congress and in academe, and especially the liberal Democrats, who had championed the claims of a strong Presidency when they liked what the Presidents—Truman, Eisenhower, Kennedy—were doing to assert American leadership and "contain Communism" in the world. It was the liberals who had scoffed when conservatives like Senator Robert A. Taft questioned the constitutionality of some of the Presidential actions and recommended fewer commitments abroad. And it was the liberals who had done battle for Eisenhower when conservatives in Congress, some motivated by distrust of a "Communist-infiltrated" United Nations, sought to tie the President's hands in the conduct of foreign policy by restricting, if not abolishing, the use of executive agreements—compacts with foreign governments that, unlike treaties, do not have to be approved by the Senate.

As late as the fall of 1961 Fulbright had written in the *Cornell Law Quarterly:*

The question we face is whether our basic constitutional machinery, admirably suited to the needs of a remote agrarian republic in the 18th century, is adequate for the formulation and conduct of the foreign policy of a 20th-century nation, preeminent in political and military power and burdened with all the enormous responsibilities that accompany such power. . . . I wonder whether the time has not arrived, or indeed already passed, when we must give the Executive a measure of power in the conduct of our foreign affairs that we have hitherto jealously withheld.[8]

His words came back to mock him now. Four years of Johnson had turned him around. His position now was more comparable to that of, say, Speaker of the House Thomas B. Reed in the great foreign policy debate of 1898–1900. Reed and the others of the "anti-imperialist" camp, all Republicans, all nostalgic for the older agrarian America of their youth, had protested against the policing of the Caribbean and the repression of the nationalist insurrection in the Philippines that had flowed out of victory in the Spanish-American War, fearing the corrupting effect of empire on American institutions and society; Fulbright had been warning recently against an "arrogance of power" linked to "the view of Communism as an evil philosophy and the view of ourselves as God's avenging angels" that had led to an overextension of world mission threatening America with ruin. Yet Reed had been as eloquent as he, as morally indignant as he, and had lost to the sway of Manifest Destiny over American minds. Could Fulbright and his disillusioned fellow liberals do any better against the mental bent of twenty-five years of Cold War?

What could they do? Repeal the Gulf of Tonkin Resolution? And repudiate the President in the middle of a war? They didn't have the votes for that, not nearly enough, and the fiasco the attempt would produce would be interpreted as reaffirmation of the resolution, the last thing they wanted to see. They were caught, all of them who now sounded belated alarm over the excess of Presidential power in foreign affairs and the Vietnam misadventure it had made possible—caught by the failure of Congress to take timely measures against the shrinkage, in practice and principle, of their own powers of decision; caught by their failure to hold a timely inquiry into the nature of the country's involvement in Southeast Asia, their rush to patriotic "yeas" when the President asked for a resolution endorsing every-thing he had done or might do in that region, the hopeless-ness of trying to recapture the moment they had let slip by. They had issued another of their blank checks that weren't really meant to be cashed, and this time the President had cashed it.

What made the whole thing even more galling was a suspicion the Senators could not openly express without impugning the Administration's very integrity—a suspicion the White House was well aware of and that underlay the testiness of Katzenbach's session with the committee. Three years after the event, they were no longer sure they had even been told the truth about the Gulf of Tonkin incident of August 4, 1964, the incident that had caused the United States to retaliate with its first air strike against North Vietnam, make its first substantial deployment of air and naval forces in South Vietnam and Thailand and, as the Defense Department's annual report for fiscal year 1965 had put it, "assume a more direct role in the conflict in Vietnam."

Was the North Vietnamese attack on the American de-stroyers wholly unprovoked? What of the report by Tom Wicker of *The New York Times* that Johnson "had been carrying [the resolution] around in his pocket for weeks waiting for the moment"?[9] Had there actually been an attack or had someone jumped to conclusions before all the evidence was in? Had the President himself been misled by his civilian or military advisers? Or had a minor incident been exploited by him to implement a prior plan to loose the bombers against the North and obtain a resolution from Congress?

For the curious fact in that August of 1967 was that all this contention over the Constitution and all these fears over the mounting price of Vietnam stemmed from a confused naval episode on a stormy tropic night three years before about which Congress and the American people still knew practi-cally nothing.

August 4, 1964 2

A ship that sets a northward course along the S-shaped coast of Vietnam enters a haunted crossroads where different civilizations met through the centuries to enrich and destroy each other. A little way up the peninsula jutting south into the ocean is the site of the legendary city of Oc-Eo, munificent outpost of Indian trade and culture in the third century A.D., sunk without a trace in the mud of the Mekong River delta. Farther up, a few temple ruins and some mountain folk of Indonesian appearance are all that remain of the glory of Champa, the seafaring kingdom that embellished the coast for seven hundred years, until obliterated in the fifteenth century by the southward expansion of the Viets.[1]

The mountains rearing up from the narrow coastal plain form a chain of forested malarial plateaus, a region peopled sparsely by the remnants of the country's aboriginal tribes and shunned by the Vietnamese of the lowlands as the land of bad water and evil spirits. Here was nature's barrier to the spread of Indian civilization, with its sensuousness, its factionalism and its religious sects. Halfway up the twelve-hundred-mile coastline the mountains run into the sea and veer inland again, and we enter a zone where the homogeneous vigor of Confucianism coupled with Chinese power have pressed down from the North for two thousand years.

A ship going up the tropic coast past blue-green lagoons and shimmering beaches fringed by coconut trees and pine, past islands where sea swallows build the nests that form a delicacy of Chinese and Vietnamese cooking—a ship that has come this far has retraced the passage taken by the earliest arrivals from the West. They were traders, missionaries, navigators—among them an American, Edmund Roberts, sent by President Andrew Jackson on a mission to the Vietnamese Emperor, Minh Mang, in 1832 and again in 1836. Though advised by some of his mandarins to reject the American's request for an audience ("Their country is cunning and crafty. . . . We shall have much trouble in the future"), the Emperor declared, "They have come from many leagues beyond the seas, thus proving their admiration for our virtue. . . . How can we reject them?" [2] But Roberts, falling ill, cut short his second visit before an audience could be arranged, and the next American to come, in 1845, was obviously ignorant of the imperial virtue. Captain John Percival, master of the USS *Constitution,* was informed while cruising Asian waters that the court in Hué planned to execute a French bishop. He landed at Danang and rounded up some high Vietnamese officials, holding them hostage. The court disavowed execution plans and the incident was settled locally, to the American government's embarrassment over the whole affair, when it learned of it. [3]

The commanders of the Franco-Spanish fleet that appeared at Danang a decade later, also in response to the persecution of Catholic missionaries and their converts, had broader concepts. They planned to sail north against Hué and all of Tonkin, the French name for the country beyond. But the monsoon winds blowing south made southward sailing easier, and so it was southern Vietnam that the French subdued and colonized (the Spanish withdrawing from the enterprise) before they proceeded, twenty years later, to the conquest of the northern half.

It was not the first time the weather had influenced history in these parts, for we are in the heart of monsoon Asia, where cool dry winds born in central Asia blow down from the north six months of the year and rain-laden air from the southern seas flows up for the other six months. For peasant and emperor the monsoon has always set the rhythm of life, with its time for sowing rice and its time for reaping, its time for war fleets to sail and its time for safe harbor. Yet respect for the tempo of the monsoon is not always enough, for its timing can vary, bringing drought when the rains come too late or flood when they stay too long.

A modern ship continuing along its northward course, against or with the prevailing monsoon, does not take long to cross the seventeenth parallel. The coast is now the coast of Communist North Vietnam. The waters are the waters of the Gulf of Tonkin.

At first the gulf is deep enough up to the shoreline, but as the coast curves in and the mountains fall away from the sea, the captain will be on the lookout for muddy patches. He is on the difficult approaches to the Red River delta, where the great river that cuts through the mountains from its source in China seven hundred miles away spills at last its red alluvial load.

Here in the delta is where the first kingdom of Vietnam arose in the third century B.C. Here, because of the fertile sediment, the agricultural population density has long been one of the highest in the world. The peasants plant their rice by hand, with the aid of primitive tools and water buffaloes. Their villages lie in the shelter of the dikes—earthen levees rising from the flatness of the plain, protecting the rice fields from flood in the months when the Red River and its sister streams are swollen with rain. When the dikes have been breached and the delta inundated, there has been famine. The peasants work unceasingly at repairing the dikes, as they have for centuries.

Navigation past the delta can be hazardous. The Vietnamese tell of what happened to the fleet of Kublai Khan

during one of his attempts in the thirteenth century to restore over Vietnam the Chinese rule imposed in 111 B.C. and
flung off a thousand years later. The fleet, traversing one of
the river mouths, found itself impaled at low tide on beds
of stakes the Vietnamese planted out of sight in the river
bed; the Chinese were then attacked and defeated. The
eighteenth-century Chinese Emperor Ch'ien Lung, though
considering himself the power center of the civilized
world, gave up on the whole attempt to bring Vietnam more
firmly inside the Chinese sphere of influence. Rejecting advice for yet another limited intervention to put down a Vietnamese rebellion against a subservient king in Hanoi, he
wrote, "Why should we take Chinese troops, horses, money
and provisions and waste them in such a hot, desolate and
useless place?" [4]

North of the delta the coast breaks into a series of jagged
inlets, with huge rocks of fantastic shape leaping up from
the water like deep-sea monsters at play. In local folklore
this is the home of a protective dragon. A ship for which
these are unfriendly waters should be wary: North Vietnamese dragons can take the form of torpedo boats, and a
coastline like this provides ideal hiding places.

Forty miles of wild beauty fade at length into a
flatter shore. Clusters of sampans herald the coastal villages.
Long bamboo poles anchored with stones and tagged with
little flags mark the stakeouts of the fishermen in their
brightly colored junks, whose catch supplements the native
diet. Red and black spheres hung from masts on the shoreline advise fishermen farther out of the expected weather.
When the shoreline straightens out from its long crescent
curve and runs due east, our ship would do better to head
out to sea. It is off the coast of the People's Republic of
China.

A vessel placed in the center of the Gulf of Tonkin will be
about sixty miles from shore in three directions—from
North Vietnam to the west, from the Chinese mainland to

the north and from China's Hainan Island to the east. If it is winter, the gulf may tremble to the touch of the northeast monsoon or dissolve in a misty drizzle or, in periods of calm, smile luminously from horizon to horizon. But in the summer the gulf's countenance darkens, and the sultry southwest monsoon wraps it in rains and storms. Vagrant typhoons may spring out of the South China Sea to lash the waters into frenzy. "The typhoon months," says the mariner's handbook of the United States Navy Hydrographic Office, "are from June to October, those which occur in August and September being considered the worst."

On the night of August 4, 1964, two American destroyers on patrol were traversing the center of the Tonkin Gulf. A storm was kicking up, the sea was choppy and the night was black.

It was 7:40 P.M.

* * *

In Washington, it was still only 7:40 A.M. of the same day.

At the National Military Command Center in the Pentagon basement, the tightly guarded, nineteen-room nerve center of a worldwide military apparatus, the day shift was taking over. Over the "hot line" to Moscow, a teletype link tested every hour to make sure it worked, the Russians and the Americans were exchanging their accustomed fare of poetry, Anton Chekhov and baseball lore. In the gold-curtained, gold-carpeted private conference room of the Joint Chiefs of Staff known as The Tank, the trays on the table were kept filled with pieces of candy, which the Chiefs liked to suck on during their discussions. In the Communications Department quarters, computers were geared to receiving, decoding and typing out radio messages from U.S. Army, Navy and Air Force units everywhere.

Just before 8 A.M. the high-priority messages from the Gulf of Tonkin began spilling in. Captain John J. Herrick, commodore of a two-ship patrol, the *Maddox* and the *C. Turner Joy,* was reporting intermittent radar contact with unidentified high-speed vessels, probably torpedo boats, about thirty miles distant. From the vessels' movements, an attack appeared imminent.

In his office three floors above, at his great oaken desk (once used by General "Black Jack" Pershing) since 7:15 A.M., his regular hour for attacking the morning pile of documents and reports in black and red binders, Secretary of Defense Robert S. McNamara received a telephone call from the command center, or War Room. He picked up a white telephone, a direct line to the President.

It was a puzzling reprise. Something just like this had happened two days before. The United States had just raised the number of its advisers in South Vietnam from 16,000 to 21,000. Was it possible that the North Vietnamese were responding by raising the level of the war? Were they trying to show that Peking was right in calling the United States a "paper tiger"?

The earlier incident had taken place on a Sunday. The messages from the Gulf of Tonkin had started coming in before dawn. Night duty officers at the War Room had roused key officials out of bed.

They met with Johnson at 9 A.M.—Secretary of State Dean Rusk; his Under Secretary, George W. Ball; the Deputy Secretary of Defense, Cyrus Vance, entering the White House through the back gate so as not to be seen from the pressroom. The President questioned them in detail. He seemed astonished by the attack. Were any of our men hurt? he asked. No, he was told. Good, he said, then we don't have to do anything. He said some people were goading him into hitting North Vietnam, and he didn't want to do it.

McNamara was on one of his rare weekend absences from Washington. While his wife and children vacationed at their cabin in the Michigan woods, he was staying with Jacqueline Kennedy and her mother in Newport, Rhode Island. The McNamaras, who were close to the Kennedy family, tried to see the late President's widow as often as they could. McNamara was taking her to church when he received word of the attack on an American destroyer in the Gulf of Tonkin. There was only one destroyer in the gulf that day, the *Maddox*. It reported being attacked in daylight, thirty miles from shore, by three torpedo boats. McNamara flew back to Washington by military plane.

President Johnson went to church too, waiting for McNamara's return. They met again at the White House shortly after noon, with the Chairman of the Joint Chiefs of Staff, General Earle G. Wheeler, joining them. Nobody had a good explanation for the rash and extraordinary attack on an American destroyer by Hanoi's mosquito fleet. There was no intelligence material suggesting any sinister move by Peking.

Johnson said he wanted that ship back in; nobody was going to run American ships off the high seas where they had a right to be.

Someone asked: Should we retaliate? The question flowed naturally from some of the options being urged on the government in regard to the larger conflict in Vietnam. On May 26, 1964, Hanson W. Baldwin, military correspondent of *The New York Times*, had reported:

The Navy and the Air Force proposed some time ago the utilization of United States planes to undertake, in conjunction with a naval blockade, token bombings with conventional weapons of thinly populated areas in North Vietnam. . . . The initial targets suggested were power plants, some key bridges and a few factories, selected to minimize loss of life.

But retaliation was discussed only briefly. Nobody was hot for the idea. It was decided to play down the affair. The announcement issued at the Pentagon did not even identify the attackers' nationality. "While on routine patrol in international waters," the Defense Department said,

. . . the United States destroyer *Maddox* underwent an unprovoked attack by three PT-type boats at latitude 19–40 north, longitude 106–34 east, in the Tonkin Gulf.

The attacking boats launched three torpedoes and used 37-mm. gunfire. The *Maddox* answered with 5-inch gunfire. Shortly thereafter four F-8 [Crusader] aircraft . . . joined in the defense of *Maddox*, using Zuni rockets and 20-mm. strafing attacks. The PT boats were driven off, with one seen to be badly damaged and not moving, and the other two damaged and retreating slowly.

No casualties or damage were sustained by *Maddox* or the aircraft.[5]

Briefing officers whose job it was to supply media correspondents with background information had little to add. Zuni rockets, they said, were pretty destructive. The boats, they indicated, were probably North Vietnamese, although they displayed no flags or identifying markings. Why didn't the *Maddox* pursue and finish them off? Well, officials said, North Vietnam, like Red China, claimed jurisdiction over waters twelve miles out to sea, and "hot pursuit" might have brought the *Maddox* within those limits. Why did the boats attack a vessel that was so much bigger and more heavily armed? Officials expressed astonishment. Units of the Seventh Fleet had been patrolling the Gulf of Tonkin for a long time, they said, checking on supplies that might be moving by sea from North Vietnam to the Communist guerrillas in South Vietnam, and there had been no incidents heretofore.

At Honolulu, a public information officer for Admiral Ulysses S. Grant Sharp, Jr., Commander in Chief of U.S. forces in the Pacific (CINCPAC), said the boats were definitely North Vietnamese. "We have information that confirms that," he said. "I can't go into details." Sharp, advised of the attack while flying back from an inspection visit to South Vietnam and Thailand, held a news conference on his return to headquarters. "This incident may well be a change in the present situation," he declared. "We have always had a policy that if somebody shoots at us, we will shoot back at them. Our ships will go wherever they need to go in international waters."

Met by newsmen at the Commodore Hotel in New York, where he arrived to address the fiftieth anniversary of the American Field Service, Secretary of State Rusk said, "The other side got a sting out of this. If they do it again, they'll get another sting."

Several members of Congress were briefed on the incident, learning little that was not in the announcement. One of them, Hubert H. Humphrey of Minnesota, Senate Majority Whip, said on television, "Our Navy defended itself in an admirable, creditable maner." Another Senator, Minority Leader Everett McKinley Dirksen, called the attack "one more item in the Communist bag of tricks." Republican Senator Thomas H. Kuchel of California called the attack "contemptible."

Then there was a surprise twist. The Hanoi radio charged on its English-language program that "the United States and . . . its lackeys in South Vietnam, on 30 July, sent warships to shell [two] islands in the DRV [Democratic Republic of Vietnam] territorial waters." Hanoi also charged that four U.S. fighter-bombers flying in from Laos had attacked a North Vietnamese border post and village on August 1, destroying many homes and much property. The broadcast, monitored by Western wire service bureaus in Tokyo, did not mention the attack on the *Maddox*. But *The Washington Post* the next morning pointed out that Hon Me was only twenty miles from the site of the *Maddox* incident.

American officials denied the Hanoi charge. They said

there had been no shelling of North Vietnamese islands in the Gulf of Tonkin. And, while conceding that American planes were flying reconnaissance missions in Laos on behalf of the Laotian government, they said they had no knowledge of any air raids on a North Vietnamese village.

In Saigon, General Nguyen Khanh, who had recently seized the Premiership in a coup d'etat and was in danger of being ousted in another coup by his army rivals, declared that the United States had to retaliate forcefully "to save face." In Newport Beach, California, where he was vacationing, Senator Barry Goldwater, the magnetic conservative who had just driven the liberal money changers from the temple of Republicanism and crowned himself the party's nominee for President, suggested that the presence of American destroyers in the Gulf of Tonkin might mean that his calls for more decisive military action in Vietnam were hardening his Democratic campaign opponent's policy. But, he asked, does this mean a real change? "Does [it] signify the possible landing of larger American ground forces? Does it mean medium bombers are going to be used to interdict supply lines?"

Johnson, who up to then had said nothing publicly, called the White House press corps into his office at 11:30 A.M. on Monday and read them the following statement:

I have instructed the Navy:

1. To continue the patrols in the Gulf of Tonkin off the coast of North Vietnam,

2. To double the force by adding an additional destroyer to the one already on patrol,

3. To provide a combat air patrol over the destroyers, and

4. To issue orders to the commanders of the combat aircraft and the two destroyers (a) to attack any force which attacks them in international waters, and (b) to attack with the objective not only of driving off the force but of destroying it.[6]

His voice boomed. "These orders will be carried out."

No questions were permitted. The newsmen filed out.

At the State Department's regular midday news briefing, the department spokesman, Robert J. McCloskey, couldn't "enlarge" on what had been said about the *Maddox* patrol. Asked about Hanoi's charge of attacks on its offshore islands, he said he had "no knowledge of any such attacks being made by anyone." He said the United States would be sending a protest to Hanoi.

The protest, the first diplomatic note the United States had ever sent to North Vietnam, was conveyed through the International Control Commission, the three-nation group (Canada, India, Poland) that was set up by the Geneva accords of 1954 to oversee reunification of Vietnam. Released by the State Department the following day, the message said:

The United States Government takes an extremely serious view of the unprovoked attack made by Communist North Vietnamese torpedo boats on an American naval vessel, the USS *Maddox*, operating on the high seas in the Gulf of Tonkin on Aug. 2.

United States ships have traditionally operated freely on the high seas in accordance with rights guaranteed by international law to vessels of all nations. They will continue to do so and will take whatever measures are appropriate for their defense.

The United States Government expects that the authorities of the regime in North Vietnam will be under no misapprehension as to the grave consequences which would inevitably result from any further unprovoked offensive military action against United States forces.[7]

Then, curiously enough, there was a crossing of signals between the State and Defense departments.

Twenty-five Senators, members of the Foreign Relations and Armed Services committees, joined by Majority Leader Mike Mansfield of Montana and Minority Leader Everett Dirksen of Illinois, met secretly in the afternoon with Mc-

Namara, Rusk and Wheeler to be briefed on further details of the incident. The Secretary of Defense had several interesting things to say.

The first was that the American patrol, consisting now of two destroyers, did at times come within eleven miles of the shore, to show that the United States did not recognize the twelve-mile limit claimed by Communist nations but was adhering to the three-mile limit that had been standard in the past.

The second was that, despite the earlier State Department denial, South Vietnamese vessels had indeed shelled points along the North Vietnamese coast.

And the third was that the attack on the *Maddox* was viewed by McNamara as a possible miscalculation or misunderstanding on the part of North Vietnamese naval authorities, who may have mistaken the American destroyer for one of the South Vietnamese vessels. At any rate, whether this supposition was correct or not, the secretaries and General Wheeler regarded the incident as an isolated one and did not expect a repetition.

To Richard B. Russell of Georgia, chairman of the armed services group, dean and chief strategist of the Senate establishment and a man who was wary of any deeper entanglement in Vietnam, the misunderstanding theory sounded plausible, and he repeated it to the press. "There have been naval operations in the Gulf of Tonkin by the South Vietnamese," he said, "and this could have confused the North Vietnamese." To his surprise, and to the surprise of reporters who were not used to seeing Russell contradicted on military matters, his suggestion was categorically rejected in the edifice at Foggy Bottom. As *The New York Times* reported the next day:

State Department officials described as highly unlikely the possibility that the North Vietnamese had attacked the Maddox thinking that the ship was South Vietnamese and not American.

The North Vietnamese know the Maddox, it is said, and know the area where she has been patrolling.

Russell did not feel free to name the source of his information, and the discordant note hung in the air for a day, until it faded.

*
* *

Now it was the morning of August 4, a second incident in the Gulf of Tonkin was in progress, and messages from the patrol commander saying both his ships had opened fire and were "under continuous torpedo attack" suggested to McNamara that the Administration's evaluation of the first attack had been wrong. He called Cyrus Vance, the Deputy Secretary of Defense; Lieutenant General David A. Burchinal, USAF, the Director of the Joint Staff, the working arm of the Joint Chiefs; and several of Burchinal's aides for a meeting in his office as an "*ad hoc* action group" to consider possible retaliation. A full-dress conference with the Joint Chiefs was scheduled for 11:00 A.M.

In the dining room of the East Wing of the White House, Johnson was having his regular Tuesday breakfast meeting with the Democratic Congressional leadership. Mansfield was there, Humphrey, Speaker John McCormack, several others. Before taking up the matter of bills pending and planned, Johnson told them in deeply worried tones of the news from the Tonkin Gulf. He said he didn't know yet exactly what had happened, but there was no doubt that another attack had occurred. This time, he felt, the Administration should make some response, and swiftly, both for its posture abroad and at home. The legislators were in accord. Johnson said he thought he ought to have Congressional support for his action. He said he'd ask Congress for a joint resolution. No one demurred. The agreement around the table was that there should be some form of retaliation cloaked in a decision of the Executive and the approval of Congress.

After the meeting Kenneth O'Donnell, a Kennedy man who had stayed on as Johnson's appointments secretary and executive director of the national committee for re-electing him in November, walked with him by way of the Rose Garden to the President's Oval Office. As O'Donnell was to write later,

he was wondering aloud as to the political repercussions, and questioned me rather closely as to my political reaction as to his making a military retaliation. We agreed as politicians that the President's leadership was being tested under these circumstances and that he must respond decisively. His opponent was Senator Goldwater and the attack upon Lyndon Johnson was going to come from the right and the hawks, and he must not allow them to accuse him of vacillating or being an indecisive leader.[8]

*

* *

In the two foreign crises that had jarred the nerves of the Kennedy Administration—the Bay of Pigs fiasco of 1961 and the Cuban missile drama of 1962—no one among the President's advisers was more sagacious or self-possessed than a pink-cheeked, young-looking man of forty-four with sandy hair, plain glasses and a way of cutting through the nonessential with swift, brusque strokes. McGeorge Bundy epitomized the new breed of foreign and defense policy administrators that John F. Kennedy had brought to Washington to fulfill his campaign promise to "get the country moving again." Coming from the same backgrounds of law, engineering, banking, business and academe that had supplied the national-security apparatus with its brains and energy since the Second World War, but regarding themselves as tougher and more sophisticated in their appreciation of international realities, the self-confident young men of the New Frontier proceeded to focus on the organization of the future after the slack Eisenhower years. Their program had two facets: on the one hand to move more boldly in negotiating what was negotiable with Russia and, on the other, to apply more expertise to the use of American power, intelligently refashioned, to prevent changes in the status quo in the Communists' favor. If this amounted to a firmer grip on the role of world policeman, they preferred the phrase of being the "watchmen on the walls of freedom," but whatever the rhetoric, the substance as they saw it was acceptance of the responsibility of the country's liberal elite for the safety and welfare of the nation in the second half of the twentieth century.

Of all the captains of the watch in the public eye in the summer of 1964, Bundy was perhaps the most accomplished. Descended on his mother's side from the Lowells of Boston, one of the great originative families of America, he had not only gone to all the right schools but had been brilliant (first in his class at Groton, the first Yale student to get three perfect scores on his college entrance exams), gregarious and sparkling, so that when—after serving as intelligence officer in London (in the planning for the invasion of France) and as consultant in Washington (for the Marshall Plan for Western Europe)—he returned to Harvard, where he had been a junior fellow, to lecture in government, he quickly acquired immense prestige. His classes were popular. "He glitters, positively glitters on the lecture platform," one colleague said. At thirty-two he was Dean of the Faculty of Arts and Sciences, a post second only to the presidency of Harvard, delighting the campus by taking steps to build a drama center, getting Lillian Hellman to teach a course in playwriting, and moving about Cambridge on a bicycle. Washington found Mac Bundy equally refreshing when he became Kennedy's Special Assistant for National Security Affairs. Despite the magnitude of his job—to cut corners in the Federal bureaucracy, get the President the information he needed when he needed it, coordinate the information, clarify the choices and help the President oversee the way his decision was being carried out, with all

the influence with the President that this entailed—Bundy
was informal, tartly witty at dinner parties, "very bright."
He was also intolerant of vagueness and could be coldly
impatient with those slow to follow his dissection of a
problem, leading some of the older hands at the State
Department to grumble that his answers were quick, orderly,
convincing—and conventional—and that he was more interested in how a problem could be solved than in why it
was a problem and whether the real problem lay elsewhere.

Though Bundy could never hope to develop with Johnson
the kind of kinship that had grown up between him and
Kennedy, his power and prestige increased, if anything, in
the months following Kennedy's death. Kennedy had drawn
ideas from half a dozen other White House aides, such as
Arthur M. Schlesinger, Jr., the historian, and from unexpected quarters around the country to complement the flow
from Bundy and his fifty-man staff. Johnson wanted all
foreign-policy advice, other than from Rusk, McNamara and
one or two others, channeled through "my intellectual" in
the White House basement, which Bundy had fixed up
into a "Situation Room" with teletype and "scrambler"
telephone links (circuits that scramble the impulses to
make the conversation unintelligible to eavesdroppers) to
the Pentagon, the State Department and the Central Intelligence Agency. More than ever Bundy was the man
who flagged the issues that required the President's attention, brought together *ad hoc* groups to consider these questions, ushered the President into the discussions at the
proper time and kept alternatives alive.

Shortly before 11:00 A.M. on August 4, a chauffeured car
drove McGeorge Bundy from the White House across the
Potomac River to the Pentagon. Bundy was on his way to
join McNamara, the Joint Chiefs of Staff and Rusk in a
conference on the new incident in the Tonkin Gulf. That in
itself was an indication of the character of the meeting.
Hitherto, when an important political-military question

was to be presented for the President's decision, preliminary meetings were held either in the State Department or the White House, with a good deal of interagency consultation and coordination to make sure the right questions would be asked and everyone would be aware of the political consequences of any given course of action. That the President's three top national-security officials should meet at once, short-circuiting the usual staff work—and meet at the Pentagon—indicated that for the Johnson Administration, facing its greatest international test to date, Vietnam was essentially a military rather than political problem.

Vietnam had become an almost exclusively military problem because of a succession of decisions going back over twenty years to a situation far removed from the origins of the Vietnam conflict. Confronted by a suddenly hostile Russia in the climate of distrust that breached the wartime alliance in 1945, American policy makers under President Truman chose to interpret Soviet conduct as motivated by ideological lust for the conquest and Sovietization of all of Europe, for which there was little evidence, rather than by traditional Russian obsession with a security belt in Eastern Europe, for which the evidence was plentiful; and out of that clash of political, economic and security interests, with its mutual fears and suspicions and, on the Western side, its revulsion against Stalin's renascent brutality, there emerged the impassioned abstractions of the Cold War that were to hold sway over an entire generation on both sides of the dividing line.[9]

The Vietnamese Communist movement was born of entirely different ferment, an Asian compound of bitterness over a century of European colonialism and fascination with Western ideas, which revolutionaries like Mao Tse-tung and Ho Chi Minh ransacked for the secret that would enable them to rejuvenate and liberate their decadent societies. But the fact that the blend of Confucianism, Marxism, Leninism, Rousseauism and "Lincolnism" that

33

formed Ho's intensely nationalistic creed was named Communism was enough for him and his movement to be damned in American eyes.[10] For by 1949 China was "lost," and the political backlash of that traumatic experience was making it politically impossible for any administration in Washington to submit passively to the "loss" of any other "free nation," even a French colony. The Truman Doctrine that had been devised for Western Europe was transferred bodily to Asian soil, which was not prepared to receive it, and with Secretary of State Dean Acheson's statement of May 8, 1950, equating the Vietnam movement with "Soviet imperialism," and the subsequent dispatch of thirty-five American military specialists to Saigon, the American involvement in the Vietnamese struggle had begun.

After 1954, the American violation of the Geneva accords that divided Vietnam into two temporary "regroupment zones" pending reunification elections within two years—and prohibited outside military assistance to either zone—was rationalized by the argument that the United States had not joined in the accords but had merely promised not to "disturb" them and was released from that promise by prior violation of the accords by covert aggression by North Vietnam. On a more sophisticated level it was argued that the French had stacked the cards against "freedom" in South Vietnam, first by withholding from the anti-Communist nationalists the grant of independence they needed to acquire a popular following of their own and then by asking them to sit still for their political extinction in an election that Ho Chi Minh, with his halo of victory, was bound to win, and that it would be overscrupulous of the United States to accept this unfair deal and see monolithic Communism make another advance at the expense of vital American security interests.

By 1963 President Kennedy appeared to be ambivalent about the Saigon leaders' inability to make better use of the arms and training provided them, saying in one of his last interviews that it was "their war" to win or lose, Americans could not fight it for them, yet intimating a week later that they could not be permitted to lose it, since "if South Vietnam went it would . . . give the impression that the wave of the future in Southeast Asia was China and the Communists"—and, according to Kenneth O'Donnell, planning privately to pull out of Vietnam once safely re-elected in 1964.[11] Presidents have a way of saying different things to different confidants as they wrestle with their problems, and no one can be sure what Kennedy would have done about Vietnam had he lived, but at the time of his assassination the Cold War was still the reigning theology, though some of the chill had been taken out of it and many Americans were finding it stale, and the Communist-led peasant rebellion against the oppressive landlord regime of South Vietnam was still viewed in terms of instigation and manipulation by Hanoi, as the spearhead of an international Communist conspiracy testing in Vietnam the techniques devised by Moscow for general use in Asia—or, rather, devised by Peking, the Chinese having replaced the Russians as the principal expansionist threat in Asia after the shock of the Korean war. That the Chinese intervened in Korea in a rather desperate bid to retain their Korean buffer against American power in the Pacific was a possibility that American scholars and Foreign Service officers with Chinese experience might have offered for public consideration—as they might have provided better understanding of the Vietnamese rebellion, with its cultural affinity to the Chinese Communist revolution—but the scourge of McCarthyism was driving most of the prominent China experts out of office or into silence, and Assistant Secretary of State Dean Rusk characterized the Mao Tse-tung regime as "a colonial Russian government—a Slavic Manchukuo on a larger scale." [12] By 1964 the eruption of political hostilities between Moscow and Peking had made an embarrassment of that Ruskian insight, but whether serving the ultimate interests of Peking or Moscow, Vietnamese Communism was still viewed as dangerously inimical to American interests, still capable of causing other Asian countries to fall like dominoes, in Eisenhower's phrase, if allowed to triumph in South Vietnam. The question for the policy makers who had been assembled by Kennedy and were now standing by Johnson was not whether the United States should continue to treat Vietnam as an extension of the Cold War but what degree of military assistance was required to prevent South Vietnam from "going down the drain." The question for McGeorge Bundy as he drove across the Potomac to the Pentagon was not whether this new threshold of intervention, this direct clash with the naval forces of North Vietnam, was a warning signal for belated political stocktaking, but how severe the American retaliation should be.

The
President 3

In reaction to Roosevelt's personalized management of the Second World War, the process of Presidential decision making in foreign and defense matters was institutionalized in 1947 by the creation of the National Security Council. With the secretaries of State and Defense and other affected agency heads as permanent members and with a provision for bringing additional officials into its meetings when necessary, the NSC formulated and debated the major decisions of the Truman years. Under Eisenhower, "the nation's highest policy-making body" became even more important, acquiring a planning board to draft decisions and a coordinating board to implement them. Kennedy found all this too overgrown and cumbersome. Stripping the NSC of its extra layers of officialdom, he proceeded to bypass it by making its staff, under Bundy, his traffic manager for needed information, while confining the NSC itself to infrequent *pro forma* meetings to approve decisions already reached. President Johnson, who had wielded his power as Senate Majority leader through secret decisions by small select groups and who had a phobia about leaks to the press, saw no reason to change the Kennedy arrangement. In the summer of 1964 neither the NSC nor the Cabinet were deliberative bodies in any real sense, though still widely regarded as such, and the fulcrum of decision making on national security affairs had shifted to Johnson's regular Tuesday lunches with Rusk, McNamara and Bundy.

On August 4 there was a scheduled NSC meeting at 12:30 P.M. on the situation in Cyprus, with its threat of Turkish military intervention in the communal fighting between Greek and Turkish Cypriots, but the attack in the Gulf of Tonkin naturally took precedence. McNamara, who had left the conference that was still going on in his office, reported on the latest information. There was a quick consensus on the need for some kind of limited reprisal relevant to the offense. The meeting was brief.

Then, with Bundy back from the Pentagon, the "Awesome Foursome," the Inner Cabinet, secluded themselves in the second-floor dining room of the executive mansion, this time with the addition of CIA director John McCone, who always wanted to be invited to the Tuesday lunches but usually wasn't. It was a room of comfortable size, not too baronial for a small group but big enough to accommodate a dozen men, wall-papered with pictures of early America, a room the President liked to use for business and for late suppers with his staff. There had still been no announcement of the new incident, so the White House press corps still didn't know that anything more than a routine NSC meeting and Tuesday lunch were on the calendar, but the word to the press later was that the proper response to the new attack was too obvious to require lengthy debate, the President and his advisers having had plenty of time since Sunday to consider what they should do if the attack were repeated in the teeth of the President's warning to Hanoi.

McNamara laid out the maps he had brought from the Pentagon meeting, showing the targets recommended by the JCS: four North Vietnamese PT bases and an oil depot. All present agreed on this form of retaliation, though Rusk, according to one version, thought the two northernmost targets a shade too close to the Chinese border. Johnson sided with McCone on hitting all five. "All right," he was reported to have said, "let's go." [1]

In her book, *A White House Diary*, Lady Bird Johnson remembers:

Today was a momentous day. . . . On Tuesday, Lyndon always has lunch with the Secretary of Defense, the Secretary of State, and McGeorge Bundy. . . . Today they stayed a long time. As McGeorge Bundy passed me in the hall afterward, he was looking extraordinarily grave. I remember asking him something which brought forth a portentous answer—one which left me apprehensive, of what, I did not know. . . . [2]

*

* *

Lyndon Johnson sat hunched forward in his black leather chair with the brass plate, "The President," on the back, a white telephone at his knee, the Secretary of State sitting on his right, the Secretary of Defense on his left. It was 6:45 P.M. Around the big eight-sided table in the Cabinet Room, with its portraits of Andrew Jackson, James Monroe and Daniel Webster on the walls, sat sixteen members of the Senate and House, including the Speaker, the majority and minority leaders, and the chairman and ranking minority members of the foreign affairs and armed services committees. They had been summoned at short notice, and asked to use the southwest gate, just as an announcement at the Pentagon confirmed a flurry of rumors on Capitol Hill of a new incident in the Tonkin Gulf. "A second deliberate attack," the Defense Department said,

was made during darkness by an undetermined number of North Vietnamese PT boats on the USS *Maddox* and the USS *C. Turner Joy* while the two destroyers were cruising in company on routine patrol in the Tonkin Gulf international waters about 65 miles from nearest land. . . . The attackers were driven off with no United States casualties, no hits and no damage to either destroyer. It is believed that at least two of the PT boats were sunk and two others damaged.[3]

The attack, Defense officials said, took place in "miserable" weather and was much fiercer than the first one. Aircraft from the carrier *Ticonderoga*, stationed in the South China Sea, joined the destroyers in defensive fire. There were perhaps six attacking boats. Asked how they knew the attackers were North Vietnamese, officials were as cryptic as Admiral Sharp's headquarters during the first incident. "We're satisfied," they said.[4]

The meeting in the Cabinet Room, which followed a second hurried meeting of the NSC to give final approval to the reprisal plan, was convened in an atmosphere of profound gravity. To be sure, this was not another Cuban missile crisis, but it would do. Coffee was served, and the President spoke in a tone of deep feeling, telling the legislators of the new unprovoked attack and of the retaliation he had ordered. Explaining that he would tell the American people of the retaliation and the reasons for it over television when the planes were over their targets, he emphasized the importance of strictest secrecy until then. If the retaliation order were revealed, the information would be relayed to Hanoi within ten minutes, and the safety of the pilots would be endangered.

Rusk spoke briefly on the political implications of the attack (were the Communists testing U.S. resolve before launching a military offensive?), and McNamara, standing before a map on an easel, gave a more detailed account of the engagement, with assistance from the JCS chairman, General Wheeler. Then Johnson spoke again.

Taft, he recalled, had criticized Truman for not going to Congress on Korea; Eisenhower, on the other hand, had obtained Congressional resolutions in support of his actions on Formosa and the Middle East. While making clear to his former colleagues on the Hill that his decision to retaliate had been made on his own responsibility as Commander in Chief, Johnson said he wanted to work in conjunction with Congress and would be sending up a joint resolution. Passed promptly by the two houses, the resolution would show the Communists that, although this was an American election year, the country was firmly behind the President in this test of its resolve; this demonstration of unity should help deter Hanoi and Peking from further acts of aggression that could widen the war.

To Fulbright, the Senate Democrats' foremost spokesman on foreign issues, there was something irregular about this whole procedure. In the eight months of the Johnson Presidency, the Senator from Arkansas apparently had begun to suspect his old friend Lyndon of trying to manipulate the Congress from the White House with a variation of the techniques he had employed to manipulate the Senate as majority leader. Johnson would call in picked groups of legislators—and even in Fulbright there was enough of the Ozark country boy to be flattered by invitations to private counsel from the most powerful man in the world—and he would tell them what he had done and ask for their comment. The Speaker, the seventy-two-year-old John McCormack, would say, Well, Mr. President, you are our leader, we stand behind you. Somehow most of the others present were always people committed to Johnson. Some of them would urge him to go even further than he had. Those skeptical of the President's course, as Fulbright sometimes was, would find it difficult to express their objections in such an atmosphere. Then Johnson would tell the press that he had consulted with the leaders of Congress and that they approved. The leaders who weren't sure they approved had their hands tied. Fulbright was beginning to regard it as undermining the Federal system, under which the Executive places its proposals before the responsible committees of Congress, and the committees, after hearing the testimony of Executive and other witnesses and making further inquiry through their professional staff, submit their recommendations to the full chamber. These White House visits were beginning to be Johnson's substitute for committee hearings. Fulbright, who was doing his best to revitalize the Foreign Relations Committee after the comatose regime of its former chairman, the nonagenarian Francis Green, did not like that at all. On the other hand, in a crisis like this. . . .

Johnson finished speaking and asked if anyone had anything to say. McCormack said he was their leader and they would stand behind him. Senator Russell, the man who was closest to Johnson personally, spoke in support of the President, concurring in his course of action. Senator Bourke B. Hickenlooper of Iowa, a Vietnam hawk, asked if there was any doubt that an attack had taken place. No, McNamara said, the evidence was clear. In that case, said Hickenlooper, he'd certainly approve cleaning out the North Vietnamese nests. Several members of Congress asked if the destroyers had gone within North Vietnam's territorial sea limit at any time during the patrol and were assured by McNamara that they had not. Dirksen, the organ-toned, said, Mr. President, we're behind you in this. No one voiced any objections. As Senator George A. Smathers of Florida was to report, "It was agreed by all present that the retaliation was appropriate." [5] The only question was how Congress could show its agreement and concern in the crisis.

In spite of his distrust of this general mode of procedure, Fulbright was not, in this case, troubled by doubts over the substance of Johnson's approach. Johnson *was* their leader, the leader of the forces of sanity that opposed any deepening involvement in Southeast Asia. He was their man who would keep the country out of war, and he needed all the support Congress could give him, including a joint resolution if he wanted it, to help him hold the line against the dangerous demands of the Republican Presidential nominee that the Air Force be unleashed against North Vietnam. Besides, Fulbright was not immune to the low fever of injured patriotism that was felt in the Cabinet Room as the President and the Secretary of Defense described this brazen new attack on United States ships on innocent passage in international waters. They were *Americans,* and they weren't about to let a bunch of North Vietnamese run them out of Southeast Asia, and it was good to know that their President was not the man, by background, temperament or conviction, to let it happen.

*
* *

Earlier that year, like a late arrival at a discussion who brings up a question assumed to have been settled, Lyndon Johnson had asked his advisers: Would the rest of Southeast Asia fall if South Vietnam did? The answer from the Board of National Estimates of the Central Intelligence Agency was: Not necessarily, and any further spread of Communism would take time, but the damage to the American position in Asia would be profound, because of the loss of prestige and the doubts that would spring up about Washington's commitments to other nations in the area.

It was enough to confirm Johnson in his determination, as he had expressed it to Henry Cabot Lodge forty-eight hours after Kennedy's assassination, "[not] to be the President who saw Southeast Asia go the way China went." [6] For by that time Asia seemed, to some who knew him, to be linked in some curious way with the memory and legend of his Texas heritage, the Texas hill country from which he had come, not the Texas of the oil and cattle barons but the earlier Texas of small cotton farmers wresting a meager living from the exhausted earth, lost between the ample past of slaveholding plantations and the technological onrush of the future, prey alike to drought and flood and Wall Street, with little to take pride in except being rugged and enduring and Texan. It was during his Asian swing in 1961 that he burst the restrictions and taboos that the powerless office of Vice President had imposed on his restless, imperious, rambunctious personality. In the faces of the crowds that massed for him in Asia's cities, of the peasants who stared at him from their hovels and their fields, of the Asian leaders who flattered and cajoled him amid the delightful settings of Asian privilege, he thought he saw the love and admiration of the common man he had always hungered for at home and never got, sensing instead the subtle patronizing of the raw Southwesterner by the elitist East. Here in Asia he could give vent to the rough extravagant eloquence of his Populist beginnings and not have a censorious young Easterner in the White House convey displeasure through his aides or have mocking columnists draw unflattering comparisons with the "Kennedy style." Here in Asia he was not the guileful master of the Senate fallen into obscurity after probably winning for Kennedy those extra Southern votes that had put their ticket across in 1960. Here in Asia he personified the United States of America in the fateful act of turning its eyes from the Atlantic to the Pacific, with all the excesses of its generous, troubled, impulsive nature forgiven him, even relished, by his fascinated hosts.

His ego expanded to fill the heroic role. The seas and archipelagos unrolling below his majestic jet linked him to yet another Lyndon Johnson, the naval reserve officer on leave from the House of Representatives in 1942, an observer on the crew of a B-26, cool under fire when their plane was machine-gunned by a swarm of Japanese Zeros over New Guinea. The rosette of the Silver Star he received for that engagement had been in his lapel ever since. The remembrance of his participation in the Pacific struggle of the nineteen forties nurtured his growing conviction that a new and even greater drama was unfolding in this teeming, important, long-neglected part of the world which the United States could ignore only at its peril. Sent by Kennedy to reassure Asian allies that the deal he had struck with Khrushchev for neutralizing Laos would not apply to them, and also to gauge the situation in South Vietnam, Johnson wrote in his report that:

the basic decision in Southeast Asia is here. We must decide whether to help those countries to the best of our ability or throw in the towel in the area and pull back our defenses to San Francisco and a "Fortress America" concept. More important, we would say to the world in this case that we don't live up to our treaties and don't stand by our friends.[7]

In 1964, as in 1961, he saw Vietnam as a crossroads of American destiny and himself as Asia's champion—a Democratic President drinking of the old Republican brew of a protective mission in Asia juxtaposed to aloofness from the affairs of a corrupted Europe. "America keeps her word," he said in a speech in June laying down the basic themes of his policy in Southeast Asia. "This is not a jungle war, but a struggle for freedom on every front of human activity." [8]

❊

❊ ❊

Passing the White House pressroom at 8:15 P.M. on his way out, Speaker McCormack conceded there had been a ninety-minute meeting with Congressional leaders but said only the President could talk about it. The other members of Congress had left by the southwest gate, unseen. They had been cautioned a second time, just before the meeting broke up, about the need for secrecy in regard to the air strike. Charles A. Halleck of Indiana, the House Minority Leader, was so affected by the admonition that "I hid out for a couple of hours," as he was to report, "and did not even answer the telephone when I finally got home."

At 8:25 P.M. George Reedy, the White House Press Secretary, announced that the President would be making a statement to the nation on television. He indicated it would come soon. Around the country, millions of Americans, knowing of the new attack in the Tonkin Gulf, waited tensely to hear what Johnson would say. A network crew set up a television camera in the Fish Room, across the corridor from the Oval Office, and the text of the statement was fed into the teleprompter, where Johnson could follow it from behind the lectern. There was a long delay. The teleprompter was unloaded and a new text put in. Outside the black cast-iron fence on Pennsylvania Avenue, crowds of tourists attracted by the blaze of kleig lights inside the Executive Mansion watched the official limousines come and go. The teleprompter was unloaded and reloaded a third time.

In his office, Johnson took a telephone call from Goldwater at Newport Beach, California. Johnson had tried to reach Goldwater three times after the Cabinet Room meeting. There was a radio-telephone link to the yacht (a converted PT boat, actually) aboard which Goldwater was cruising, but the connection was so poor each time that Goldwater told the President he'd call him back from shore. When he did, at 10:07 P.M. Eastern Daylight Saving Time, Johnson read him his television statement.

White House reporters, who had missed dinner waiting for the statement, sensed the rising tension in the executive offices. There was no explanation for the continued delay. At 10:40 P.M. Mrs. Johnson insisted that her husband, Bundy and Jack Valenti, the President's factotum on domestic affairs, have dinner with her.

Whatever the President and his aides were waiting for arrived at last. At 11:37 P.M. Johnson stood behind the lectern, and the networks interrupted their programs to announce the President of the United States.

Johnson's solemn manner underscored the grave import of his statement.

As President and Commander in Chief, it is my duty to the American people to report that renewed hostile actions against United States ships on the high seas in the Gulf of Tonkin have today required me to order the military forces of the United States to take action in reply.

The initial attack on the destroyer *Maddox* on August 2 was repeated today by a number of hostile vessels attacking two U.S. destroyers with torpedoes.

Two of the attacking boats were believed sunk. There were no U.S. losses.

But repeated acts of violence against the armed forces of the United States must be met not only with alert defense but with positive reply.

That reply is being given as I speak to you tonight. Air action is now in execution against gunboats and certain supporting facilities in North Vietnam which have been used in these hostile operations.

In the larger sense, the President went on, this new act of aggression brought home the importance of the struggle going on in Southeast Asia. The determination of all Americans to carry out their commitment to the people of South Vietnam would be redoubled by this outrage.

Yet our response for the present will be limited and fitting. . . . We still seek no wider war.

He had met with the leaders of both parties in Congress, he said, and they had assured him of prompt and overwhelming passage of

a resolution making it clear that our government is united in its determination to take all necessary measures in support of freedom and in defense of peace in Southeast Asia. . . . And just a few minutes ago I was able to reach Senator Goldwater, and I am glad to say that he has expressed his support of the statement that I am making to you tonight.

It was a solemn responsibility, the President concluded, to have to order even limited action by forces as vast as those of the United States.

But it is my considered conviction, shared throughout your government, that firmness in the right is indispensable today for peace.

That firmness will always be measured. Its mission is peace.[9]

＊

＊　＊

"Its mission is peace. . . ."

Johnson did not want to be the President to lose Southeast Asia, but he was not spoiling for a fight either. The military's proposals for bombing North Vietnam left him skeptical. "If one little ole general in shirt sleeves can take Saigon," he was said to have remarked, referring to General Khanh's recent coup, "think about two hundred million Chinese coming down those trails. No, sir, I don't want to fight them." [10]

Johnson was no great reader of books, but he was a close questioner of men and an intense observer of events, and he had an idea he could handle old man Ho. These Asians, they weren't so different from the Mexicans in Texas. "I know these Latin Americans," he said to a group of reporters when rioting in the Panama Canal zone disturbed the early days of his Presidency. "I grew up with Mexicans. They'll come right into your yard and take it over if you let them. And the next day they'll be right up on your porch, barefoot and weighing one hundred and thirty pounds, and they'll take that too. But if you say to 'em right at the start, 'Hold on, just wait a minute,' they'll know they're dealing with somebody who'll stand up. And after that you can get along fine." [11]

The Vietcong and the North Vietnamese weighed one hundred and thirty pounds and Johnson was prepared to get along fine with them—once he had his way. The Johnson Treatment, with its virtuoso range of reasoning, forthrightness, subterfuge, blandishment, entreaty, warning, the appeal to self-interest, the unexpected blow and the threat of worse to come—it had worked in the Senate and it would work in Vietnam. And afterward—reward! Johnson in victory was prepared to be generous. He was, he liked to tell people, a river man, a power-dam man. He remembered the day in 1961 when he stood in the Mekong River valley and visualized the reservoirs and power lines that could make of this great waterway a cornucopia for the people of the whole Indochinese peninsula, North Vietnam included, if North Vietnam would only give up trying to take over South Vietnam. He had done it for Texas, getting the bills and the money to harness the Colorado River and the Pedernales, bringing water and crops to dried-up farmland and removing forever the fear of floods, and he could do it for Vietnam. This was what he wanted to bring the Vietnamese—not war. Besides, war would encumber his Presidency. He had other plans.

Lyndon Johnson, handed by an assassin the office he had coveted and despaired of winning, knew he was about to be elected in his own right as the thirty-sixth President of the United States. The Republicans' choice of an extremist like Goldwater made a Johnson victory certain. But he wanted more than a victory. He wanted an overwhelming popular mandate that would raise him up as a new FDR and enable him to do what he wanted to do in the years ahead.

Beneath the tarnish deposited on his reputation by a single-minded pursuit of wealth and influence, there was in Johnson a simple and unspoiled belief in what America should and could be that was even more powerful than his belief in standing up to world Communism. It was something that went back to the hard times in Texas when his father, Samuel Ealy Johnson, by turns farmer, businessman and state legislator, lost his money in the agricultural depression of the 1920s; something that struggled to be heard over the din of a 1964 Democratic fund-raising gathering in Chicago ("We have been called upon—*are you listening?*—

to build a great society of the highest order"); something that finally, in an address in Ann Arbor, Michigan, was endowed by a Kennedy speech writer, Richard Goodwin, with words to make the nation listen:

For a century we labored to settle and to subdue a continent. For half a century we called upon unbounded invention and untiring industry to create an order of plenty for all of our people.

The challenge of the next half-century is whether we have the wisdom to use that wealth to enrich and elevate our national life, and to advance the quality of our American civilization. . . .

For in your time we have the opportunity to move not only toward the rich society and the powerful society, but upward to the Great Society.[12]

The Great Society. After the New Deal, the Fair Deal, the aborted promise of the New Frontier, this would be the banner of the next advance of the American republic, attacking the long-neglected problems of poverty amid plenty, racial injustice, inadequate education, urban blight. But for that he needed a landslide. Marked by the painful experience of 1948, when he got into the Senate by a mere 87 votes out of 988,295 cast, amid allegations of fraud that were to shadow his first years as Senator, Johnson has always craved election walkovers, not just victories. "Have you voted for me yet?" he asked a fellow Texan, Pat Holt, a consultant on the staff of the Foreign Relations Committee, right in the middle of a brink-of-war committee hearing on the Berlin crisis of 1954. Holt, startled, said he was a Maryland voter now, and besides from what he heard Johnson didn't need his vote to be re-elected. With a look of scorn, as though dismissing a traitor, Johnson exclaimed, "The hell I don't! I need every vote I can get!"

He needed every vote he could get in 1964. He sensed that the support given him in the awful wake of Kennedy's death was, in his own words, "like a Western river, broad but shallow." He knew that in the back of people's minds there was distrust of him as a shady operator that could easily be tapped by some untoward development and weaken his election mandate. He was absorbed with proving to the American people that, his flaws and his virtues taken together, he was a national leader in the authentic mold. And in domestic affairs he was succeeding beyond his expectations. By exploiting the mood of national contrition over Kennedy's death, he was drawing from Congress all the progressive measures that had been bottled up during the last year of the young President's life because of rising white resentment of rising black unrest. If people were still unsure about Johnson, it was in regard to his competence in foreign affairs. With Goldwater out to make a major issue of the Democrats' failure to heed military sentiment for bombing North Vietnam and their alleged lack of the purpose and leadership required to "win," the biggest problem in his campaign was to appear neither infected by Goldwater's warmongering (which would be suicidal) nor vulnerable to Goldwater's accusations of being soft on Vietnam (which would be damaging) but to seem firm and restrained at the same time. On August 4, 1964, with the Gulf of Tonkin incidents certain to have political impact, Vietnam for Johnson was as much a domestic flank to be defended as a foreign involvement to be sustained.

How well he defended his flank that day was made evident when Goldwater issued a statement saying, "I am sure that every American will subscribe to the actions outlined in the President's statement. I believe it is the only thing that he can do under the circumstances." And Richard Nixon, who had assailed Johnson's "equivocal" Vietnam policy when he was still an unannounced contender for the Republican nomination, said the President should have bipartisan support in dealing with the situation.

*
* *

After the President's six-minute speech, McNamara came

on the television screens, relaxed and animated, complete with maps and pointer, in a post-midnight news conference at the Pentagon. He couldn't name the targets until the action was completed (no, Hanoi wasn't among them), but some of the targets had already been struck by aircraft from the carriers *Ticonderoga* and *Constellation*, and certain reinforcements (no, not combat troops) were already being moved to Southeast Asia from bases in the Pacific. Any idea why the North Vietnamese did this? No, none. "I am going to stay in the building tonight," McNamara said, "and receive reports every half hour from CINCPAC."

Spokesmen at the Pentagon and the State Department provided additional guidance. No, there had not been time to consult allied governments, since the attack on the destroyers was a calculated move that had to be answered promptly, lest the North Vietnamese misread American intentions in Southeast Asia.

No, there had been no use of the hot line to Moscow, nor any effort to contact the Communist Chinese.

Yes, the President and his advisers had weighed the danger of Communist countermoves and had decided to go on.

No, there was no question that the President, as Commander in Chief, had the right to use military power as he had used it, without a declaration of war by Congress.

The Manager   4

The room was said to have been used as a post office when the Capitol was built and Washington was beginning to sketch its geometric pattern across open fields and muddy unpaved streets, and something of the casual serviceability of early America still inhabited its high-ceilinged, well-proportioned interior, though its crystal chandelier and gilt-framed mirrors gave it a glowing rococo appearance now, and it was one of the most famous rooms in the city. A tourist group bold enough to try the tall white double doors would be welcomed by a woman secretary, who would show them the Senators' name plaques on the big green-baize oval table and answer any questions they might have. This was where the Senate Committee on Foreign Relations held its private closed-door meetings. On matters of extreme importance involving both foreign policy and defense, it met here together with the Senate Committee on Armed Services. Starting with the Dumbarton Oaks proposals of 1943 to regulate the world's postwar economy, no important undertaking requiring Senate approval had been acted on by the United States without passing through this room.

At 8:55 A.M. on August 6 a tall pug-nosed man with rimless spectacles, black slicked-down hair and a purposeful stride entered Room S-116 for a joint hearing of the two committees. Robert Strange McNamara was making one of his formidable appearances on the Hill. The President had sent a message to Congress the previous day urging prompt passage of the resolution he had requested "to give convincing evidence to the aggressive Communist nations . . . that our policy in Southeast Asia will be carried forward." Senator Dirksen had proposed that committee hearings be waived in the interest of speed—the Formosa Resolution of 1955 had taken days to pass and the Middle East Resolution of 1957 had tied things up for weeks—but for Fulbright and others this was going too far. Due process would be preserved, though with dispatch. The hearing was set for the unusually early hour of 9:00 A.M. The Secretary of Defense, accompanied by General Wheeler, was there to answer any questions the Senate might have on the incidents in the Gulf of Tonkin.

Fulbright met them at the door, a doyen of the Senate club welcoming distinguished visitors, and took them into a side office for a chat while the Senators, more than a quarter of the entire Senate membership, took their places around the table. Rusk, there to testify on the substance of the resolution, had already arrived. The women secretaries were banished, their desks occupied by members of the two committees' professional staff. Fulbright ushered the three witnesses to their chairs. Russell moved that Fulbright preside. Saying he hoped the Senators could limit their questions to five minutes apiece, Fulbright called on Rusk to speak first.

Before each Senator lay a copy of Senate Joint Resolution 189, "to promote the maintenance of international peace and security in southeast Asia." As slimmed down and simplified by the State Department the previous day, at Fulbright's suggestion, the resolution read:

Whereas naval units of the Communist regime in Vietnam,

in violation of the principles of the Charter of the United Nations and of international law, have deliberately and repeatedly attacked United States naval vessels lawfully present in international waters, and have thereby created a serious threat to international peace; and

Whereas these attacks are part of a deliberate and systematic campaign of aggression that the Communist regime in North Vietnam has been waging against its neighbors and the nations joined with them in the collective defense of freedom; and

Whereas the United States is assisting the peoples of southeast Asia to protect their freedom and has no territorial, military or political ambitions in that area, but desires only that these peoples should be left in peace to work out their own destinies in their own way: Now, therefore, be it

Resolved by the Senate and House of Representatives of the United States of America in Congress assembled, That [Sec. 1. The] Congress approves and supports the determination of the President, as Commander in Chief, to take all necessary measures to repel any armed attack against the forces of the United States and to prevent further aggression.

Sec. 2. The United States regards as vital to its national interest and to world peace the maintenance of international peace and security in southeast Asia. Consonant with the Constitution of the United States and the Charter of the United Nations and in accordance with its obligations under the Southeast Asia Collective Defense Treaty, the United States is, therefore, prepared, as the President determines, to take all necessary steps, including the use of armed force, to assist any member or protocol state of the Southeast Asia Collective Defense Treaty requesting assistance in defense of its freedom.

Sec. 3. This resolution shall expire when the President shall determine that the peace and security of the area is reasonably assured by international conditions created by action of the United Nations or otherwise, except that it may be terminated earlier by concurrent resolution of the Congress.[1]

Rusk's comment was brief. The language of the resolution, he said, was similar to that of the Formosa, Middle East and Cuba resolutions of 1955, 1957 and 1962. Its primary purpose was to "make it quite clear to the entire world that we are prepared to take the steps that may be required to ensure the security of those to whom we are committed." [2] Fulbright thanked him and called on the Secretary of Defense.

*

* *

If Bundy epitomized academe in the service of national security, McNamara was harder to categorize. He was a businessman—yes, president of the Ford Motor Company for forty-two days, when Kennedy made him the engineer of a breathtaking remodeling of the entire United States defense structure—but a businessman who had nonplussed his fellow executives by making his home in the cloistered university suburb of Ann Arbor rather than the company acres of Detroit, belonging to cultural discussion groups, offending Republican regularity by voting for good Democrats when they came along, contributing to the NAACP, collecting art, reading Toynbee. Something of the pedagogue in him too: his years at Harvard had been, by his own account, the happiest years of his life. A mixture of the two, really—something new in the executive firmament, a high priest of the cult of quantification, the technocrat supreme.

A native of San Francisco and a graduate of the University of California at Berkeley, he was the mathematics genius of his Harvard Business School class when he came across a series of articles written in 1924 in the magazine *Management and Administration* by Donaldson Brown, a General Motors executive. Experience and intuition were no longer enough, Brown had written, for establishing tight rein over the huge corporation that was becoming the exemplar of the American economy; rational choices between alternate forms of production could be made only on the basis of numerical data that showed what was actually happening, rather than what was assumed, through habit and hunch, to be happening. The words bit into young Bob McNamara's concepts. Here was an idea that had been a little ahead of its time, but whose time had come.[3]

McNamara did so well at the Harvard Business School that he stayed on to teach, but when the Second World War put him in uniform he joined a small group of other young disciples of the new creed in an innovative exercise in statistical control that enabled the Air Force, though swamped by wartime aircraft production, to get the right number of planes and the right number of men to the right places at the right time, all this when the age of computers was barely dawning. They were the Air Force's Whiz Kids, and after the war they were packaged and sold as a team to the highest bidder, which proved to be Henry Ford, 2d, who needed some kind of overhauling to arrest his decline in the car market in relation to General Motors. The Whiz Kids did the job and McNamara outpaced them all in promotions, but just making cars and money was never enough for him, and giving up the presidency and the Ford stock was no sacrifice when measured against the opportunity to manage the defense establishment of the United States.

McNamara bowled Washington over. Energy flowed from his vibrant voice, his robust frame kept hard by physical exertion on the squash courts and, during vacations, on mountain trails and ski slopes. Whatever the occasion, McNamara gave it all he had. If it was a question of proving his anti-Communism before a Congressional committee, he could compete with the late John Foster Dulles:

There is no true historical parallel to the drive of Soviet Communist imperialism to colonize the world. . . . Soviet communism seeks to wipe out the cherished traditions and institutions of the free world with the same fanaticism that once impelled winning armies to burn villages and sow the fields with salt. . . . If the free world should lose to communism, the loss would be total, final and irrevocable.[4]

If it was testifying on the defense budget or a new weapons program, he would dazzle his questioners with his presentations that made everything so clear, so definite, so comprehensive—all backed up by an array of statistics and a memory for figures that made one Congressman observe that "if we would ask the Secretary for the number of nuts and bolts in warehouse number one, drawer seven, Fort Dix, he most probably could tell us." If it was socializing on the New Frontier, hostesses would be surprised to find him a party star with a bouncy interest in the arts and stimulating conversation for the women placed next to him at the dinner table, a quantifier with a copy of the collected poems of Yeats on his Pentagon desk and a penchant for warm Irish laughter. He was the wonder of Washington, Kennedy's greatest find. And a tougher Secretary of Defense than the generals thought they'd ever get.

In what he and Kennedy set out to do—establish for the first time since the war a coherent defense policy, with a complementary role assigned to each service—there was no place for the poky practices of the Eisenhower era, when old Ike would place an arbitrary ceiling on the defense budget and let the four services divide the money between themselves. There would be no toleration under McNamara of a state of affairs in which different services would prepare for wars of different duration, each with its own, often duplicating, equipment. McNamara set out to shape the budget around distinct missions cutting across service lines —so much money for nuclear missiles, whether the Army's Minuteman or the Navy's Polaris, so much for conventional weapons—with whatever money it took to fund each mission adequately. Instead of relying on the threat of massive retaliation to deter the Soviet Union from disturbing the status quo, the United States would acquire a vastly increased store of conventional weapons as the cutting edge of American power, while at the same time making a quantum jump in missile strength, giving the country a range of options from counterinsurgency action against Communist-inspired aggression or subversion in Asia (or Africa or Latin

America), to deployment of conventional troops against Soviet brinkmanship in Europe, to "controlled response" with nuclear weapons, if it ever came to that. No longer would the United States be faced with a choice between overreaction with nuclear bombing and loss of territory to the Communists for lack of conventional forces for limited war—as was the case when the French position in Indochina was collapsing in the spring of 1954 at Dien Bien Phu. No longer would Khrushchev be able to send chills into the Western alliance with his rocket rattling or his threats over Berlin. Buoyed up by their besting of Khrushchev in the Cuban missile crisis of 1962, the Kennedy team moved confidently toward their goal of stabilizing the peace on a foundation of American capability to respond flexibly to any Communist challenge—to fight a guerrilla war, a limited war and a general war at the same time. And the man translating the vision into reality was Robert S. McNamara.

How was he doing it? By running the Defense Department as he had run Ford, taking the power of decision away from the service chiefs and centering it in his own office and his own band of initiates in the arts of "systems analysis," substituting "cost effectiveness" for the military's "feel" of what they needed, working a twelve-hour six-day week with an intensity of concentration that was amazing, learning more about the problems on the generals' desks than the generals did—and, everyone said, bringing the Defense Department for the first time under civilian control.

Control. Management control. That was the essence of the McNamara phenomenon. That was the quality that came most strongly across as his whittling down of the uniformed professionals brought him into conflict with the chairmen of the armed services committees and other allies of the military on Capitol Hill. Whether cutting billions of dollars from the service chiefs' "wish lists" (he once said the military think of weapons the way women think of perfume) or defending his controversial decision to save costs by having the Navy and Air Force develop an aircraft, the F-111, of common design for their differing missions (the Navy was complaining that the resultant jet was too heavy for takeoffs from carriers), his mastery of the Pentagon jungle of 7,000 offices, 150 staircases, 17 miles of corridors and 25,000 daily inhabitants was something he asserted with a coldness and, occasionally, a passion that allowed of no questioning. Any implication that his management of any program was less than total would bring out the schoolboy debater in him, the bright boy of the class who hated to be worsted in an argument—and also, at times, the dissembler evading a direct answer or leaving out a pertinent fact, like a Ford dealer bringing out the car's best features but not its shortcomings.

In the summer of 1964, McNamara's reputation was at its height. "I thank God every night for Bob McNamara," Johnson was supposed to have said. Awed by him in Kennedy's day, Johnson spoke of him as the ablest man he had ever seen in public life and backed him up to the hilt in his tussles in the Pentagon and on the Hill. On everything from budgetary priorities to issues of foreign (and sometimes even domestic) policy, McNamara was clearly the most trusted and warmly regarded of Johnson's advisers. Only on Vietnam was McNamara's luster beginning to dim.

Taking on the Vietnam problem for Kennedy after the 1961 decision to bolster Diem with "advisers" and military hardware, he had established a set of indexes for measuring the progress of the war and testing alternate courses of action. How many actions per month were initiated by the government troops? By the Vietcong? What was the ratio of Vietcong killed to government killed? Of weapons losses by both sides? Of prisoners taken? Of desertions? What was the proportion of territory controlled by the two sides? Returning in 1962 from his first visit to Vietnam, McNamara said, "Every quantitative measurement we have shows we're winning this war."[5] After another trip in 1963 he and General Maxwell D. Taylor, then Chairman of the JCS, reported to Kennedy that "the major part of the U.S. military task can be completed by the end of 1965, although there may be a continuing requirement for a limited number of ... training personnel."[6]

McNamara had his critics, and with the reversal of the withdrawal process in 1964, as the situation began to deteriorate again, the murmurings grew louder. It was suggested that there were other factors in Vietnam that were not being fed into his computers, that he was more interested in precision of data than in its validity, that some officials with Vietnam experience had told him they were instinctively opposed to his whole approach. It was suggested that instinct in others was precisely what he could not accept, because he had suppressed it in himself in conformity with his lifelong managerial credo. Could it be, some asked, that Robert McNamara, rattling off figures to the last digit (sometimes incorrectly), was a victim of his reputation as the human computer, embellishing his evenings with art and ideas but committed in his real daytime world to the mathematical magic that had turned him from nobody to Secretary of Defense, clinging to it so fiercely because without it he would feel out of his depth?

The Hearing 5

With precision, economy and the inevitable map, the Secretary of Defense disposed of the first incident, the one of August 2, in a matter of minutes. The *Maddox* was *here*—his finger traced the ship's course thirty miles off the North Vietnamese coast—when in the early afternoon she came under torpedo and machine-gun attack from three PT boats. Evading two torpedoes and suffering no damage or injury among her crew, the *Maddox* believed she destroyed one of the boats with fire from her five-inch guns, while the other two boats were destroyed either by the *Maddox* or by planes from the carrier *Ticonderoga* stationed *here*—the finger moved downward—at the mouth of the Tonkin Gulf.

The second incident, the night attack of August 4, was the more serious one. It showed that the first one had not, after all, been a miscalculation or misunderstanding by the North Vietnamese.

By nightfall on August 4, the Secretary testified, the *Maddox,* joined after the first incident by the *C. Turner Joy,* began reporting radar contact with vessels paralleling their track. At 9:30 P.M. Tonkin Gulf time, these vessels began to close on the patrol at speeds in excess of 40 knots.

Within the next hour, the destroyers relayed messages stating that they had avoided a number of torpedoes, that they had been under repeated attack, and that they had sunk two of the attacking craft. By midnight local time, the destroyers reported that, even though many torpedoes had been fired at them, they had suffered no hits nor casualties and that the defensive aircraft from the *Ticonderoga* were illuminating the area and attacking the enemy surface craft. . . . The *Turner Joy* reported that during the engagement, in addition to the torpedo attack, she was fired upon by automatic weapons while being illuminated by searchlights.

Finally, after more than two hours under attack, the destroyers reported at 1:30 A.M. that the attacking craft had apparently broken off the engagement.[1]

The President decided that this deliberate, preplanned attack sixty miles from shore required a military response.

These reprisal attacks, carried out by naval aircraft of the United States Seventh Fleet from the carriers *Ticonderoga* and *Constellation,* were limited in scale . . . sixty-four attack sorties against four North Vietnamese patrol boat bases and their boats and against a major supporting oil storage depot.* . . . [All] targets were severely hit, in particular the petroleum installation where ten percent of North Vietnam's petroleum storage capacity was ninety percent destroyed. Smoke was observed rising to fourteen thousand feet. Some twenty-five North Vietnamese patrol boats were destroyed or damaged.

Our losses were two aircraft destroyed and two damaged. One of the pilots is believed to have crashed with his plane between two PT craft he had under attack. Another pilot reported that he was ejecting from his downed aircraft. His whereabouts is at present listed as unknown.[2]

Bearing in mind that the best way to deter escalation is to be prepared for it, the President and his principal advisers decided to make certain military deployments to the area, including transfer of an attack carrier group from the Pacific Coast and movement of fighter-bomber aircraft into South Vietnam and Thailand. "In the meantime, U.S. destroyers with protective air cover as needed continue

* A sortie is one mission by one plane.

their patrol in the international waters of the Gulf of Tonkin."

"Well, gentlemen," Fulbright said, "I don't wish to ask any questions. I only want to make a very brief statement. The promptness and decision which all of you exhibited on this occasion was commendable, and I also think the restraint with which you used overwhelming power in the area is a new attitude on the part of a great power that is extremely beneficial and I think will be effective."

With that Fulbright turned to Russell, and the questioning began.

The Georgian was brief. How was petroleum delivered to North Vietnam? Principally by sea, McNamara said. "It could be cut off then?" Yes, sir, it could be. "I have nothing further."

Hickenlooper wanted to know why all the targets weren't struck simultaneously; the newspapers indicated the strikes were spread over a period of time. McNamara explained that the planes from the *Constellation* had a longer distance to go, but that all the aircraft were picked up by North Vietnamese radar when they were launched, so no element of surprise was sacrificed. "I only want to say that I think the United States had no other recourse," Hickenlooper said. "I certainly support the necessity of vigorous and immediate retaliation in this situation."

John Stennis, Mississippi Democrat, Hollywood's picture of a courtly Southern grandee and Russell's heir apparent on the Armed Services Committee, was interested in the size of the North Vietnamese navy. Somewhere in excess of forty patrol boats, said General Wheeler—before the reprisal took place, of course.

Any evidence of Red Chinese participation or prompting in the PT-boat attack? No evidence of their participation, McNamara replied. "What their counsel may have been . . . I can't say."

Leverett Saltonstall of Massachusetts, ranking Republican

on the Armed Services Committee, had no questions. "I believe the action of the President was essential to defend the prestige of our armed forces. . . . I intend to support this resolution wholeheartedly and with my best efforts."

Wayne Morse, Democrat of Oregon: "Mr. Chairman, I am unalterably opposed to this course of action which, in my judgment, is an aggressive course of action on the part of the United States."

❋

❋ ❋

Everyone agreed that Wayne Lyman Morse was a brilliant fellow. He was probably the Senate's ablest expert on labor law, he could be sweet reason itself, shepherding an education bill or arbitrating a labor dispute for the White House, and he could take on all comers arguing the Constitution. When he arrived in the Senate in 1945, lean, unsmiling, a teetotaler, a Populist in Republican clothing ready to chastise his party's conscience on unionizing rights and the public interest in natural resources and other causes appropriated by the Roosevelt Democrats, his immense energy and his shrewd and overpoweringly logical speeches quickly raised him to a national figure, the latest in a line of progressive scrappers in the image of Nebraska's late Senator George W. Norris. His apostasy in 1952, when he quit the party in disgust over candidate Eisenhower's surrender, as he saw it, to the GOP reactionaries, infuriated the Republican leadership, but the Democrats rewarded him with even better committee assignments when he joined their ranks, and Morse's reputation as a courageous if cantankerous man of the people who followed only his own sense of right was enhanced.

But somewhere along the way the Morse legend began to sour. The relish for argumentation that had carried the Wisconsin farm boy to debating honors at the University of Wisconsin and salted his courses as law professor at the

University of Oregon was billowing into garrulousness. Senators hearing his gravel voice rise in anger over some issue of consequence were apt to remember that it rose just as wrathfully the previous day over his refusal "on principle" to agree to some minor accommodation to the Senate's convenience. People began saying that Wayne lacked a sense of proportion. He was the record holder for the longest continuous oration in the Senate's history—a twenty-two-hour and twenty-six-minute speech in 1953 against a tidelands bill that put offshore oil deposits under state control—but that was a lonely stand on a major issue, something the Senate could understand. What his colleagues found tiresome was his insistence on mounting speeches that were increasingly pedantic and self-righteous and interminable on every issue that came along. He began to be regarded as an eccentric. The press began to ignore him. As one committee member put it, "If Morse was questioning an American Ambassador to Brazil and suddenly asked, 'How many times have you had intercourse with the Brazilian President's wife?' the other Senators would just shrug and say to themselves, 'Well, that's Wayne.'"

In the summer of 1964 Morse was clearing the Senate chamber with the efficiency of a fire alarm by rising almost daily to pour vituperation on "McNamara's War" in Vietnam. A number of other Senators were becoming restive over the cheerless prospects of the American intervention, some calling for more, some for less, involvement, and the fact that an esteemed liberal like Ernest Gruening of Alaska had joined Morse in calling for withdrawal had given Morse comfort, but the tendency to discount whatever Morse said was robbing his speeches of the weight they would have if they had come from a smaller but more conventional figure.

Just the previous day, on the floor of the Senate, after the clerk had read out the President's message on the proposed joint resolution, Morse had breasted the first tide of praise for the President's decisiveness and moderation with robust dissent. The incident that inspired the resolution, he charged,

is as much the doing of the United States as it is the doing of North Vietnam. For ten years the role of the United States in South Vietnam has been that of a provocateur, every bit as much as North Vietnam has been a provocateur. . . .

The American effort to impose by force of arms a government of our own choosing upon a segment of the old colony of Indochina has caught up with us. Our violations of the Geneva accord have caught up with us. Our violations of the United Nations Charter have caught up with us.[3]

According to press reports, Morse said, U.S. naval vessels were patrolling the Tonkin Gulf during a South Vietnamese naval attack on coastal targets. "Was the United States Navy standing guard while vessels of South Vietnam shelled North Vietnam?"

Under Article 1, Section 8, of the Constitution,

the power to declare war is vested in Congress. . . . No President has the legal authority under the Constitution to send American boys to their death on a battlefield in the absence of a declaration of war. . . . I shall not support any substitute which takes the form of a predated declaration of war . . . a delegation of the duty of Congress to determine an issue of war or peace.

He would vote against the resolution.

The Senate, after hearing him out, resumed consideration of a bill for sundry minor appropriations. And now, as Morse disturbed the harmonious flow of the hearing in Room S-116, the sensed reaction of the other committee members was one of irritation and impatience. Let Wayne have his five minutes, which he'll probably stretch to ten, and we'll get on with the business at hand.

What no one in the room knew was that Morse had had a telephone call after 11:00 P.M. from an officer in the Pentagon he had met while serving on the Armed Services Committee. The caller, whose identity Morse will not disclose, said he supposed Morse would oppose the resolution requested by the President.

Yes, Morse said, he certainly would oppose it.

The caller said that since he was in uniform he could not tell the Senator anything specific. But he could tell him that what the Administration was saying about the situation did not include all the facts. He suggested that the Senator question the Administration on the location of the *Maddox* and on its true mission. If all the facts were known, they would reveal that the United States was playing a provocative role in the Tonkin Gulf.

Morse had attended the August 3 briefing at which McNamara had conceded knowledge of the South Vietnamese shelling of two North Vietnamese offshore islands. The telephone call heightened Morse's suspicion that the *Maddox*'s presence in the general vicinity at the time was not entirely unconnected with the South Vietnamese raids.

Fixing McNamara with his green tigerish eyes under the bushiest pair of eyebrows in the Senate, he blurted his suspicions into the decorum of Mr. Fulbright's reception for the secretaries of State and Defense.

Such boorish questioning of his command of the facts, if not his truthfulness, was more than McNamara had had to put up with in his worst moments on the Hill. Like a weapon wheeling on a pestiferous target, he fired an obliterating volley.

"First, our Navy played absolutely no part in, was not associated with, was not aware of, any South Vietnam actions, if there were any. I want to make that very clear to you.

"The *Maddox* was operating in international waters, was carrying out a routine patrol of the type we carry out all over the world at all times. It was not informed of, was not aware of, had no evidence of, and so far as I know today has no knowledge of any South Vietnamese actions in connection with the two islands that Senator Morse referred to. . . . I say this flatly. This is a fact."

Did *you* know about it? Morse asked.

No, not at the time.

Were the boats that struck the island supplied by the United States?

"The boats that may have struck at the coastal areas of North Vietnam may have been supplied by us. We have been helping South Vietnam arm itself. I do not know about the specific boats. I personally think this is a perfectly legitimate and proper way to defend oneself from the kind of aggression South Vietnam has been subjected to for years."

Some sort of fog was still sticking to those South Vietnamese operations. The sequence of information on them had been as follows:

August 2—Hanoi radio reports attacks on Hon Me and Hon Ngu by ships of the United States and its South Vietnamese "lackeys."

August 3—McNamara confirms in a closed-door Senate briefing that there had been such a South Vietnamese naval attack and suggests that the North Vietnamese, in attacking the *Maddox* on August 2, may have mistaken her for one of the South Vietnamese raiders.

August 3—State Department officials adamantly deny that any such misunderstanding could have occurred when Russell raises that possibility publicly.

August 5—The State Department retreats into silence on the issue. A Department spokesman says, "I can neither confirm, deny nor discuss any such reports." [4]

August 5—McNamara seems unwilling to discuss them publicly either. At a news conference called to report on the results of the American reprisal, the following exchange occurs:

Q. Mr. Secretary, how do you explain these North Vietnamese attacks?

A. I can't explain them . . . our vessels were clearly in international waters. . .

Q. There have been reports that South Vietnamese vessels were . . . taking some sort of action against North Vietnam approximately at this time.

A. No, to the best of my knowledge, there were no operations during the period I was describing last night.[5]

And now McNamara, appearing before the same committees he had briefed on August 3, was being strangely slippery about the South Vietnamese actions, using phrases like "*if* there were any," "the boats that *may have* struck."

Morse did not press him further. But apparently McNamara himself felt that some further explanation was necessary. The committees should understand, he said, that the South Vietnamese have been trying to stop the infiltration of men and weapons from the north by sea. The United States has helped them in organizing a force of about five hundred paramilitary junks, some of them motorized, for patrolling the coast. Lately this operation has been taking the junk force farther north. "As part of that, as I reported earlier to you this week, we understand the South Vietnamese sea force carried out patrol action around these islands and actually shelled the points they felt were associated with this infiltration. Our ships had absolutely no knowledge of it, were not connected with it, and in no sense of the word can be considered to have backstopped the effort."

If the committee had delved into the question of infiltration, they might have established that, by the Administration's own figures, the movement of men did not amount to more than several thousand a year; that these were South Vietnamese, former Vietminh guerrillas who had transferred north under the terms of the Geneva agreement, expecting to return to their homes after the 1956 election; that the bulk of this infiltration was overland, along the Ho Chi Minh trail; and that whatever the degree of northern control over the peasant revolt against Diem that sprang up in 1958, the Vietcong's weapons were still old French matériel or American equipment captured from the South Vietnamese army. But apart from Morse's expostulation that "you have never been able to produce a scintilla of evidence" of "any organized military operation of North Vietnam going into South Vietnam," the committee passed over this subject in silence.

Saltonstall asked if there were any American advisers aboard those junks. To the best of his knowledge, McNamara said, no. Aiken wondered if the U.S. Embassy in Saigon knew of the South Vietnamese attack ahead of time. McNamara presumed it did.

And that finished off Senator Morse—for that morning at least.

*

* *

Clifford P. Case, the liberal Republican from New Jersey, wanted "to associate myself with those who gave their hearty support to the actions taken by the President and the Secretary." But why wasn't the *Maddox*, with help from the aircraft, able to sink more than one boat during the first incident? General "Bus" Wheeler, whose smile had been compared to moss on granite but whose background in logistics and troop training made him more of an administrator than a warrior, replied that the two other boats were heavily damaged, so the overall result was quite satisfactory.

Frank J. Lausche, a big tousled Democrat from Ohio, an emotional superhawk ever ready to scatter flurries of doves obscuring the light, came down on an important point. In that first action of August 2, it was correct, wasn't it, that "the *Maddox* did nothing until it was actually fired upon?"

What happened, Wheeler said, was that when the PT boats approached within 9,000 yards, the *Maddox* fired three warning shots.

"Despite the warning shots," Rusk contributed, "the PT boats continued to close at high speed."

Then, said Lausche, "the torpedoes were set into motion, and it was *then* that you began your firing."

"That is correct, sir," Wheeler said.

Lausche looked around the table, as though to demand, *Now* who can say the United States is following an aggressive course?

Daniel K. Inouye, Democrat of Hawaii, was moved to wonder if Uncle Sam was being too chivalrous in such encounters. "Does this mean that from now on we will have to await until the adversary fires either a burst of machine gun or fires a torpedo before we respond?"

McNamara assured him that "the commanders have been instructed to defend themselves if there is an indication of hostile intent."

Anyone present who had given a careful reading to the Defense Department's chronology of the August 2 incident, printed in *The New York Times,* might have been nonplussed. The chronology included the following sequence (the times are for the Tonkin Gulf):

2:40 P.M.—Maddox reported being approached by high-speed . . . craft. . . .

3:08 P.M.—Maddox reported being attacked by the torpedo craft. Opened fire with 5-inch battery after three warning shots failed to slow down attackers.

3:08 P.M.—The boats continued closing maneuvers, and two closed to 5,000 yards, each firing one torpedo.[6]

This suggested that the *Maddox* fired both the warning shots and the shots aimed in earnest *before* the boats had launched their torpedoes. But few newspaper readers, busy Senators in particular, have time for the fine print. No one at the hearing pointed out the apparent discrepancy, not even Morse.

Karl E. Mundt, Republican of South Dakota, whose Vietnam stance combined martial fervor with native caution, asked what "our intelligence" had reported on Hanoi's reaction. Nothing of any consequence, Wheeler said.

The previous day, in its first comment on the August 2

incident, Hanoi radio claimed that the *Maddox* had been within North Vietnamese territorial waters when it was approached by coastal craft and "chased" away. As for the incident of August 4, *the North Vietnamese claimed it never happened!* It was a "sheer fabrication," they said, aimed at "covering up illegal acts" against North Vietnam such as the violations of the territorial limit, the attacks on the coastal islands and the air strikes that followed.[7]

But no one at the hearing asked about any of that.

George Smathers, dapper suntanned Democrat of Florida, probably the only man to have campaigned actively for the title of "Best Dressed Senator," wanted "to commend the President and the Secretaries and the Joint Chiefs of Staff for the decision which they made, its decisiveness, its effectiveness, and its prudence." But how were the governments of Japan and the Philippines reacting?

With wholehearted support, Rusk replied. "We have had that right around the world, a high degree of understanding of the necessity for counteraction, and also a hope that it will not escalate."

According to the newspapers, Free World reaction to the quickest and most unexpected major American move in eighteen years of Cold War was mixed, at best. Most of the allied Western governments expressed their support for the reprisal in carefully worded statements that betrayed misgivings about its justification and its possible consequences. Even in Britain, the one European ally to provide vigorous backing, there was an undertone of apprehension. Canada urged Washington to avoid steps that could precipitate a war. The French government was morosely silent.

Thailand, Australia and the Philippines expressed support in varying degrees. The Chinese Nationalist officials in Taiwan said they believed the attacks on the American ships had been directed by the Chinese Communists. In Saigon *The New York Times* reported "enthusiasm bordering in some quarters on the delirious." The Tokyo government

73

called the American action "unavoidable under the circumstances," but the Japanese Foreign Ministry was reported to have been "shocked." In Turkey, the *Times* reported, "popular feeling appeared to be that the United States had done precisely what it had prevented Turkey from doing—striking back at an 'aggressor' [in Cyprus]." The Latin Americans had little to say. The Vatican expressed disquiet. The neutrals were critical, saying United States warships had no business in the Tonkin Gulf. The Indian government was "distressed." There were minor anti-American demonstrations in New Delhi, Tokyo, Stockholm, Glasgow, Toronto, Melbourne and Algiers.

At the United Nations, where the Security Council had convened the previous day at Washington's request to hear a report on the affair, without being asked to do anything about it, "many countries," according to a *Manchester Guardian* correspondent,

appear to question the U.S. account of the events in the Hanoi Straits and are wondering whether the United States has not been deliberately trying to encourage a clash with North Vietnam. The most widespread comment heard is that the United States should have gone to the Security Council first if it had proof of North Vietnamese aggression and only acted afterwards.[8]

Why the United States retaliated so swiftly, "without taking time even to notify our allies," was a question put to Rusk in an interview on the National Broadcasting Company television network the previous day. "Well, in the first place," Rusk replied,

we had some ships in the Gulf of Tonkin who were under attack, and they were dodging torpedoes. . . . We had to strike immediately because we didn't expect to ask those ships to run a continuing gauntlet of torpedoes on their way back to the Gulf of Tonkin. . . .

Further than that, if under these attacks there had not been an immediate and appropriate response, then Hanoi and those who might be standing behind Hanoi in this might well have come to a very formidable mistaken judgment about what is possible in the Southeast Asian situation.[9]

But the Senators did not choose to go into any of that either.

In the same NBC interview Rusk was asked how he could explain the North Vietnamese attack.

I haven't been able, quite frankly, to come to a fully satisfactory explanation. There is a great gulf of understanding between that world and our world, ideological in character. They see what we think of as the real world in wholly different terms. Their very processes of logic are different.

Margaret Chase Smith, trim white-haired Maine Republican who took pride in having made her way in Congress in such masculine areas as armed services, aerospace and appropriations, put a variation of the question to McNamara. The Secretary had originally evaluated the August 2 incident as an isolated event; was that because of a lack of intelligence information or an error in judgment? Because he regarded the attack on the destroyer "a form of suicide," he said, "and I didn't expect them to undertake that."

Which disposed of that puzzle as well.

Henry M. "Scoop" Jackson, Democrat of Washington, known also as "the honorable Senator from Boeing" for his championing of aerospace contracts, wanted to know what the Chinese Communist air force was like. Pretty deficient in spare parts and modern jets, McNamara said, as a result of the 1960 cutoff in Soviet supplies. And the ground forces? Well, "they have a tremendous advantage of large numbers of men."

Did the Administration "take into consideration the possibility of war with Red China?" George D. Aiken, Republican of Vermont, inquired.

Bombing a country of the "Socialist bloc" had been an unprecedented challenge to the Soviet Union, but Khru-

75

shchev was clearly wary of military involvement in Indochina, and it was uncertainty over Peking's response that was reported to have been keeping American officials on edge. The intelligence estimate given to the President, it was said, had been that China, though blustering about "not sitting idly by," would not enter the conflict unless her own borders were imperiled. Nevertheless, according to *The New York Herald-Tribune*, Johnson had awakened with a start at 3:30 A.M. August 5—the hour when the American aircraft, having struck the three patrol-boat bases of Quang Khe, Loc Chau and Phuc Loi and the petroleum storage depot at the port of Vinh, were scheduled to hit their northernmost target, the base at Hon Gay, only fifty miles from the Chinese border.[10]

The first Chinese reaction, though harsh in tone, was sufficiently vague to be reassuring—Moscow's initial protest was even milder than expected—but tension over the Chinese enigma was still high, and texts of the Peking radio's broadcasts were still being speeded to Washington the minute they were monitored.[11] Aiken's question was one of the critical ones.

"We have contingency plans, Senator Aiken, which take account of that," McNamara said.

"You are fully prepared then?"

"Yes, sir."

And that settled that.

Mike Mansfield of Montana, the tall, gaunt, mild and likable Majority Leader, the Asian scholar more interested in history and in his study missions to the Orient than in the political authority thrust on him by the departing Johnson, the pipe-puffing former marine, miner and professor who had a way of disconcerting interviewers with answers like "Yes" and "No," had no questions.

Stuart Symington, Democrat of Missouri, the elegant former Air Force Secretary and Presidential aspirant, the Senate's official interpreter of the military wisdom, addressed himself to General Wheeler with brisk professionalism. What type of antiaircraft weapons did the North Vietnamese use? Did any of the American planes fly two sorties? What were the characteristics of the F-86 Crusader? What kind of automatic weapons were fired against the *Turner Joy?*

"These were probably three-inch or something of that size on the Swatow and/or PT-4 boats," put in McNamara, not one to take a back seat on expertise.

"May I ask why you didn't go for more of their petroleum?"

Their other petroleum depots weren't associated with the patrol boats and therefore weren't relevant targets.

Symington, satisfied, left the hearing for pressing business elsewhere.

Russell Long, son of the Louisiana demagogue Huey Long, said it seemed to him that in carrying out the reprisal "we achieved about the kind of surprise on their navy that the Japanese achieved in Pearl Harbor."

"I think that is exactly true," said McNamara.

Long commended them for striking back as soon as they knew they were attacked. "As much as I would like to be consulted with on this kind of thing, the less time you spend on consulting and the quicker you shoot back the better off you are."

Strom Thurmond of South Carolina, the dour prophet of the Dixiecrat schism and ramrod-straight Major General in the U.S. Army Reserve, wanted to know if "we have a policy to win." If General Khanh wanted to eliminate Communism there by going to the source of it, in North Vietnam, would the Administration object?

Rusk didn't think now was the time to enlarge the war.

Well, Thurmond said, there's going to be a stalemate in Vietnam "unless we go ahead and strike at the heart of the trouble," and "I think we ought to have a *victory. . . .* I think if we are firm with the Communists, that we can *win.*"

Frank Church, liberal young Idaho Democrat, rose to his President's defense. "I think it would be the height of folly to believe that an American war on the Asian continent, particularly for a Western nation against Asians, could have any durable result."

Frank Carlson, Republican of Kansas, was interested in the occasional reference in the press to reverse infiltration in Vietnam—from South to North.

"This is such a highly classified subject, Senator Carlson, it is difficult for me to answer your question fully," McNamara said.

"I will not ask you to discuss it then."

Robert C. Byrd, Democrat of West Virginia, a former kleagle, or organizer, of the Ku Klux Klan and no kinsman of the Byrd dynasty of Virginia, wanted to know if there was any indication that the Russians were violating the nuclear test-ban treaty, which was exactly one year old. No, Rusk said, none.

John Sparkman of Alabama, a falling star since his selection as Adlai Stevenson's running mate in 1952, was glad to see that the resolution before them appeared to recognize "the constitutional right of the President to take these actions"—that it appeared to be merely "confirmation or a ratification by the Congress of the action taken and a pledge to lend all support that may be necessary."

But Sam Ervin, the North Carolina Democrat whose small-town-lawyer folksiness camouflaged a first-rate legal mind, had a less sanguine view of Presidential actions, particularly lately, in Vietnam. "Is there any reasonable or honorable way we can extricate ourselves without losing our face and probably our pants?"

"If the North would leave the South alone," Rusk replied, "there is no problem."

*
* *

The questioning had gone around the table. "Does that complete the hearing?" Fulbright asked.

Morse had another question. McNamara had said at the August 3 briefing that the destroyers were permitted to approach to within eleven miles of the coast to show that the United States did not recognize the twelve-mile limit, "but I think," said Morse, "[the record] will show at some times we were less than eleven miles, but beyond three miles," the limit recognized by the United States.

The secretaries had to leave to testify on the resolution before the House Foreign Affairs Committee, but McNamara asked Wheeler to stay behind "for a few minutes" to answer any further questions.

Wheeler reiterated that the destroyers were under instructions to go no closer than eleven miles.

"It is still too close," Morse said.

FULBRIGHT: The committee is open to a motion.
SMATHERS: I so move.
LAUSCHE: I second it.
MORSE: I ask for a roll call.

The motion before the meeting was:

The Committee on Foreign Relations and the Committee on Armed Services . . . having had under consideration Senate Joint Resolution 189 supporting the President's determination to repel any armed attack against U.S. forces in southeast Asia and to prevent further Communist attacks, report the resolution favorably and recommend that it be passed by the Senate.[12]

The staff called the roll. "Mr. Sparkman?" "Aye." "Mr. Humphrey?" "Aye." "Mr. Mansfield?" "Aye."

Hubert H. Humphrey, the Minnesota Democrat, was waiting on tiptoe to be chosen by Johnson for the Vice-Presidential slot and had not been able to attend the committee meeting, and Mansfield had had to leave before the voting, but both had given their proxies to Fulbright, who answered for them.

"Mr. Morse?"

"*No!*"

"Chairman Fulbright?" "Aye." "Mr. Smathers?" "Aye." "Mr. Hickenlooper?" "Aye."

With twelve members absent from the hearing (out of the combined membership of thirty-six) but with eight of the absentees leaving their proxy votes, the count was 31 to 1.

The committee recessed. The time was 10:45 A.M. The hearing had lasted one hour and forty minutes.

＊

＊　　＊

At the hearing of the House Committee on Foreign Affairs, the secretaries presented the same statements they had submitted on the Senate side. There were thirty-one members, and each was given three minutes for questioning. Chairman Thomas E. Morgan, Democrat of Pennsylvania, was under instructions from the House leadership to "move it," and he did. "It was a go-go type of session," he recalls.[13]

There were a few questions about the purpose of the patrol. The answer was that the ships were in international waters, checking on infiltration from the North. There was no mention of the South Vietnamese raids. The vote was 29 to 0, with two members, Republicans H. R. Gross of Iowa and Edward J. Derwinski of Illinois voting "present," which was a way of avoiding being recorded either for or against. The hearing took an hour and a half.

The committee system of the United States Congress had outdone itself in expeditious response to an urgent request from the President.

The Senate 6

Now that time had blurred Bill Fulbright's husky cleft-chin handsomeness, the first thing people noticed about him was his voice. It was a voice that caressed the mind like the purl of a sweet-water creek of his native Ozarks, low and calm and clear, with a play of light and shadow, making one feel that here was one Senator who had managed to stay a natural human being in an atmosphere that turned so many into pompous poseurs. It was a voice to be enjoyed, but to be on guard against as well, because it made what he said seem so reasonable and so right, and what if it wasn't?

In the early afternoon of August 6, other business having been pushed aside, Fulbright's urbane voice rippled over the Senate chamber in the cause of speedy endorsement of the resolution requested by the President of the United States. The facts of the August 4 incident were clear, he said: The attack on the American destroyers "was without any doubt a calculated act of military aggression." The American response was "an act of self-defense wholly consistent [with] the United Nations Charter and . . . the international law of reprisal." Its most notable feature was its great restraint. In approving the resolution that morning with only one dissenting vote, the two committees headed by him and by the distinguished Senator from Georgia concluded, as the Senators could read in the mimeographed reports before them (the usual printed report having been dispensed with to save time), that "In the circumstances, the United States could not have done less and should not have done more." [1]

It was not one of the Senate's great debates. The air of crisis that had surrounded the summoning of Congressional leaders to the White House and the President's television address had been largely dissipated, and the chamber was not even one third full as Fulbright completed his opening statement and asked the presiding officer, Daniel B. Brewster of Maryland, a lawyer and grain-and-cattle farm owner, for permission to insert a number of editorials in the *Congressional Record.* Yet if the questions that had been glossed over or ignored in the perfunctory committee hearings that morning were to be raised, it would have to be in the Senate, with its sprinkling of independent-minded liberals of both parties; the House, a far more conservative and cautious body, could not be expected to produce a challenge, and the press showed little promise of critical inquiry into the affair.

Few major dailies took as zestful a view of the situation as *The* (New York) *News,* which wrote that "it is reassuring to see our Far East forces get set for whatever may grow out of the episode. It may be our Heaven-sent good fortune to liquidate not only Ho Chi Minh but Mao Tsetung's Red mob at Peking as well." But fewer still shared the alarm of *The New York Post:* "Where are we heading in Vietnam? Are we being sucked into a dark tunnel from which there may be no egress?" [2]

The general editorial reaction was that the President's response was well suited to the objective of deflecting Hanoi and Peking from whatever new aggressive plan lay behind their outrageous provocation. The editorials selected by Fulbright were representative.

Thus, *The Philadelphia Inquirer:*

President Johnson has called upon the American people to meet the test of courage and determination that has been thrust suddenly and irrevocably upon us all by a treacherous foe.

The Washington Post:

President Johnson has earned the gratitude of the free world as well as of the nation for his careful and effective handling of the Vietnam crisis. . . . The counterattack smashed the "paper tiger" myth, proving U.S. readiness to use whatever means necessary to stand up for its interests in the Far East.

The New York Times:

[A] provocation—twice repeated—now has brought a response that has been, in the President's words, "limited and fitting." . . . The President has rightly asked that the [Congressional] resolution express a determination that "all necessary measures" be taken.[3]

They were a faithful reflection, these editorials, of public opinion across the country, as nearly as one could tell (a Harris poll was to report in the next few days that 85 percent of the American people supported the air strike), except that Americans generally were less occupied with Vietnam than editorial writers and even more confused as to the character and objectives of the protracted involvement. The counsel of the pundits was sharply divided. On the one hand there was Walter Lippmann, calling the intervention a "mistake,"[4] and *The New York Times,* saying, "We must confront the Communists with options short of unacceptable defeat,"[5] and on the other hand there were exhortations for more drastic action, such as a major article in *Fortune* proposing that the United States "inject its own forces into the battle" and consider "extending the war into North Vietnam." Perhaps a measure of the general state of mind was that the liberal Catholic lay magazine *Commonweal,* which was to anathematize the war later on, regarded South Vietnam as an "auspicious place for the free world to make a stand."[6]

Yet the vague unease that seemed to haunt Fulbright's approving editorials was present in the national—and Congressional—mood as well and was, if anything, accentuated in the Senate that day, since the Senators were being asked once again to do something that had engendered a certain controversy in the past: give the President advance approval of action he might find necessary to take some time in the future without quite knowing what that action might be. Fulbright's presentation had dealt almost entirely with the President's response to the attacks on the American vessels and hardly at all with the resolution's endorsement of future action in Vietnam. But Fulbright, having concluded, was still on his feet as the Administration's floor manager and spokesman for the resolution, stocked by the Administration with answers to any questions the Senators might have. And Brewster had the key question: Would the resolution authorize sending a large American army to Vietnam?

"It would authorize whatever the Commander in Chief feels is necessary," Fulbright replied. "Whether or not that should be done is a matter of wisdom under the circumstances that exist at the particular time it is contemplated. . . . Speaking for my own committee, everyone I have heard has said that the last thing we want to do is to become involved in a land war in Asia."

"Am I to understand," asked Gaylord Nelson, Wisconsin Democrat and a recent convert to the dovish camp, "that we are saying to the Executive branch, 'We agree now, in advance, that you may land as many divisions as deemed necessary, and engage in a direct military assault on North Vietnam, if it becomes the judgment of the Commander in Chief that this is the only way to prevent further aggression [against South Vietnam]'?"

"If the situation should deteriorate to such an extent that

the only way to save it from going completely under to the Communists would be action such as the Senator suggests," Fulbright replied, "then that would be a grave decision on the part of our country. . . . I personally feel it would be unwise under any circumstances to put a large land army on the Asian continent."

Nelson was not satisfied. "I would be most concerned if the Congress should say that we intend by the joint resolution to authorize a complete change in the mission we have had in South Vietnam for the past ten years."

"I do not interpret the joint resolution in that way at all," Fulbright said. It neither limited nor expanded "the President's power to use the armed forces." It was aimed primarily at deterring the Communists from further attacks on American vessels.

How close to the North Vietnamese coast, Nelson asked, were the destroyers patrolling?

"It was testified that they went in at least eleven miles in order to show that we do not recognize a twelve-mile limit."

What purpose is served by that, considering how sensitive North Vietnam must be about its territorial limit?

"Why should the United States be so careful about the sensitivities of North Vietnam?" Fulbright demanded. "We were there for the purpose of observation of what went on in that area, because our people felt it necessary as a part of our activities in protecting and helping to protect South Vietnam."

"It would be mighty risky, if Cuban PT boats were firing on Florida, for Russian armed ships or destroyers to be patrolling between us and Cuba, eleven miles out," Nelson suggested.

"I do not see how the case is analogous."

"It would be a risky thing for Russia to be out there testing our viewpoint about their patrols within eleven miles of our coast."

"I do not deny that it is risky. The whole operation is risky. It is full of risks."

The discord in liberal Democratic ranks was doubly ironic since the issue raised by the questioners—delegation of authority to the President for use in circumstances Congress could not foresee—had troubled Fulbright himself in the past. When in 1955 the Chinese Communists intensified their war of nerves against Taiwan and President Eisenhower asked for a resolution authorizing him to employ the armed forces "as he deems necessary" to protect Taiwan against attack, Congressional fears that the JCS might be encouraged to foment preventive war against China brought an assurance from Eisenhower that the decision to use force would be his alone, and even then three Senators, including Morse, and three Representatives voted "nay." The issue of delegated powers came up again in 1957, when Dulles felt the need for a Congressional resolution approving use of armed force to defend Middle Eastern nations against aggression by "international Communism." Some believed then, as now, that the President had those powers already as Commander in Chief, and that even if he didn't he could do anything he wanted overseas anyway, as long as Congress voted him the funds and the armed forces remained disciplined. Even so—and this central question of the President's powers was gingerly skirted—approving action in advance would tie the hands of Congress in case the venture took an unfortunate turn. Fulbright was among those who opposed the Middle East Resolution on that ground, though he was absent when the resolution was passed (two months after being requested) by a vote of 72 to 19 in the Senate and 350 to 60 in the House. (The Cuba Resolution, expressing determination to prevent Cuba from becoming a Soviet base, was somewhat different from the other two, in that it was pressed on President Kennedy, who felt no need for it, by a Congress that wanted to help, and in that it did not specify use of armed force, an omission that enabled

Morse to vote for it when it was passed, 86 to 1, in the Senate and 337 to 7 in the House, the sole Senate "nay" coming from a Vermont Republican, Winston L. Prouty, for whom the resolution was not specific enough.)

So Fulbright in past years *had* recognized the danger of encouraging military entanglement by Congressional resolution. Yet when Brewster and Nelson pointed up this danger now, he seemed to find their concern misplaced, just as he seemed to find it perfectly reasonable for American warships not at war with North Vietnam to hug the coast in an area of South Vietnamese naval operations. George S. McGovern, liberal Democrat of South Dakota, who was beginning to attract attention by strong views temperately expressed, was ranged against him. "If this is broad enough for the Commander in Chief to commit us to fighting on the land," McGovern said, "I would not support the resolution."

Now the Republican liberals joined in.

John Sherman Cooper of Kentucky, former Ambassador to India, returned to the "distinction between defending our own forces and taking offensive measures in South Vietnam."

"I know," he said, "that a progression of events for ten years has carried us to this crisis. Ten years have passed, and perhaps the events are inevitable now, no one can tell. But as long as there is hope and the possibility of avoiding with honor a war in Southeast Asia, with consequences one can scarcely contemplate today, I hope the President will use this power wisely."

He hoped, specifically, that the President would consult with other participants of the 1954 Geneva conference on the possibility of a peaceful settlement.

The President had an opportunity two weeks previously to do just that. President Charles de Gaulle had proposed a reconvening of the Geneva conference to re-establish the 1954 agreement, with the proviso that "this time it would be respected" by all parties, and Russia and China had indicated their acceptance. Johnson cut down the proposal with one sentence: "We do not believe in a conference called to ratify terror." [7] And the introduction of U.S. Air Force jets into South Vietnam after the Tonkin Gulf incidents—the only American piloted warplanes there hitherto had been helicopters for ferrying South Vietnamese troops into battle and a small number of propeller-driven fighter bombers—violated the Geneva arms prohibition on yet another level.

The resolution, Fulbright responded to Cooper, gave clearance to the President to use his discretion. "We all hope and believe that the President will not use this discretion arbitrarily or irresponsibly. . . . I have no doubt that the President will consult with Congress in case a major change in present policy becomes necessary."

Will he utilize the United Nations? asked Jacob K. Javits of New York, who was said to have ambitions of becoming the nation's first Jewish President.

Johnson had "utilized" the United Nations, in a manner of speaking, already. Reached on a vacation island off Maine after the August 4 incident, Adlai Stevenson, serving as UN Ambassador, was brought back by boat and air force jet to place his eloquence in the service of the President's justification of the reprisal. "[These] acts of aggression by the North Vietnamese in the Gulf of Tonkin," Stevenson told the Security Council,

make no sense whatsoever standing alone. They defy rational explanation except as part of a larger pattern with a larger purpose. . . .

The attempt to sink the United States destroyers in international waters is much more spectacular than the attempt to murder the mayor of a village in his bed at night. But they are both part of the pattern, and the pattern is designed to subjugate the people of Southeast Asia to an empire ruled by means of force of arms, of rule by terror, of expansion by violence.[8]

He did not ask for any action by the Security Council.

He was merely authorized to make a report—for public relations' use.

Stevenson's new career had lost him much of the idolatry he had earned with his heart-lifting speeches of 1952. The man who had exclaimed, "Let's talk sense to the American people, let's tell them the truth," had ended up telling official lies, without knowing it, about the Bay of Pigs. The man who had always viewed force as a last resort and believed that the influence of America was her example continued speaking up for a foreign policy militarized by a national-security establishment far less established in the American tradition than he was. Why, some of his more liberal admirers asked, didn't he resign? Because service to the party was part of his code of playing the game? Because he was afraid of the emptiness of life without a public mission? Or because his new role did not cause him as much inner turmoil as his admirers supposed, since he was, after all, persuaded of the necessity of resisting Communism? No one knew, but the feeling that he deserved better of the Presidents he served seemed to exclude him personally from the criticism, by the neutrals and some of the allies, of some of the policies he enunciated.[9]

On August 5, 1964, Stevenson's defense of the American air strike as a "limited and measured response" evoked sardonic references in the delegates' lounge to his statement four months earlier—when the British forces in southern Arabia had struck at border raiders in Yemen—that the United States disapproved "of retaliatory raids, wherever they occur and by whomever they are committed" and condemned "use of force by either side as a means of solving disputes, a principle that is enshrined in the Charter." The British, tolerant of the Americans' occasional wavering under the burden of empire they had taken over from Whitehall, were the only ally to speak in support of the United States on August 5.[10]

In point of fact, the charter principles that were to have

been the cornerstone of a new world system devoid of the use of force had long since been quietly buried by the superpowers, as the onset of the Cold War rendered the United Nations inoperable as a peace-keeping organization except in disputes between the smaller countries. The charter provisions outlawing "threat or use of force" and requiring all parties to a dispute to "refer it to the Security Council" if they failed to settle it by negotiation had long since stopped being taken seriously in disputes involving Washington and Moscow. At no time did the United States make any real effort to secure United Nations support for its course of action in Vietnam, much less invite arbitration, and Russia did not bother with the United Nations at all in her military intervention in East Germany and Hungary. In justifying its reprisal in the Gulf of Tonkin under Article 51 of the charter, which recognized the inherent right of self-defense against attack until the Security Council took steps to restore peace, the United States was resorting to legalistic artifice. Article 51 was meant to apply to an attack on a country or group of countries bound by geographic, ethnic and historical ties, and then only in conformity with the Nuremberg principle that the need for self-defense be overwhelming and leaving no moment of deliberation. Sixty-four sorties after two incidents involving destroyers sent ten thousand miles across the ocean to survey the coasts of a hostile nation in the throes of civil war were not exactly what the authors of Article 51 had in mind.[11]

Fulbright, primed with arguments by the State Department's legal section, answered Javits with a rationale that was part of the Administration's Vietnam policy. Though he was sympathetic to the idea of "bringing the United Nations into it . . . it is not timely, when one is in dire straits, to turn over a situation such as this to a body which is not equipped to assert the kind of power I believe to be necessary to stabilize the area. . . . I believe that we have to establish some sort of stability before we can say to the United Nations, 'You take it.'"

*

*   *

"Mr. President."

Russell rose from his seat. Stennis inquired solicitously whether the Senator from Georgia wished to suggest the absence of a quorum, enabling Russell's friends to round up absent members while the clerk called the roll, but Russell said, "I do not think so. I thank the Senator, however, for his thoughtfulness."

With his face of a Roman proconsul who had seen what there was to see of nobility and meanness and good and evil, Richard Brevard Russell, a lonely man with neither wife nor child nor any life outside the Senate, a kingmaker who would never be king, acted on notions of right and wrong that were, in essence, rather simple. It was wrong, he felt, for one section of the country to try to change the mores of another part by Federal *Diktat;* he was, in consequence, the generalissimo of the Southern counteroffensive against the new march of civil rights (or "civil wrongs," as he called them) legislation being spurred on by, of all people, a Southern President, and he remained in gallant command of his forces even after realizing that slowing their retreat was the best he could do. It was wrong, he also felt, for the republic to waste its substance on treacherous ground far away; though the pillar of the military in the Senate, assuring them all the weapons they wanted and more, he conceived of American power as something to be husbanded for use *in extremis* and, more to the point, for its deterrent effect on Moscow (and, lately, Peking). When President Eisenhower decided to increase the thirty-five-man American military mission in Vietnam by sending several hundred additional training officers, Russell told Thruston B. Morton, now a Senator from Kentucky and then an Assistant Secretary of State, "I think you are opening up a trail today that will be costly in blood and treasure to this country, and that where there are two hundred and three hundred in Vietnam today, there will be thousands there tomorrow." [12] But once committed, American forces and American military prestige were to be backed up. That was enough to put Russell, in 1964, on the side of the Vietnam hawks. He was, in short, an orthodox Southern conservative, but his integrity, his occasional wisdom and the size of the issues associated with his name made him, even in his enemies' eyes, a big man.

"Mr. President." This was the voice of the Southern Democratic patriarchy, assured of re-election after re-election in the one-party South and in control, through seniority and alliance with conservative Northern Republicans, of the key committees and hence the Senate. The bustle in the chamber, as Senators entered or left the cloakroom or exchanged whispered remarks, was stilled. This would be the principal speech on behalf of the Gulf of Tonkin Resolution, the one that would carry the most weight.

Russell began by reminding the Senators of the qualms they had had about the Formosa, Middle East and Cuba resolutions. But what had happened to the power they had granted then? It was still in existence, in President Johnson's hands. Held in reserve during those three crises, it had done the job. And the same kind of power, granted today, would do the job again.

He didn't have to remind the Senators, Russell went on, about his own grave doubts about the original decision to go into Vietnam. But it would do no good to dwell on those doubts today. Second guesses were not involved in the question before the Senate. What was involved was the nation's right to operate its vessels on the high seas. Involved also was the national honor.

"Our national honor is at stake. We cannot and we will

not shrink from defending it. No sovereign nation would be entitled to the respect of other nations, or, indeed, could maintain its self-respect, if it accepted the acts committed against us without undertaking to make some response."

As for the resolution, no action could be taken in today's world that did not involve some danger. "It is not our purpose to escalate the war, but if events require a more vigorous response, this nation has the power, and I believe our people have the will to use that power. There is much more danger to turn tail and run."

Short as the speech was, it released in the chamber a spurt of that raw, satisfying patriotism that had been held in check by the intellectualizing of the liberals. At the same time it provided the balm of reassurance that the abstract hazards the liberals were harping on were not real-life ones. Maybe the resolution *was* a predated declaration of war, as Morse said it was, but then so were the earlier resolutions, and the Presidents then had not used them as such, and neither would Johnson. In fact, the word was that Johnson had been telephoning people on the Hill and assuring them he had no intention of sending troops to Vietnam.

Symington, a member of Russell's committee as well as of Fulbright's, voiced the general reaction to the Georgian's speech in his response: "It is a privilege to be on the floor of the Senate and hear my chairman once again express his pride and confidence in the future of America. It is also a privilege to associate myself with his remarks."

"From the beginning of the nation," Saltonstall declaimed, "Massachusetts men have always gone down to the sea in ships. We are proud of our Navy. Its prestige and the prestige of our country in the eyes of the world is at stake."

"I have always felt," said Hickenlooper, "that it was a little bit silly, if a fire started in one of the main buildings of a town or in someone's house, to call a meeting of the town council to determine whether the fire department should be called. Someone must get a bucket or a hose and put out the fire."

"Ominous and ugly," said Thomas H. Kuchel, Republican of California, "are the threat and thrust of Communism in Southeast Asia. Let friend and foe alike understand that we—America—shall keep the faith. Our country stands together in the face of danger. This is the clear meaning of our message."

"Our flag and our men have been fired upon," said Stennis. "Many hundreds, if not thousands, of our naval personnel could have lost their lives had the torpedoes been more accurately aimed. Either we must stand our ground or run away. Our honor, our safety and our security are at stake."

And so it went—one Senator after another rising to support the resolution (the President's hand had to be upheld, the prestige of the United States had to be protected, its commitments had to be honored), the chamber remaining no more than one third full as members took time off from other business to come in, speak briefly and leave. The resolution, it was clear, would pass by an overwhelming majority. So that it was with an air of resignation that the white-haired Ernest Gruening, former editor of the liberal weekly *The Nation*, former Governor of Alaska, rose from his seat.

It was always difficult, he said, not to accede to a request from a President of the United States couched in terms of high principle and national interest. But the Senate had a duty to advise and consent. This was not America's war. Americans were wholly misguided in picking up the burden abandoned by France ten years before. They were defending not freedom in South Vietnam but a series of corrupt and unpopular dictatorships, each owing its temporary sojourn to American support. The incidents in the Gulf of Tonkin were an inevitable development of the steady escalation of the American military program. Yet no threat to America's security was involved. "All Vietnam is not worth the life of a single American boy. We have lost altogether too many American lives already. Unless we reverse our policy, their number will steadily increase."

The sad sincerity of the quietly spoken speech had an effect. Frank Church confessed to his own doubts about American policy in Vietnam—"more the product," it seemed to him, "of our own addiction to an ideological view of world affairs than a policy based upon a pragmatic view of our national interests." He would vote for the resolution, but "with a heavy heart."

And Albert Gore, Democrat of Tennessee, silver-haired product of Southern Populism, a man of "really country" stock who had studied law nights in the Nashville YMCA, taught school and become one of the Senate's most telling debaters, said he had his doubts too. (They were not strong enough apparently, to have made him, a member of the Fulbright committee, attend that morning's hearing.) But he too would vote for the resolution, relying on the President's prudence.

＊

＊　＊

Mansfield, whose contribution was that of a loyal Majority Leader ("The President has acted with a cool head and a steady hand. . . . He asks for and he will have, in this endeavor, the support of Congress and the people of the United States") had a proposal. It was getting on to 6:00 P.M., and the debate wasn't going to be wound up that evening. He moved that the Senate resume debate the next day at 10:00 A.M., with a time limitation—two hours for the senior Senator from Oregon and one hour for all other Senators who wished to speak—and a vote at 1:00 P.M. The Senate gave unanimous consent.

But that did not mean that the Senator from Oregon was going to forego an opportunity to speak that evening.

"Mr. President!" Wayne Morse was on again. He had called the United States the previous day a "provocateur" in the Tonkin Gulf: "I repeat it tonight." A "snow job" was being done by the Pentagon and the State Department in regard to that South Vietnamese bombardment. Lausche, who objected that "our government had no knowledge" of that attack, was told that apparently he had not been "hearing very well" at the morning meeting. (It was a restrained rejoinder for Morse, who had once violated the rules on courtesy in floor arguments by calling a Senator a "tub of rancid butter," agreeing finally to retract the word "rancid.")

Yet McNamara at that very moment was giving public support to Lausche's position and undercutting Morse. At a 5:00 P.M. news conference at the Pentagon at which McNamara provided final details on the air strike, this exchange took place:

Q. Have there been any incidents that you know involving the South Vietnamese vessels and the North Vietnamese?
A. No, none that I know of.[13]

One more indication of McNamara's unwillingness to admit in public what he had conceded in private to the Senate committees as early as August 3. Why? The question was never raised by the only people outside the Executive branch who knew enough to raise it—the committee members.

Intervening in the Morse-Lausche argument, Joseph L. Clark, liberal Pennsylvania Democrat, said he disliked having to tell it to the distinguished Senator from Oregon, but the resolution would pass. "The resolution will pass," Morse retorted, "and Senators who vote for it will live to regret it. . . .

"Mr. President," he ground on, "we either believe in settling disputes by resort to the procedures of international law or by resort to war. After the second attack, we should have immediately laid our case before the Security Council. Bombing those sites was not necessary for self-defense at that point. At that point, the United States was guilty of an act of aggression."

After dealing at some length with principles of international law, the origins of the American involvement in Vietnam, the alleged hypocrisy of American claims to be seeking peace there, the language of the resolution and other salient points, the senior Senator from Oregon confessed bafflement over the wrongheadedness of those in high places who were responsible for this policy.

"I cannot understand what is happening to my country," he said. "I cannot understand what makes people think that way. If the yellow race has not made clear to the white man that Asia is not his fort, I do not know what the white man has to learn by way of an additional lesson. I do not agree with the North Vietnamese. I do not agree with the Vietcong. But they too have their international rights, and the place to settle the controversy is not on the battlefield but around the conference table. It is so easy to say that these things should not be said, that they create disunity and misunderstanding. So long as there is any hope to win a peace and stop a war, the senior Senator from Oregon will state the facts as he honestly believes them to be."

He stopped and glared around the almost empty chamber.

❋

❋   ❋

The House met to consider the Gulf of Tonkin Resolution at 11:00 A.M. the next morning. Time, by advance agreement, was apportioned with meticulous exactitude. Some members who wished to speak were allocated one and a half minutes. Others were given two minutes. The more important members got three. Majority Leader Carl Albert of Oklahoma got all of five.

This, said Albert, was "the most serious military confrontation since the Cuban missile crisis of 1962." "The American flag has been fired on," said E. Ross Adair, Indiana Republican. "We will not and cannot tolerate such things." William S. Broomfield, Michigan Republican, said that unless the line in Southeast Asia was held, "that part of the world could quickly swing from the side of freedom to the half-life of a Red puppet state," and "our main line of defense in the Pacific would be forced to fall back thousands of miles to Hawaii." Robert R. Barry, New York Republican, reminded the House that the Chinese "have been eyeing the rich rice paddies to the south for years." Clement J. Zablocki, Wisconsin Democrat, said, "The Communist campaign has moved into a new dimension." "These attacks," said J. Edward Roush, Indiana Democrat, "represent as real and distinct a threat to our freedom as attacks made on our frontier outposts when our nation was young." The only thing worrying Melvin R. Laird, Wisconsin Republican, was whether the President's new-found firmness really meant a strengthening of commitment "to take whatever steps are necessary to win the war." [14]

A half-dozen speakers resisted the tide. Bruce Alger, Texas Republican, warned that the resolution could make it possible for the President to bypass Congress in case he decided later to involve the nation more deeply in Vietnam. George E. Brown, Jr., California Democrat, asserted that to the mass of peasants in South Vietnam, "the Vietcong are the voices of freedom," however mistaken that view may be, while "we are but a continuation in their eyes of a hundred years of foreign oppression." James Roosevelt, California Democrat, one of the late President's four sons, wanted to remind the House that "the first principle of our foreign policy is peace." But their caveats were scarcely noticed.

What did cause a stir was a question raised by a Texas Goldwaterite, Ed Foreman.

It had been generally assumed that when Johnson told his nationwide television audience on the night of August 4 that "air action is now in execution" in reprisal for the naval attacks, he meant that the aircraft were then over their targets. But an official chronology of the air action two days later disclosed that the first strike had occurred at 1:15 A.M. August 5, Washington time—an hour and a half after the President's broadcast.[15] Goldwater's campaign strategists, chagrined at finding themselves boxed in on Vietnam, saw a chance to break out.

"I say to the House," Foreman cried, "what is this? What is this when we give an hour and a half notice of our attack upon the Communists?"

Alluding to the charge that Goldwater was irresponsible and shot from the hip, Foreman asked, "Can this kind of nationwide television appearance during prime viewing time be termed publicity-happy, political irresponsibility? Could such action be called 'shooting from the lip'?"

A chorus of boos from the Democratic side of the aisle drowned his words. "The parents, the wives and the families of the American boys that were killed in these air strikes," he proclaimed over the hubbub, "are going to be asking a very grave and penetrating question: 'Would we have our son or husband or daddy if the Communists had not been warned an hour and a half ahead of time?'"

Word of the flare-up was flashed to the White House. Reedy, the Presidential press secretary, issued an immediate statement. The President, he said, had not spoken until advised by the Secretary of Defense that "the planes had left the carriers." And McNamara followed up with a statement at the Pentagon saying he had recommended that the President schedule his announcement for 11:40 P.M. for the following reasons:

1. By that time, United States naval aircraft had been in the air on their way to the targets approximately one hour.

2. Hanoi, through its radar, had then received indications of the attack.

3. The time remaining before the aircraft arrived over their

targets would not permit the North Vietnamese to move their boats to sea or to alert their forces.

4. It was important that the people of the country learn of the manner in which their Government was responding to the attacks on its vessels from their President rather than from Hanoi, which was expected to announce the attack at any moment.

5. It was desirable that the North Vietnamese Government and others be told as soon as possible the character of the attack.

(The "others" were the Chinese Communists. The Administration, officials explained, wanted to make it clear to the Chinese, who had good radar facilities on Hainan Island, that the raid was directed against North Vietnam and not against them.)

As you know, the North Vietnamese Government did not have time to move their forces. Our attacking aircraft found the torpedo boats at their docks. The attack was highly successful.[16]

*

* *

The senior Senator from Oregon was indignant. An editorial in that morning's issue of *The Washington Post* had commended Congress for its prompt support of the President and had scored the "reckless and querulous dissent of Senator Morse." The senior Senator from Oregon was dissecting the Gulf of Tonkin Resolution to show that the *Post*'s approval of what it called this newly established "mechanism for meeting an emergency with a united front" was based on an unenlightened view of the Constitution. If Senators would only read his speech in 1955 on the Formosa Resolution, or his summation in his speech in 1957 on the Middle East Resolution, he would not have to summarize again his analysis of these resolutions as end runs around Article I, Section 8, of the Constitution—an article under which wars cannot be declared *in futuro* to meet hypothetical situations yet to arise, but only in relation to situations existing at the time when the declaration of war is sought. Which was why this resolution providing blanket authority to wage war was a surrender of prerogatives Congress ought jealously to guard.

"A constitutional principle is involved," Morse said to a Senate chamber filling up for the last three hours of debate. "It is dangerous to give to any President an unchecked power, after the passage of a joint resolution, to make war. Consider the procedural complications that could develop if Congress decided that the President was making serious mistakes in the conduct of a personal war—for it would be a Presidential war at that point. How would the President be stopped? He could not be stopped.

"What is wrong with letting the Constitution operate as written by our constitutional fathers? . . . Why this indirect amendment of the Constitution? . . . Why should we give arbitrary discretion to mere men who happen to hold office at a given time, when the American people and their lives are at the mercy of the discretion of those mere men?"

If he had sat down then, the blunt directness of his view, agree with it or not, would have had an impact. But Morse was just warming up. For another hour or more he would smother his major points under a weight of prolixity, amplification, digression, repetition. "Senators will remember that in 1955 and again in 1957 the senior Senator from Oregon made clear that . . ." He congratulated himself on his consistency, quoting anonymous Senators who had told him that he was, as always, right (while they, inferentially, were too craven to follow his example.) He vowed that the senior Senator from Oregon (unlike others) would not succumb to hysteria. Though yielding to no one in his aversion for Communism, he despaired of the shortsightedness of meddling in an Asian civil war and the immorality of doing it outside the framework of international law. On and on he grated, thinning out his audience yet another time. No matter. He was satisfied that "at the grass roots of America the people are overwhelmingly with the Senator from Alaska and the Senator from Oregon." His mail after his earlier two speeches was running more than a hundred to one in support of his position. The *Congressional Record* that day had ten pages of telegrams—a cross-section of the flood he had received—all favorable except for two, which "questioned the human source of my paternity." It was the other Senators, not he and Gruening, who were out of step with the people. The Senate was about to give the President warmaking powers in a procedurally unsound manner. "I believe that future generations will look with dismay upon a Congress which is now about to make such a historic mistake."

＊

＊　＊

Among the other Senators who hurried to record their support of the President in the last hour of debate, there was one holdout. Nelson had given further thought to his brush with Fulbright, and he proposed an amendment to allay the previous day's fears that the resolution would authorize an expanded involvement in Vietnam. Expressing approval and support of the President's action in bringing the Vietnam problem to the Security Council and of his pledge to keep response to provocation "limited and fitting," the amendment stated:

Our continuing policy is to limit our role to the provision of aid, training assistance and military advice, and it is the sense of Congress that, except when provoked to a greater response, we should continue to attempt to avoid a direct military involvement in the Southeast Asian conflict.

Would the distinguished Senator from Arkansas accept the amendment?

Fulbright seemed to hesitate. The amendment was unobjectionable, he said. It was a fairly accurate statement of

what he understood to be the President's policy. However.
...

Behind the scenes, Johnson had impressed strongly on Fulbright that no amendments should be accepted, "not even the Ten Commandments." A Senate-House conference to resolve the difference between the two versions could take days. The impression of national unity behind the President in the Tonkin emergency would be impaired.

Fulbright's indecision on Nelson's move was only momentary. The Senator's amendment, he said, was an enlargement of the resolution and would require a conference. It would confuse matters. It would cause a delay. He was sorry, but he could not accept it.

Just then a Senate clerk read a message from the other side of the Capitol. After forty minutes of debate the House had passed the resolution, 416 to 0. Fulbright said he hoped the Senate would approach that unanimity; it would have "a strong psychological effect upon our adversaries, wherever they may be." Dirksen joined him in a show of bipartisan unity. He was proud, the Minority Leader intoned, that at the Tuesday night briefing at the White House "every Republican who responded said he would support the President in his determination to meet the crisis now before us."

"I believe," declared Fulbright, summing up, "the joint resolution is calculated to prevent the spread of war, rather than to spread it, as has been alleged by some critics. I have considered every possible alternative, and I still have to come back to my own conclusion that the action that was taken, the joint resolution adopted in committee, and all our actions in this connection are best designed to contribute to the deterrence of the spread of war."

The vote, after a two-day total of six and a half hours of debate, was 88 to 2. (Ten members were absent.) No one joined Morse and Gruening in their lonely "nays," not even Nelson, whose attempt to clarify the resolution had been summarily rejected, or McGovern, who had said he "would not support the resolution" unless it were clarified, or Cooper, who had been troubled by the same imprecision, or Brewster, who had raised the issue, or Javits, whose hope that the resolution would be complemented by resort to the United Nations had been dismissed by Fulbright, or any Senator, such as Church or Gore, whose doubts about the nation's course had been sorrowfully confessed. Why?

Later, much later, when the question began being asked, a Senate aide who was in the midst of the proceedings during those two days recalled, "There were different opinions about the incidents in the Gulf of Tonkin, but Morse and Gruening were the only ones who reacted within the context of a general world view. Everyone else was on a much lower level of policy consideration—that is, Goldwater. The resolution was sold to the Democrats on the basis that it would help with the election. 'The North Vietnamese have shot at us, and we've shown them, but we mustn't let Goldwater get a free ride out of this.' As to the Republicans, they were stuck with it. The resolution was in line with what Goldwater was demanding. And the Republicans had always been more gung-ho anyway.

"Fulbright? He trusted Johnson not to use the resolution that way. He thought it would help deter the Communists from escalating the war. And it would put Johnson in a stronger position to resist Goldwater's campaign demands for escalating *our* role in the war. He really believed it."

❈

❈ ❈

"My fellow Americans—"

Once again Lyndon B. Johnson spoke for television from the White House, this time seated at a table in the East Room. It was August 10, and the "Joint resolution to promote the maintenance of international peace and security in southeast Asia" lay before him to be ceremoniously signed.

104

"One week ago, half a world away, our nation was faced by the challenge of deliberate and unprovoked acts of aggression. . . ."

Standing around him in the glare of the kleig lights were the members of the Cabinet, McNamara and Rusk in the foreground, the Joint Chiefs of Staff, the Congressional leaders—Mansfield, Dirksen, McCormack, Morgan, Russell, Fulbright—the men who had won him this victory. McGeorge Bundy, discreet assistant, favored the penumbra, but everyone knew how important his work had been.

The resolution before him, the President read from his formal statement, was the product of committee action and free and serious debate in both Houses of Congress. It had been passed by a combined vote of 504 to 2.

"Thus, today, our course is clearly known in every land. There can be no mistake—no miscalculation—of where America stands. . . .

"Americans of all parties and philosophies can be justly proud—and justly grateful. Proud that democracy has once again demonstrated its capacity to act swiftly and decisively against aggressors. Grateful that there is in our National Government understanding, accord and unity between the Executive and Legislative branches, without regard to partisanship. . . ."

"It is everlastingly right that we should be resolute in reply to aggression. . . . But it is everlastingly necessary that our actions should be careful and should be measured. . . . So, in this spirit, and with this pledge, I now sign this resolution."

The Chairman

7

Success came naturally to James William Fulbright. It was as though the gods conspired, when a fourth child was born to a country banker and land dealer named Jay Fulbright, that the boy would have health (living out the legend of the rugged halfback whose touchdown wins the big game of the season, as his did for the Arkansas Razorbacks against SMU was as wild a glory as any seventeen-year-old American can experience) and wealth (Jay prospered and added lumber and a newspaper to his holdings) and looks and a good mind, not a bookworm's mind or a dreamer's or crusader's, for no side of him was to be developed to excess (he went through the University of Arkansas on B grades, president of the student body, member of all the better clubs), but a mind capable of patrician independence ("Is it not strange that we should be so harsh toward Russia?" observed young Senator Fulbright in his maiden speech. "As I read history, the Russian experiment in socialism is scarcely more radical, under modern conditions, than the Declaration of Independence was in the days of George III") and happiness (he courted and married Elizabeth Williams, a vivacious Philadelphia Main Line brunette, and took her back to a log house in Arkansas, and wherever they lived after that, they and the two daughters she bore him, their days were unclouded and full) and accomplishment.

Remarkable accomplishment, remarkably soon.

Copping a Rhodes scholarship award for 1924 wasn't too difficult, and rugby and tennis opened as many doors to student clubs in Oxford as football and tennis had in Fayetteville, Arkansas. (But keeping up with his British peers writing critical papers for the Johnson Society meant some serious reading, which he had hitherto managed to avoid.) Bill Fulbright acquired polish and a not inconsiderable measure of knowledge at Pembroke College, and both were buffed by an interlude amid the salons and political cafés of Vienna under the patronage of the omnipresent Hungarian émigré M. W. (Mike) Fodor, correspondent for *The Manchester Guardian* (there was Walter Duranty holding forth at the Café Louvre on Wipplinger Strasse, and Dorothy Thompson and John Gunther and William L. Shirer, and "I remember people would come in there from *The New York Times* and other papers, big papers in the U.S., and have long conversations with Fodor"), and by the time he was established back in Fayetteville, president of the University of Arkansas at thirty-four ("Many remarks have been made about my youth. I mean no offense by it, and am confident that definite progress is being made every day to correct it"), it required only a nudge to launch this hometown cosmopolite on a political career. His mother Roberta provided it. A former country schoolteacher who had had to take over the family business when she was widowed in 1924, and who had found in the family-owned Fayetteville newspaper an outlet for self-expression on public affairs, Roberta said some unkind things in her column, "As I See It," about the winner of a gubernatorial contest, whose response was to make it plain that he would be pleased—since his new appointees controlled the university's board of trustees —if Mrs. Fulbright's boy resigned. The boy said they'd have to fire him first, so they did, and the Fulbrights' friends ran him for the House of Representatives in Washington, D.C., and he won.[1]

It was 1943 and Washington was the spinning capital of the allied world, and Fulbright no sooner arrived there than he found himself a national celebrity. Clare Boothe Luce, the beauteous consort battleship of Henry Luce, publisher of *Time* and proclaimer of the "American Century," was elected to the House the same year and used her maiden speech for an acid attack on the "globaloney" of the Roosevelt Administration's plans for cooperating with Russia and Britain in the postwar organization of the world. Fulbright, who had spoken at street corners during his campaign on the theme he felt most strongly about next to education, the importance of using the war against the Fascists as an opportunity to create a new world, a new League of Nations, feeling foolish addressing his earnest message to the sleepy country air, decided to make his own maiden speech a rebuttal. With his wife sitting in the galleries, he punctured Mrs. Luce's "imperialistic arguments" with a nice irony and bested her in an exchange of repartee. Now it was the liberals who laughed, and Fulbright was adopted by the liberal Eastern establishment as one of theirs, though he was to try them sorely and often down the years.

World repute came just as swiftly. A short resolution he introduced in 1943, "favoring the creation of appropriate international machinery with power adequate to prevent future aggression and to maintain lasting peace," fell in perfectly with FDR's designs, and the "Fulbright Resolution," along with a similar one in the Senate, helped to make the United Nations possible. A simple notion that occurred to him in 1946—since a scattering of American jeeps, trucks and other war surplus lay rusting in Europe and Asia, and the local governments wanted to buy it but didn't have the dollars, why not let them pay with their own currencies and use the money to enable Americans to study abroad and foreigners to study in the United States?

—led to the Fulbright educational exchange program, making the Senator from Arkansas (he was Senator by now) godfather to a generation of "Fulbright scholars" in two hemispheres, even if in some of the remoter reaches of Asia and Africa the grants seemed to have been attributed to the largesse of a recluse American billionaire.

He probably could have been Secretary of State. Kennedy wasn't planning to let control of foreign policy out of his own hands, but he wanted a good counselor and articulator and he liked Fulbright's civilized tone on foreign affairs. The Senator was at the top of his list of possible appointees. But Fulbright, who was chairman of the Foreign Relations Committee by then, the post having come to him in 1959 through swift attrition of aging members, preferred to stay in the Senate, which he found congenial, and asked Russell to ask Kennedy not to ask him, since it would be hard to refuse. Kennedy, who must have weighed the strengths of such a choice against the weaknesses, foremost among them being Fulbright's orthodox Southern voting record on civil rights, respected his wishes.

Civil rights. How were his liberal admirers to reconcile his enlightened speeches with his votes against any and all bills for racial equality? One explanation heard was that he had made an unspoken arrangement with the white voters of Arkansas under which he would not disturb their prejudices if they would keep him in Washington to do what he wanted on foreign affairs—a deal rendered less painful to his conscience, perhaps, by the rationale that prejudice is curable not by legislation but by education (he supported Federal aid to schools). Others thought that this theory owed more to the liberals' own wish to believe that such votes hurt Fulbright's conscience than to the Senator's outlook. Though no racist himself, Fulbright, they thought, had the Southern gentleman's tolerance of Southern racial attitudes and a generally pessimistic view of the perfectibility of human nature.

At any rate, the liberals forgave him for it, even when he signed the "Southern Manifesto" attacking the Supreme Court on school desegregation in 1956 while Albert Gore and Estes Kefauver of Tennessee refused to sign and survived. (Johnson, as Majority Leader, was spared the test.) They forgave him his votes for the power and natural gas interests, explaining it as the expediency forced on any Arkansas Senator by the moneyed plantations of the state's eastern flatlands. They forgave him his conservative record on labor legislation, conceding that there was a lot of the country-squire conservative (as distinct from reactionary) in him and that he was hard to pigeonhole in American political terms. They forgave him his votes for the Mundt-Nixon Internal Security Act and other "antisubversive" legislation of the nineteen fifties—as well they might, for many a certified liberal voted the same way in the anti-Communist fervor of the time. Why Fulbright, who did not share in the liberals' crusading zeal and seemed unpanicked by Communists abroad, should have nevertheless joined the general voting pattern on this issue—when even dyed-in-the-wool conservatives like Stennis and John McClellan, the other Arkansas Senator, opposed one or two of the measures as subverting the Bill of Rights—is an interesting question. One answer may be that he did not, at that time, care deeply enough about the principles involved to take an independent stand.

When some issue did stir him up, his independence of mind quickly asserted itself. He would hole up in his book-strewn office and read everything his staff could find him on the subject, much as he had swotted over his presentations at Oxford, and emerge an eloquent loner. He crossed Truman as early as 1945, deploring the dropping of the atomic bomb on Hiroshima, the seizure of Cold War initiatives and, generally speaking, the abandonment, as he saw it, of FDR's road to a more peaceful world, until Truman was goaded into calling him an "overeducated, Oxford s.o.b." He hurt the Democratic party's 1952 election prospects with an exposure of influence peddling within the Reconstruction Finance Corporation, appending the moral that corruption in government was a greater threat than the Russian Bolsheviks. He dared to attack the "swinish blight" of McCarthyism, and when Joe McCarthy's final blackmailing of his own Senate colleagues induced the Club to destroy him, Fulbright wrote the bill of particulars for the censure motion that did the job. He held hearings in 1957 which stripped bare the State Department's attempt to make travel abroad a privilege to be granted or withheld by government bureaucrats acting on secret information, paving the way for the Supreme Court's dismissal of this novel—for Americans—philosophy. He castigated the policies of John Foster Dulles, as grounded in a simplistic "fear of the deviltry of Communism," and opposed the secret Bay of Pigs invasion plan, though he did so in a private memorandum to the new President, the whisper of a dissenting courtier, rather than as chairman of a Senate committee established to exercise a check, in full light of day, on the Executive. (Influencing Executive decision making by private memoranda had, in fact, become Fulbright's preferred *modus operandi* with the Democrats' return to power. It was in a memorandum to Kennedy and McNamara that he accused the Pentagon of trying to brainwash the country by promoting business and community "seminars" under right-wing auspices. The accusation broke into public print, where it did the most good, only when Thurmond revealed it, thinking to hold Fulbright up to public censure.)

In December, 1965, Senator Fulbright withdrew into another personal cram course—on Vietnam.

He had not been, up to then, overly concerned with Indochina. "I was entirely preoccupied with Europe. I don't recall we ever had a hearing on Vietnam." He supported the policy that seemed to be sucking the United

States ever deeper into Vietnam because, as he told his aides, he could not think of a better one. The report his committee submitted to the Senate after the Gulf of Tonkin hearing was the straight State Department version of the conflict as a simple case of aggression from the north.

Now he began looking into it more seriously. Books on the origins of the Vietnam struggle by (mostly French) journalists and scholars were beginning to appear, and he read them, as well as Han Suyin's *The Crippled Tree*, a book published in 1965 that provided some poignant insights into China's (and, by extension, Vietnam's) sense of humiliation at the hands of the West, and had long talks with Bernard B. Fall, whose masterwork, *The Two Viet-Nams*, was breaking new ground in American thinking on Indochina. The key question for him was whether this was outside aggression, a tidal advance of international Communism endangering American interests, or a nationalist revolution under indigenous Communist leadership—a civil war, in short, in which, as Morse and Gruening kept insisting, the United States should not have interfered. For he had decided by now that on Vietnam Lyndon Johnson was no longer to be trusted.

All the fears that had been voiced during the Senate debate on the Gulf of Tonkin Resolution had come true—and all of Fulbright's reassurances that the fears were groundless had come back for him to eat, bitter as wormwood.

He had assured the Senate that Johnson had no intention of sending a combat army to South Vietnam—and Johnson had done just that.

He had assured the Senate that Johnson would go back to Congress if, all expectations to the contrary, he found it necessary to change the nature of the American mission—and Johnson had not.

He had assured the Senate that the essential purpose of the resolution was to deter the North Vietnamese from attacking American ships and prevent a widening war,

rejecting the Nelson amendment that would have made
that explicitly clear, and now Johnson was carrying a copy
of the resolution in his inside pocket, his "504-to-2 resolution," as he called it, his Congressional authority for his
new Vietnam course, reading it out to anyone who voiced
reservations, responding heatedly at a news conference,
"That language, just as a reminder to you, said, 'The Congress approves and supports the determination of the President as Commander in Chief to take all'—*all*—ALL—'necessary measures to repel any'—*any*—ANY—'armed attack
against the forces of the United States.'"

He had made himself Johnson's agent, to help him repel
Goldwater and Goldwater's demands for bombing North
Vietnam, and had followed up by assailing Goldwater and
campaigning for Johnson and seconding his nomination at
Atlantic City ("I commend Lyndon Johnson to this convention and to all our people as a man of understanding,
with the wisdom to use the great power of our nation in
the cause of peace"), and now Johnson was putting the
Goldwater program briskly into effect.

He who was the Senate's institutional watchdog on foreign policy had unwittingly guided the Senate into a hasty
and unintended sanctioning of a dangerous foreign adven-
ture. Whether he knew that some were suggesting collusion
between him and Johnson in 1964, the thought that such
suspicion was likely to arise could not have escaped him.
Nothing in his well-ordered career had prepared him for
this cavernous pitfall. He felt he had been deceived.

*

*　　*

Johnson's 1964 campaign statements were those of a
President who had punched the Commies in the nose when
they challenged him but who wasn't about to be rattled into
any foolishness:

We don't want our American boys to do the fighting for Asian boys. We don't want to get involved in a nation with seven hundred million people and get tied down in a land war in Asia (*September 25*).

We are not going north and we are not going south; we are going to try to get them to save their own freedom with their own men (*September 28*).

We are not about to send American boys nine or ten thousand miles away from home to do what Asian boys ought to be doing for themselves (*October 21*) .

The crowds cheered. Johnson was the peace candidate, the Commander in Chief in firm and prudent command, his standing high in the polls he carried in his pocket. Goldwater's halfhearted attempt to revive the "soft-on-Vietnam" issue was a dud.

On September 18, 1964, there was another Gulf of Tonkin incident. Two American destroyers on patrol engaged in a night battle with four radar contacts that was remarkably similar to that of August 4. The Administration clamped a tight lid on all details, and within a few days Defense officials were saying the radar blips might have been "ghosts" formed by atmospheric conditions or crests of waves.

Two days before the election, Vietcong mortars hit a South Vietnamese air base. Six U.S. B-27 bombers were destroyed; five Americans were killed. Johnson let it pass.

"It seems that I have spent my life getting ready for this moment," said Johnson on election eve, and the moment surpassed even his Texas-sized dreams: a landslide, more than 60 percent of the popular vote, the largest share in the country's history, and lopsided Democratic majorities in the House and Senate.

Just before the inauguration the Vietcong struck at an American officers' billet in Saigon. Johnson let it go.

But when the Vietcong mortared an American military barracks and airfield at Pleiku on February 7, 1965, killing

8 Americans and wounding 108, the White House announced an immediate retaliatory air strike

in response to provocations ordered and directed by the Hanoi regime . . . [and] made possible by the continuing infiltration of personnel and equipment from North Vietnam. . . . As in the case of the North Vietnamese attacks in the Gulf of Tonkin last August, the response is appropriate and fitting. . . . [W]e seek no wider war.

With map and pointer McNamara identified the "staging areas" above the seventeenth parallel struck by the forty-nine aircraft from carriers in the South China Sea.

The air strike occurred while the new Soviet Premier, Aleksei Kosygin, was visiting Hanoi as part of a Soviet-led effort to arrange for negotiations. Arthur Krock, columnist and former chief of the *New York Times'* Washington bureau, reported on February 10 that the strike had been prepared in advance, to be implemented the next time American forces were attacked. Escalation followed.

February 10—The Vietcong blow up a U.S. barracks, killing nineteen Americans. U.S. aircraft in greater numbers retaliate against North Vietnam.

February 18—American-piloted planes for the first time attack Vietcong positions in South Vietnam.

March 2—The United States for the first time bombs North Vietnamese installations not as an act of reprisal but because they are "being used by Hanoi to support its aggression."

March 8 and 9—Some 3,500 marines, the first American combat troops to be sent to Vietnam, wade ashore to guard the U.S. air base at Danang.

March 19—The bombing of North Vietnam begins on a continuous basis. The ninety-four warplanes moved into Vietnam and Thailand immediately after the Tonkin Gulf incidents join the carrier-based aircraft in the wider war.

This totally unexpected turn of events sent deep political currents flowing. One was a shift of Goldwater supporters to Johnson's side and a drop of support among liberals and moderates. Another was a rallying of Congressional conservatives of both parties behind the President, and a painful confusion among liberals and middle-of-the-roaders who were enthusiastic about Johnson, the fashioner of the Great Society, but alarmed by the emergence of Johnson, the Asian cowboy. The sense of shock was felt most keenly in academic circles, which had been particularly active in mobilizing campaign support for Johnson, and a phenomenon called the teach-in—day-long student-faculty discussions on Vietnam, sometimes in place of regular classes—made its zealous and often vehement appearance on campuses from coast to coast. But in the country as a whole, Johnson's polls assured him, confidence in him remained solid. Each new step into Vietnam, such as the piecemeal buildup on the ground that raised the number of combat troops to 34,000 by May, was presented as an isolated decision made in response to the other side's escalation of the conflict. The general reaction in the country was: What else can the President do?

The President, having used the stick, offered the carrot. While declaring in a speech at Johns Hopkins University that "We are there [in Vietnam] because we have a promise to keep," [2] he also held out before North Vietnam the promise of unstinting economic aid within the framework of a Mekong River development project to dwarf even the Tennessee Valley Authority, if only North Vietnam would leave South Vietnam alone. "In the countryside where I was born," he said, "I have seen the night illuminated, the kitchens warmed and the homes heated where once the cheerless night and the ceaseless cold held sway." All this happened because of rural electrification. All this and more he would give the North Vietnamese with a billion-dollar appropriation by Congress, if only they would make it possible for him to do so. He offered, for the first time, "unconditional discussions" of a peaceful settlement.

Hanoi's answer was scornful defiance. The President

turned his attention to the muttering on the Hill. He wanted his "504-to-2" resolution reaffirmed. So, though he had plenty of transferable unspent funds in other programs, he sent Congress a special request for an additional $700,000,000 "to meet mounting military costs in Vietnam," appending these words:

This is not a routine appropriation. For each member of Congress who supports this request is also voting to persist in our effort to halt Communist aggression in South Vietnam. . . .

A quarter century ago it became apparent that the United States stood [in Asia] between those who wished to dominate an entire continent and the peoples they sought to conquer. . . . The consequences of our determination was a vast war which took the lives of hundreds of thousands of Americans. Surely this generation will not lightly yield to new aggressors what the last generation paid for in blood and towering sacrifice. . . . The Communist aim in Vietnam is not simply the conquest of the South. . . . It is to show that American commitment is worthless. Once that is done, the gates are down and the road is open to expansion and endless conquest. . . .

I deeply regret the necessity of bombing North Vietnam. But we began those bombings only when patience had been transformed from a virtue into a blunder—the mistaken judgment of the attackers. . . . We then decided we could no longer stand by and see men and women murdered and crippled while the bases of the aggressors were immune from reply.

But we have no desire to destroy human life. Our attacks have all been aimed at strictly military targets. . . .

Our conclusions are plain. We will not surrender. We do not wish to enlarge the conflict. We desire peaceful settlement and talks. And the aggression continues. Therefore I see no choice but to continue the course we are on. . . . Nothing will do more to strengthen your country in the world than the proof of national unity which an overwhelming vote for this appropriation will clearly show.[3]

The House voted 408 to 7 with little discussion, but only after hearing George E. Brown, Jr., California Democrat, address words to Johnson the House had not heard before. "Mr. President, you are on the wrong path. You are gambling the welfare of the United States on the illusion that liberty, democracy and the peace of mankind can be won by the slaughter of peasants in Vietnam." [4]

In the Senate, which voted 88 to 3 after an agitated five-hour debate, with Nelson joining Morse and Gruening in opposition, the senior Senator from Oregon concluded, "I say sadly and solemnly, but out of deep conviction, that today my Government stands before the world drunk with military power." [5]

Members of Congress, including Fulbright, who remonstrated with Johnson privately, were perturbed by his mood. Keyed up and defensive, living off his store of nervous energy as he stayed up past midnight until "my boys" had returned from his targets for the day (he selected them personally from the JCS list), he subjected his visitors to harangues and hours-long briefings by subordinates, justifying his policies when other arguments failed by saying they didn't have the intelligence information he had. Johnson was, in fact, trying desperately to avoid a decision that he knew would drastically affect the nature of his Presidency, hoping against hope that something—a victory in the field, Uncle Ho crying quits, *anything*—would come along to make it unnecessary.

His Presidency thus far had been one in which everything except Vietnam yielded to his touch. The 1964 crop of Great Society legislation—the Keynesian tax cut for stimulating the economy, the civil rights bill he won without the compromises sought by the South (even though he had to humble Dick Russell to do it), the new measures on Federal aid to education and to mass transit—all this was only prelude to the harvest being gathered in 1965. Free medical care for the aged, Federal protection of Negroes' voting rights, a Federal-state program for cleaning out the nation's deep pockets of poverty, regional integration of economic growth, a start on rescuing the nation from industrial pollution—one by one, the bills left over from the renovating season of the New Deal rolled from Congress to the White House for Lyndon B. Johnson's signature. By the summer of 1965 he was expanding the horizons of the New Deal. His dream for America was coming true. But his stand in Asia was under threat. And he didn't have to be a seer to know that what he did about the second would affect the first.

South Vietnam had a 500,000-man army, but it was demoralized and stretched thin. With about 20,000 men infiltrated from the North since 1958, the guerrilla force was now estimated at 100,000. On April 27, 1965, Mc-Namara announced confirmation within the previous month of the presence of a battalion (about 500 men) of the regular North Vietnamese army—an ominous new factor in the equation. A secret report from the American commander, General William C. Westmoreland, warned of a summer offensive by the Vietcong to cut South Vietnam in two.[6] Westmoreland predicted the collapse of the Saigon regime within months unless the American forces, grown by mid-July to 75,000 men, with essentially defensive duties, were augmented by 100,000 men by the end of 1965 and another 100,000 in 1966 and thrown into offensive operations. McNamara, who had brought the estimate back after another visit to South Vietnam, joined in the recommendation, as did the Joint Chiefs of Staff.

Averse since Korea to land wars on the Asian continent and distrustful of military advice from his earliest days in Congress, but forced to admit after six months of bombing that neither his stick nor his carrot were having any effect on his unfathomable adversary, Johnson appears to have gone through an excruciating week, pacing the back corridors of the White House, presiding over daily conferences in the Cabinet Room, deadly calm on the surface, as he always was in a crisis, but under obvious internal stress— and, finally, accepting the recommendation though rejecting the proposed call-up of reserves. On the evening of

July 27 he summoned Congressional leaders of both parties to the Cabinet Room. He told them he had decided to send 50,000 more men to South Vietnam—without revealing that another 150,000 would follow in the months to come—and appealed for bipartisan support, as he had done in that same room at the time of the Tonkin Gulf incidents. McCormack said he was their leader and they'd stand behind him. But Mansfield, who had told President Kennedy in a special 1963 study that "there is no interest of the United States in Vietnam which would justify the conversion of the war in that country into an American war" and who now saw that conversion taking place, read a three-page typed statement of disapproval, while assuring the President that he would support him publicly. The only other dissenter at the meeting was Fulbright.

＊

＊　＊

Poles apart though they were in many ways, there had always been an affinity between Fulbright and Johnson, Southerners to the marrow yet standing apart from the South, both of them, in the national cast of their perspectives. "Bill Fulbright is *my* Secretary of State," Johnson used to say when he was Majority Leader, and Fulbright thought Kennedy would be "as good a President as he makes use of Lyndon Johnson's political genius." At the beginning of April, before the President seemed wholly committed to his new course, Fulbright wrote a memorandum to Johnson, urging the viewpoint that the danger in Asia was not Communism so much as Chinese imperialism, and that a strong and independent Vietnamese regime, even one that called itself Communist, would be a better bulwark against China than weak anti-Communist regimes propped up by American troops and money. He went over the memorandum with McNamara, who was noncommittal, and handed it to Johnson at a White House dinner. The President took it without comment. Fulbright never heard of it again.

But Johnson *had* accompanied the step-up in military pressure with an offer of peace talks, and when he asked Fulbright in June to help him maintain what he explained was his middle position, in the face of pressures for irresponsible withdrawal on the one hand and steeper escalation on the other, Fulbright responded with a speech assuring the Senate that the President remained "committed to the goal of ending the war at the earliest possible time by negotiations without preconditions." A month later Johnson announced the dispatch of 50,000 more men.

It was Fulbright's hardening suspicion that Johnson was pulling the wool over his eyes that was the catalyst for the break that occurred over an event in an entirely different region. Closed hearings held by the Foreign Relations Committee in July, 1965, into Johnson's military plunge into the Dominican Republic that April produced evidence of such overreaction to the "Communist" danger, such unblushing exaggeration on Johnson's part (the "fifteen hundred innocent people . . . murdered and shot and their heads cut off" proved to be a figment of the imagination), as almost to vindicate Morse's charge that the President was becoming power-mad. If Johnson was ready to intervene in Latin America against any revolt in which even the smallest Communist role was suspected, he would restore to the United States the role of the hated policeman of the Western Hemisphere that Roosevelt had abjured by solemn treaty. After brooding over it for more than a month, Fulbright denounced the Dominican intervention in a major Senate speech. Not since William E. Borah's attack on Coolidge's intervention in Nicaragua in 1927 had a chairman of the Foreign Relations Committee defied a President of his own party as Fulbright did that day. He sent Johnson an advance copy of the speech, together with a letter submitting that "constructive criticism" was sometimes the best service a Senator could render a President, but Johnson was in no mood for such subtleties. Coldly and immediately, he cut Fulbright off.

The buildup in South Vietnam continued steadily—almost 200,000 men and no sign of a stop. The "conventional option" fashioned by McNamara was proving itself logistically in its first major test. But the divisions at home were widening. The teach-ins were exploding into off-campus demonstrations. The war backers were exhilarated and loud. Richard Nixon, observing the substantiation of his Vice-Presidential warning of 1954 that "putting our boys in" to prevent Communist expansion in Indochina was a step that might have to be taken, called for "two or three more years of intense activity to win military victory," now that the policy of drift had at last been abandoned.[7] Somewhere between the two extremes stood the older patriotism of men like Richard Russell, who declared in the midst of the buildup, "I don't think it [Vietnam] has any value strategically,"[8] but added on another occasion that "the flag is there, United States honor and prestige are there, United States soldiers are there," so South Vietnam could not be permitted to fall.[9]

In November an interesting disclosure leaped into the headlines. Johnson had said that "there has not been the slightest indication that the other side is interested in negotiations or in unconditional discussions, although the United States has made some dozen separate attempts to bring that about."[10] It now developed that just before his fatal heart attack in London in July, Adlai Stevenson had told Columbia Broadcasting System correspondent Eric Sevareid that in the fall of 1964 Hanoi had accepted a proposal by U Thant, Secretary General of the United Nations, that American and North Vietnamese emissaries meet in Rangoon, Burma, for peace talks—and that the proposal had been rejected by the United States.[11] A State Department spokesman explained that Rusk's "antenna" had not detected any sign that Hanoi was prepared for "serious" talks—or, as Rusk elucidated, that "the other side is prepared to stop trying to impose their will by force on South Vietnam." [12] Johnson's trumpeted offer of "unconditional discussions" thus turned out to be conditioned on North Vietnamese agreement to retire from the struggle. He was ready to talk if Hanoi was ready to give in.

Partly to counteract the unfavorable impression created by these headlines, but also because he hoped it would produce results, Johnson mounted a diplomatic rodeo on a world scale, suspending the bombing for thirty-seven days while six high-ranking officials cantered off to thirty-four capitals to find someone who might prevail on Ho Chi Minh to submit to the Johnson Treatment. He also asked Congress for another special appropriation of $415,000,000, the bulk of it for Vietnam, leaving it to Henry Cabot Lodge, who was back in Saigon as Ambassador, to underline its significance with the telegram: "A vote for the appropriation is [an] utterly indispensible act if one supports U.S. policy in Vietnam." Testifying on behalf of the request at a public hearing of the Senate Foreign Relations Committee, Rusk was explaining that Hanoi's refusal to respond to the latest search for peace left the United States with no alternative to "meeting force with force" when he was raked by a broadside from Fulbright. Why did the United States go into Indochina on the side of the French? Exactly what is the American commitment to Saigon? Why did the United States encourage Diem to violate the Geneva agreement to hold elections? Didn't the Communist-led insurrection begin only after that? What is the American objective now? [13]

Encouraged by their chairman's sudden militancy, Gore and a few others joined in. Rusk appeared gradually to realize that he had misjudged the committee's temper. "Senator," he said, "I regret that I did not, in the words of the House of Commons, have notice of this particular questioning. I would need to review the record and be much more briefed and detailed on it."

All right, Fulbright said, let the Secretary prepare himself and appear before the committee again. But, he said, the committee would be hearing from others as well. Its discussion of the issue thus far had been "rather superficial." It was the committee's duty to clarify the nature of the Vietnam involvement and what it was leading to and whether the objective justified the sacrifice in lives and treasure. There would be public hearings—in depth.

The lines were abruptly drawn. An appropriation bill that was to have served Johnson as yet another confirmation of Congressional support on Vietnam was seized on by Fulbright as legislative basis for a public challenge of the President's course. Stung by the *fait accompli* put over on him by his former Texan confidant, J. William Fulbright, writer of private memoranda, participator in White House tête-à-têtes, taker of prescient independent positions and preserver of Congressional-Presidential unity in moments of crisis, none of it of any perceptible influence on decision making within the Executive, was ready for the first time to substitute the Senate's judgment for the President's on an issue of war or peace and to use his committee as an instrument for arousing public opinion to the dangers of the President's policy. Late in life and after much hesitation, J. William Fulbright was outgrowing himself.

Collision   8

On the first two days of testimony CBS canceled its
commercial fare to televise the hearings live. When the
financial sacrifice involved drove the network management
back to a rerun of *I Love Lucy* on the third day of the
hearings, the head of its news division, Fred Friendly,
resigned, precipitating a *cause célèbre* on network responsibility to the public. By then NBC was doing what CBS had
started to do, so that between them the two networks gave
the country an unbroken view of a rare, unheralded and
gripping drama on Capitol Hill. In town and city, work
slowed down or stopped as employees coagulated around
the office television set. In many localities high-school classes
were let off on the five days between February 4 and 18,
1966, when the hearings were on. An estimated twenty-two
million Americans watched.

Johnson tried to divert attention from the hearings by
throwing together a Honolulu "summit meeting" with Premier Ky, the jaunty, scarf-sporting Air Vice Marshal who
had replaced General Khanh as South Vietnam's transient
savior. The obviousness of the attempt only succeeded in
dramatizing the public collision between the President and
the Senator. Returning, Johnson watched the hearings in his
Oval Office, bluing the air.

There had never been anything like it. Right in the middle of a war, the war was put on trial in the Senate. The courtroom spectators and ultimate judges were the American people. The witnesses for the prosecution led off.[1]

General James L. Gavin (retired). Military bearing, sincere face. Led paratroopers in the invasion of France. Former Army Chief of Plans and Operations. Opposed sending troops to Indochina in 1954. Opposes current buildup in Vietnam. Regards this supposed sideshow as hurtling out of control, leading to possible war with China. Proposes that the 200,000 men already there establish coastal enclaves. Dig in for the long pull. See what happens.

George F. Kennan. Country's most distinguished scholar diplomat, looks it—and sounds it. Master of words. Author of the containment doctrine. Feels it's been distorted. Never thought all Communists should be contained everywhere. Always assumed it was understood some areas are more important than others. Vietnam not one of them. No reason to have become involved. Communist regime in South Vietnam would be fairly independent of Peking and Moscow. Disorderly withdrawal now would be bad, but Vietcong can't be uprooted, except at a cost in civilian life and suffering he wouldn't like to see his country be responsible for. Goodwill of other peoples already being lost.

"I would submit that there is more respect to be won in the opinion of the world by a resolute and courageous liquidation of unsound positions than by the most stubborn pursuit of extravagant and unpromising objectives."

He quotes words spoken in Washington by John Quincy Adams on the Fourth of July, 1821:

Wherever the standard of freedom and independence has been or shall be unfurled, there will be America's heart, her benedictions, and her prayers. But she goes not abroad in search of monsters to destroy . . . She well knows that by once enlisting under other banners than her own, were they even the banners of foreign independence, she would involve herself beyond the power of extrication in all the wars of interest and intrigue, of individual avarice, envy, and ambition, which assume the colors and usurp the standards of freedom. The fundamental maxims of her policy would insensibly change from liberty to force. . . . She might become the dictatress of the world. She would no longer be the ruler of her own spirit.

Morse is ecstatic. Lausche is flustered. Hickenlooper is puzzled. What happened to "the international Communist theory of world dominion?" It's still there, Kennan says, but it's a quasi-religious tenet they profess, the respectable thing for good Communists to do. That doesn't mean they act on it for today or tomorrow, any more than the Moslems and Christians did in the Middle Ages. As for the Chinese, they haven't been particularly aggressive, except rhetorically, for reasons of face, and if the United States stopped encircling China militarily and excluding her from the world's councils, agreements with China could be reached too.

Witnesses for the defense.

General Maxwell D. Taylor. Author in the nineteen fifties of the doctrine of less-than-nuclear wars to preserve American interests. Served as Ambassador to Saigon after retirement as chairman of the JCS. President's special military adviser now. Fresh from the Honolulu summit. Nice-looking man. Nice smile. Says we're making good progress on the ground. Good hope that with this, and the bombing, the people in Hanoi will decide it's in their interest to halt their aggression. It's a contest of wills. They hope ours will break first. They remember they won more in Paris than at Dien Bien Phu. They hope to be as fortunate in Washington.

Morse bridles. This is the Administration line: The hearings are serving Hanoi's purpose. It is his recollection that, as the French people turned against the Indochina war, Pierre Mendès-France stood for office on a pledge to end it.

MORSE: If the [American] people decide that this war should be stopped in Southeast Asia, are you going to take the position that is weakness on the home front?

TAYLOR: I would feel that our people were badly misguided. . . .

MORSE: Well, we agree on one thing, that they can be badly misguided. You and the President have been misguiding them for a long time in this war.

Burst of applause from the spectators crowding the big, marble-columned, plush-curtained Caucus Room of the Old Senate Office Building and lining the walls three deep. Fulbright gavels it down. Russell Long, the new Democratic whip and the Senate's most impassioned defender of the escalation, takes over.

LONG: General. . . . Do you think we are the international bad guy or the international good guy?

TAYLOR: I hope we are the international good guys.

LONG: Would you like to see Old Glory pulled down over the First Marine Division or the 101st Airborne and a white flag of surrender run up there?

TAYLOR: No, sir.

LONG: Do you think those young men over there want to be brought home on anything less than honorable terms?

TAYLOR: They would deeply resent any settlement which nullified their gallant efforts.

LONG: If I had a son and he died in Vietnam, would you feel that boy died in vain?

TAYLOR: No, sir.

LONG: Do you have a son, General?

TAYLOR: I am very proud of having a captain in the infantry, in the 101st Airborne Division.

LONG: He is in Vietnam fighting for his country right now?

TAYLOR: Yes, sir.

The room is very still.

Symington says he visited a Vietnamese village where

the Vietcong had disemboweled the four children of the village chief, right before their mother's eyes, then disemboweled the mother before her husband's eyes, then the village chief himself. "Could you imagine in your wildest dreams any groups of Americans pulling a stunt like that?"

"No, sir, I cannot."

FULBRIGHT: Can you imagine in your wildest dreams of a Secretary of the Air Force agreeing to napalm a great city . . . resulting in the death of thousands of people? Can you imagine any President ordering the burning of these little children right before the eyes of their mothers?

TAYLOR: I am not sure of the situation.

FULBRIGHT: Isn't it a fact we did just that in Tokyo?

TAYLOR: The fire raid?

FULBRIGHT: Didn't we?

TAYLOR: I am not familiar with the details.

In a war, Fulbright says wearily, people use what they have. Knives or planes. Taylor objects: The war in Vietnam is a *limited* war with a *limited* objective, and one of the objectives is to protect the civilian population, "which we are trying to rescue and not destroy." Fulbright dismisses that. You say your objective is limited but you're asking the other side to surrender.

TAYLOR: No, sir.

FULBRIGHT: I don't understand this play on words. Maybe I am much too stupid to understand what it means when you say, "We are going to do what it takes to make them come to the conference table." This to me means they are going to have to, as they used to say in Ozarks, holler "Enough" or say "Calf rope." I would think a limited war would be where our real efforts are to seek a conference and propose a compromise.

TAYLOR: How do you compromise the freedom of fifteen million South Vietnamese, Senator? They are either free or not free.

FULBRIGHT: You can extend that reasoning and say, "How

do we compromise the freedom of two hundred and fifty million Russians?" Why don't we go over there and free *them?*

Next day: Dean Rusk.

*

* *

Colonel Rusk was happy in the army. Twenty years later, when the Vietnam war was Americanized, he still liked to follow military tactics. He'd say, "I don't see how they could have done this. You should have had your scouts out." Or, "I'd rather blow up a supply train than risk the life of one of my men." He was a man of great personal decency and integrity who had given up a good deal of money—which is different for someone who grew up dirt poor, as he did, than for someone born to wealth—to be Secretary of State, but he did see most issues with the uncomplicated practicality of an army pro charged with getting his outfit with a minimum of loss from here to there.

Some thought his World War II experience in the China-Burma-India theater had left him with a Yellow Peril view of China that came to full bloom in Vietnam, but those who worked closest with him said there was nothing racial about this—it was the old Communist peril in his eyes; it had simply exchanged a white skin for a yellow one when Mao Tse-tung proclaimed his doctrine of Wars of National Liberation, just as the Nazi peril had become the Soviet one at an earlier phase. There were forces of aggression abroad in the world that it was America's job to arrest, once and for all. Once the United States demonstrated to Peking (and Moscow) that the national-liberation war wheeze couldn't work, they'd give up on it and the world could have some peace. But if the idea were allowed to succeed it would be applied on a larger scale, and in Europe too, which is where the big game was. (Rusk was too clear-sighted to be an Asia-firster conceptually, though he may have been one emotionally.)

It really boiled down to the question of whether America kept her word. If her word was no good in Southeast Asia it was no good anywhere, the allies would lose faith in American commitments and the Communists wouldn't be deterred, and it would become a much more dangerous world, with a new world war, the last war for mankind, waiting in the wings. Some Administration figures who approached this apocalyptic vision in their public statements would confess to some pragmatic amendments in private, but not Rusk. His public and his private thinking were the same. In a private talk he could say things like "I just believe that when the American people put their shoulder to the wheel, we'll come out all right," as though he were making a confidential statement.

The high mission, implicit since the Truman years, of organizing a Pax Americana for disordered mankind found the most congenial residence in the breast of Dean Rusk. His boyhood on a hard-scrabble Georgia farm—his father, an ordained minister, eked out a living growing cotton and teaching school when a throat ailment prevented him from preaching—was spent in an atmosphere of moral striving. "We were under constant admonition to excel," one of his brothers recalls, "to go out in the world and do something." Dean did. He was a straight-A high school student in Atlanta, worked two years in a law office to earn money for college, supported himself through college working in a bank and waiting on boardinghouse tables, graduated magna cum laude, won a Rhodes scholarship, received the B.S. and M.S. degrees at St. John's College in Oxford, studied at the University of Berlin during summer vacations, was taken on in 1934 as assistant professor at Mills College, Oakland, California, and became faculty dean. (He also married one of his former students.)

Those who worked with him when he rose to the post of General Joseph ("Vinegar Joe") Stilwell's deputy chief of staff in India and, after the war, to the post of Assistant

Secretary of State for Far Eastern Affairs remember him as affable and reliable, if somewhat bland, but then there occurred the one indiscretion of his career, a lapse from cautiousness that gave a glimpse of the pugnacity smoldering underneath. Against the background of the showdown between President Truman and General Douglas MacArthur, who had wanted to expand the Korean war into Communist China, Rusk, speaking at a dinner arranged by Henry Luce, called for a new policy of fomenting rebellion against the Peking regime. (That was when he called the Mao government not Chinese but a branch office of Moscow.) The liberals were outraged, the MacArthur camp was exultant, Secretary of State Dean Acheson seemed bewildered and in 1952 Rusk left the State Department to head the Rockefeller Foundation.

Some reports were that he had been eased out to a soft berth. If so, eight years at the foundation, during which he directed the spending of $250,000,000 to promote the "well-being of mankind throughout the world," earned absolution, and Acheson recommended him highly to Kennedy for Secretary of State (while deprecating Fulbright as a dilettante), as did the banker Robert Lovett, a seigneur of the Eastern liberal establishment. The only other thing Kennedy knew about this obscure technician was an article of Rusk's in *Foreign Affairs* on the primacy of the President's role in making foreign policy; Kennedy liked that. The secretaryship he offered Rusk, after summoning him for one brief chat, paid $25,000 a year; Rusk was making an estimated $50,000 to $75,000 at the Rockefeller Foundation, but he didn't hesitate.

His years under Kennedy were not particularly happy ones. Among the flashing spirits of the New Frontier, this bald, moonfaced, hulking six-footer (he once said with one of his gentle smiles that he looked like "your friendly neighborhood bartender") was put down as a self-effacing hack, his one contribution to the mystique of Camelot the phrase attributed to him during the Cuban missile crisis: "We're standing eyeball to eyeball, and the other fellow just blinked." His major talent lay in setting out a problem in all its aspects and keeping them all in skillful order while palavering with foreign diplomats, but his reluctance to choose among alternatives and follow up on decisions once made appears to have exasperated Kennedy and led to thoughts of another Secretary of State for the second term.

It was under Johnson, more appreciative by temperament and background of the plain devotion of a self-made Georgia boy and more dependent on Rusk's sure grasp of the surface events of modern diplomatic history, that he came into his own as the articulator and shaper of policy—particularly after the decision to escalate in Vietnam. That decision Rusk was prepared to defend on Capitol Hill, in speeches and in news conferences, patiently, courteously, doggedly, grittily, emotionally, becoming the Administration's principal spokesman for the war, even though the liberals in 1965 began attacking him as a turncoat and a simpleton and the strain of the contention seemed to make him work even longer into the evenings and come in even more often on Sundays when there was no need—for on that decision, he fervently believed, and on the determination to stay with it, the future hinged.

✿

✿   ✿

"Why are we in Vietnam?"

The question that caught him off guard three weeks before is the question he makes his own this time, to catch the attention not so much of the committee facing him as of the millions on the other side of those television batteries. He proceeds with the answer.

Before the guns were silent in World War II, many governments sat down and wrote their ideas of a peaceful world order into the United Nations Charter. But the Communists returned to their demand for world revolution. They are now pursuing that objective through what they call wars of liberation. We are in Vietnam to prevent them from extending their power through such a war. Commitments to that end were made by Presidents Eisenhower and Kennedy. North Vietnam has sought to confuse the issue by making its aggression appear to be an indigenous Southern revolt. No one should be deceived. The war in Vietnam is as much an act of outside aggression as though Hanoi had sent an army across the seventeenth parallel rather than infiltrating armed forces by stealth. If Hanoi were prepared to call off its aggression, peace would come in almost a matter of hours. That is the simple message the United States has been trying to convey to Hanoi. But Hanoi and Peiping (Rusk never refers to that capital by its historic name, Peking, restored by the Communists) have rejected our proposal for unconditional discussions. They insist on prior acceptance of certain points, whose effect would be to deliver South Vietnam to Communist domination. And that we cannot do.

Fulbright doesn't thank him for his statement. There is a minimum of civilities. The soft Georgia accent and the Arkansas drawl are not enough to conceal a mutual antipathy. Fulbright says he wishes things appeared as simple to him as they did to the Secretary. He calls for questions.

Aiken takes the Pentagon's latest figures on the Vietcong. Killed since 1960, 112,000. Present strength, 225,000. Total, 337,000. Subtract the 63,300 infiltrated from the North since 1960. That leaves 273,700 guerrillas recruited and trained in the South. Doesn't that indicate "civil war aspects to this struggle, and that the appeal of the Vietcong to his fellow countrymen in South Vietnam is quite strong?"

Rusk concedes "elements of civil war in this situation." But the heart of the problem is external aggression. And when the United States has undertaken a commitment to resist aggression, it is duty-bound to meet that aggression.

134

AIKEN: That would include what, about eighty or ninety countries in the world?

RUSK: No, sir. This would include just over forty countries.

AIKEN: Only forty?

Fulbright asks if he'd have to vote against the new appropriation request if he disapproved of the policies being followed in Vietnam, since the Secretary told the committee during his last appearance that approving foreign-aid programs was a form of commitment. Rusk says he hopes the chairman would think carefully before turning aside from the declaration of policy embodied in the Gulf of Tonkin Resolution. Morse asks if the Secretary thinks the vote on the resolution would have been the same if the Senate had contemplated that it might lead to 200,000 or 400,000 or 600,000 American troops in South Vietnam. Rusk says he doubts the vote would have been much different. Morse says we'll see; he is offering a motion of repeal. Besides, he says, Eisenhower in 1954 committed himself to economic aid to Saigon, nothing more.

Rusk draws on the lessons of his younger days:

Hitler could see that the Japanese militarists in Manchuria were not stopped. He saw that Mussolini was not stopped in Ethiopia. This encouraged him. Now what happens here in Southeast Asia if Peiping discovers that Hanoi can move without risk or can move with success? What further decisions are they going to make? What difference will that make in Moscow about what would happen to our commitments elsewhere. . . ?

He tells the committee of the great debate in the Oxford Union in 1933, when he was an undergraduate there, on the motion "that this house will not fight for King and Country." The motion was moved by the great philosopher C. E. M. Joad, and passed, and Hitler quoted it as an indication that Britain wouldn't fight and he could pursue his ambitions.

But just a few years after that debate, C. E. M. Joad issued a statement saying to the young men who were in the Union that night, "Sorry, lads, but this fellow Hitler is different. Now get out there and fight." And a battalion of the Black Watch charged Nazi Panzers at Dunkirk with naked bayonets in order to help a few of their comrades get off the beach.

Church wonders if the analogy stands up. This recent treatise of Marshal Lin Piao, the Chinese army commander, is it really an Asian version of Hitler's *Mein Kampf*, a blueprint for Chinese conquest, as Rusk has been intimating, or is it, as some scholars say, a kind of "do-it-yourself kit" outlining the Chinese revolutionary experience as an example for others? Rusk concedes that "in practical terms thus far it takes on the shape of a do-it-yourself kit," but "that does not necessarily provide a guarantee for the future." And the situation in Asia, Church persists, isn't it quite different from the threat posed by Hitler? Rusk says there are differences but there are also similarities. And Ho Chi Minh is just an agent of Mao Tse-tung, is he? "Not entirely, not entirely." Then he is independent enough to come to a conference table even if Mao objected? Rusk is not sure.

Long is steamed up over the very idea of not voting to give the troops in Vietnam whatever extra money the Administration is requesting. He asks Rusk for assurance "that you are going to give them whatever help it takes to see that they are not cut off and surrounded and decimated as those people were at Dien Bien Phu." Rusk assures him the men will be backed up.

LONG: Mr. Secretary. You spoke to the American Legion. They tell me that those men stood there and applauded so long that people wondered if you were ever going to get a chance to make a speech at all. Have you ever in your whole lifetime found a much warmer reception anywhere?

RUSK: No, sir. On occasion I have found the other kind of reception.

LONG: Mr. Secretary, don't you think this is somewhat significant, that the men who have fought for their country in years gone by were proud to see a Secretary of State speaking for the President of the United States who is not the kind of fellow who believes in rolling over and playing a dead dog when the Communists take him on?

RUSK: Well, Senator, my duty, under the direction of the President, is to carry out the great stated policies of the United States.

LONG: I am going to ask that we send for men who have been to Vietnam. . . . Those boys know what it is to fight for the country and get hurt, and most of them don't regret it for a moment. They are proud that they served their country, even though they lost arms and legs and got shot to pieces. . . . I have a paper here that shows in these so-called peace demonstrations we have been having—not in front of them but always in the crowd—there is a bunch of Communists. They are the guys who lead the applause and start the cheering going for the speakers . . . those are the people we have been hearing so much about!

Gore says the troops in Vietnam are there not of their own choice but on government orders and will be backed up with all the supplies they need—that's not the issue. The issue is the decision to send them there. President Kennedy gave assurance to the American people that combat forces would not be sent to Vietnam. President Johnson, two days after the Gulf of Tonkin Resolution was approved, said he wasn't taking the advice of "some others" that he "supply American boys to do the job that Asian boys should do." How could the commitment to South Vietnam be as binding as Rusk claims if Kennedy and Johnson promised not to send combat troops there?

At the end, Fulbright makes "a few observations of my own." The struggle began as a war of liberation from the French. The Vietnamese nationalists were led by Communists, "most unfortunately, from our point of view." These "nationalistic Communists" were twice betrayed, once by the French in 1946, when they thought they had an independence agreement, and later in 1956, when Diem with American support refused to hold unification elections. After 1956, the struggle became a civil war between Diem and the Vietcong, the nationalistic Communists remaining in South Vietnam. So it's oversimplifying to say it's a case of aggression by North Vietnam. As for our efforts to negotiate, the real trouble lies in our peace terms. There's a lot of complicated talk about their points and our points, but we have never made it clear we would support an election under international supervision and abide by the results, or allow the National Liberation Front, as the Vietcong call themselves, to participate in a new government, and until we do we leave them no alternative except surrender or annihilation. Of course, if we put enough troops there, we can kill them all. All these questions should have been discussed during the debate on the Gulf of Tonkin Resolution. He regrets that he did not discharge his duties properly at that time. All he is trying to say now is that Vietnam is not the kind of test that will lead to a collapse if the United States accepts a compromise.

But how do you arrange a compromise, Rusk asks, if the other side won't talk? There must be something wrong with our approach, Fulbright says.

"Senator, is it just possible that there is something wrong with *them?*"

Fulbright pauses reflectively before answering. "Yes, there is a lot wrong with them. They are very primitive, difficult, poor people who have been fighting for twenty years, and I don't understand myself why they can continue to fight, but they do."

*
* *

The phones never stopped ringing in the offices of the Senate Foreign Relations Committee while the hearings were in progress. The calls came from all over the country. "Tell Senator Fulbright to ask him . . ." "Ask Senator Gore to ask if . . ." Mostly they were people calling to express their interest and gratitude. The flood of telegrams and letters continued after the hearings ended. The staff counted more than twenty thousand, a rare outpouring. They were heavily for Fulbright and against the escalation.

The Vietnam hearings, however unfocused and inconclusive, "broke through the official screen," in Walter Lippmann's words, "and made visible the nature of the war and where our present policy is leading us." For the first time, some of the fundamentals of the Vietnam struggle were uncovered before a national audience and presented for public debate. For an uncounted number of Americans who had harbored misgivings or opposition to the war but felt they did not have sufficient factual information for an independent judgment—or, having reached a judgment, felt isolated and helpless in the close atmosphere of conventional support for the President and the flag—the hearings were a breath of fresh air. This was not "the kids" flaunting their unkempt, new-found radicalism in the face of American moderation or the older peace demonstrators who could be dismissed by a State Department spokesman as constituting "an infinitesimal fraction of the American people." It wasn't just Morse and Gruening, their strident appeals reduced to a few sentences at the end of a newspaper story from Washington. This was the Senate moving. Fulbright the Sensible, with his national influence that far exceeded his influence in the Senate and with the power of television fleetingly in his hands, had made opposition to the war respectable. And the response was profound. Alienation from the deepening commitment in Southeast Asia began to grow in the Senate and even in the House and most noticeably in the nation—a response that came not so much from any new clarity about the nature of the involvement or any general idea of how the involvement could be terminated as from an inchoate feeling that in the piecemeal beginnings and abrupt enlargement of a war for which the people's clear support had never been sought, some essential compact between the government and the governed had been violated.

Deadlock 9

Lyndon Johnson was not comfortable with the suggestion that his 504-to-2 resolution, which visitors said had become dog-eared with handling, was a fraudulent document, so Rusk discovered the Southeast Asia Collective Defense Treaty (SEATO) as a legal basis for the war. "It is this fundamental SEATO obligation that has, from the outset, guided our actions in Vietnam," Rusk told the Senate Foreign Relations Committee during the Vietnam hearings,[1] as though forgetting that he had told the same committee at the time of the Gulf of Tonkin incidents that "we are not acting [in Vietnam] specifically under the SEATO treaty."[2]

SEATO was a leaky vessel for so heavy a load. It was virtually inoperative from the outset (1954) because of disinterest on the part of other members (Britain, France, Pakistan, Thailand, the Philippines, Australia and New Zealand) in joining the United States in fighting subversion in South Vietnam, the primary purpose for which it was devised. Hence, instead of acting in meaningful "consultation with others" as provided for by the treaty, the United States had been going it alone. It had now, in 1966, decided unilaterally that South Vietnam had come under "armed attack" within the meaning of the treaty—a deci-

sion it made on the basis of its own 1964 "interpretation"
of the text as permitting action by one member without
consulting the others in the absence of a dissenting vote.[3]
Even "armed attack" obligated a member to nothing more
specific than action "to meet the common danger in accordance with its constitutional processes." In the case of the
United States, as the Senate was assured in 1954, that
meant approval by Congress. When, the critics in Congress
now asked, had Congress given its approval? Why, said
Rusk, in the resolution of August, 1964.

So Johnson was cast back on his flawed resolution ("I
continue to be guided in these matters by the resolution of
the Congress approved on August 10, 1964—Public Law
86–408—by a vote of 504 to 2").[4] He would also, at times,
suggest that he really needed no authorization beyond his
own powers as Commander in Chief ("We stated then
and we repeat now, we did not think the resolution was
necessary to do what we did and what we're doing").
But Johnson wasn't as sure of his constitutional powers as
he made out, for even as he began building up his expeditionary force in the spring of 1965 and planning to move it
from guard duty to offensive combat operations he was
consulting his aides on whether he needed fresh Congressional authority for his new course of action. Nicholas
Katzenbach, who was then Attorney General, advised him
in a June 10, 1965, memorandum that he could go ahead
on his own authority as Commander in Chief provided he
did not go so far as to wage all-out war against a foreign
state, for he would then be infringing on the prerogative
of Congress to "declare war." Short of that, Katzenbach
said, Congress had already given him all the backing it
could in the Gulf of Tonkin Resolution; to go back for another expression of support would only make it seem that
the President lacked confidence in his legal position or in
public approval of his policy; he recommended against it.

As the insatiate demands of General Westmoreland's

search-and-destroy strategy burst the confines and man-power ceilings of the spring of 1965, the President was caught in a bind. He wanted to ask Congress for renewed support for the wider war it had not counted on, but he was constrained from doing so by his own Attorney General—who added the warning that another Congressional authorization, short of a declaration of war, could place restrictions on his freedom of action that he would find difficult to ignore. Johnson, of course, could have taken Morse at his word and asked for a full-fledged declaration of war. He might have obtained it, too, though not without a donnybrook, but that would have meant wage and price controls and a general political upheaval, and Vietnam was supposed to be an exercise of America's new McNamara-given ability to fight a limited war without mobilizing the resources that would be required for accepting the challenge of a general war at the same time.

It was a limited war, all the same, like no other before it. The aerial offensive against industrial and communications targets in the North was sizable enough—a greater tonnage of bombs dropped by the end of 1967 than on all of German-occupied Europe during the Second World War—but it was far exceeded in the scale of destructiveness by the operations in the South. The Kennedy-phase infatuation with counterinsurgency (Green Berets, elite adventurers, living among the people, speaking their language, eating their food, healing their sick, fighting the guerrilla with his own methods) was pushed aside by the regular army with its regular-army maxims: seeking out the enemy's main forces, and firepower. Firepower on an American scale against an enemy embedded in the peasantry meant devastation of the countryside: leveling of villages, creation of "free fire zones" where anything that moved was a fair target, decimation of forests by B-52s, poisoning of cropland, creation of a moonscape of craters, four million refugees (a third of the rural population) and no one knew how many hundreds of thousands of civilians dead and wounded by the end of 1967. And, in spite of all this, stalemate. An American army of half a million pitted against an estimated force of 250,000 "main-line" and part-time guerrillas and 50,000 North Vietnamese regulars (Hanoi's response to Johnson's escalation) was able to produce comparatively little in the way of enemy manpower fixed and destroyed, and areas cleared by American offensives reverted to the enemy after the Americans withdrew. (The South Vietnamese army had been relegated to rearguard duties.) Some of the military, Hanson Baldwin reported, were saying it would take one million Americans to do the job.

At every point in the Vietnamese tragedy when political alignments in the southern half of the country made accommodation feasible, American power and American methods had stepped in to upset the balance with a new investment for victory, American-style. Diem might have been forced to cooperate with the Vietminh and pro-Vietminh nationalists (who were not all Communists by any means) if Eisenhower's pledges had not encouraged him to turn instead to those domestic elements that had backed the French and to mount a campaign of rural terror against the Vietminh and all their real or fancied supporters. The revolt he precipitated might have produced a viable coalition between the Vietminh and those segments of the rural and urban population that, given the South's economic, cultural and religious distinctness, were not nearly as susceptible to the Vietminh's claim to the Mandate of Heaven as the more impoverished and Confucian North. But Kennedy threw more support behind Diem. By the time Johnson assumed the Presidency the Vietcong had gone so far in appeasing the land hunger of the Southern peasantry and winning or exacting their support that the ability of the non-Communists to rival them politically had probably been undermined, but there was still a chance of a coalition of non-Khanh Vietnamese and the Vietcong—of the middle and the Communists, instead of the right and the Communists—in which the Communists would be forced into political accommodation with the Buddhists and other groups. Johnson's escalation swept the cards off the table. The Hanoi government and its leadership cadres in the South were now so deeply committed to the struggle, with large-scale help in weapons and supplies from Russia and China, that whatever remained of South Vietnam after the war would either be Communist-dominated or a virtual American colony. The deadlock was symbolized by an exchange of letters between Johnson and Ho Chi Minh in which Ho agreed to negotiate if Johnson stopped bombing North Vietnam and Johnson said he would stop the bombing if Ho stopped infiltrating men and supplies into South Vietnam.[6]

The unpremeditated barbarism of the war that glanced across the front pages and television screens of America piled shock on top of opposition. It wrung a cry on the Senate floor from Robert Kennedy. "We're killing women, we're killing innocent people . . . because they're twelve thousand miles away and they might get eleven thousand miles away. Do we have the right here in the United States to perform these acts because we want to protect ourselves?"[7] The implacable investigator of the nineteen fifties, who had said on a 1962 visit to Saigon, "We are going to win in Vietnam; we will remain here until we do win,"[8] had changed since his brother's assassination. Aware now of the dark underside of the shining endeavors in which he had played so large a part, he was groping painfully to a repudiation of his own Vietnam past, to Johnson's dismay, now that Johnson had made it his present. Gore, in October, 1967, went further than any other Senator until then in proposing that the United States "extricate" itself by accepting neutralization of Vietnam. Thruston B. Morton, one of the Senate's most influential Republicans, created a sensation with a hawk-to-dove speech in which he re-called Eisenhower's parting warning about the dangers of too much power and influence in the hands of the "military-industrial complex" and added:

I believe that President Johnson was brainwashed by this power center as early as 1961. . . . I believe he has been mistakenly committed to a military solution in Vietnam . . . so have I. . . . In early 1965, when the President began to escalate the war, I supported the increased military involvement. I was wrong.[9]

As far as the military were concerned, however, they were operating under restrictions in the North, since they were not being permitted to bomb certain remaining in-dustrial and communications targets in the heart of the Hanoi–Haiphong complex and on the Chinese border or mine the harbor of Haiphong; and in the Senate Strom Thurmond demanded that the Administration drop these restraints, while from retirement in California General Cur-tis LeMay, the former Air Force Chief of Staff, said, "We must be willing to continue our bombing until we have de-stroyed every work of man in North Vietnam." [10] But these voices were now clearly in the minority in the Congress and in the country, if still a sizable minority. The majority viewpoint, according to the polls, was one of continued support for the President, but a support shot through with qualification and doubt.

The peace activists were becoming rapidly more vocal. *The New York Times* in 1967 came out with a series of powerful editorials calling for an end of the bombing and the beginning of talks. Other important newspapers began taking a similar line. The Luce publications were waver-ing. Antagonism toward the war mounted the stage in a succession of off-Broadway hits. Draft resistance spread. Drawing on a tradition of radical-liberal attack on the contradictions between the American promise and the

American reality, a new generation inspired by the Southern Negro civil-rights movement burst the mental barriers erected by the Second World War and the Cold War and was channeled by Vietnam into a nationwide surge of peace demonstrations. In October, 1967, an estimated 150,000 persons, mostly young, conducted an unprecedented "March on the Pentagon."

Johnson's initial reaction was one of pained forbearance. Likening his role to President Lincoln's during the Civil War, he said in a speech, "Sad but steady—always convinced of his cause—he stuck it out. Sad but steady, so will we." [11]

"There will be some Nervous Nellies," he said in another speech, "and some who will become frustrated and bothered and break ranks under the strain, and some will turn on their leaders, their country and our own fighting men." [12] As for him, he had "a sacred promise" to keep. [13] Always there was the inspiration of the brave Texans at the Alamo. "Just like the Alamo, somebody damn well needed to go to their aid. Well, by God, I'm going to Vietnam's aid." [14]

He led a caravan of five giant jets on a 26,000-mile political campaign across the Pacific, capping it with a seven-nation "Asian summit" in Manila and following up with an unscheduled descent on a surprised assembly of American fighting men in Vietnam ("I thank you, I salute you, may the good Lord look over you and keep you until you come home with the coonskin on the wall"). [15] He brought General Westmoreland back for a spine-straightening oration before a televised joint session of Congress, the first time an American battlefield commander had been recalled for such a purpose. [16] He conferred in Canberra with President Nguyen Van Thieu, South Vietnam's latest savior, working in another stopover at Camranh Bay, South Vietnam, on the way back, as well as a secretly arranged call on Pope Paul VI at the Vatican. [17] It all fell flat. The "watchmen-on-the-walls-of-freedom" rhetoric that soared when Kennedy

spoke it came leaden out of Johnson's mouth. The words
("We did not ask to be the guardian at the gate, but there
is no one else") [18] were often the same. But the times had
changed.

At the entrance to the White House pressroom there
hung a glass case with a row of pens and the inscription,
"With these fifty pens President Lyndon B. Johnson signed
into law the foundations of the Great Society." But of his
Great Society program, starved by Vietnam of funds and
attention, little more than titles remained, and the blacks
whose hopes had been raised by Johnson's antipoverty
speeches were venting their resentment in a debauch of
rioting, burning, sniping and looting in the cities. He no
longer carried the latest polls in his pockets. His personal
direction of the bombing campaign became increasingly
obsessive. One summer night, when the gradual broadening
of the industrial-target list was to come close for the first
time to the center of Hanoi and Haiphong, he told his
daughter Luci, "Your daddy may go down in history as
having started World War III," and accompanied her to
a nearby Roman Catholic church (she was a convert to
Catholicism) to pray.[19]

McGeorge Bundy had left—not because of any disagree-
ment over Vietnam ("you have set a course there that is
both right and brave," he wrote in his letter of resignation) [20] but, apparently, because of personality difficulties.
Bundy, who seems to have had ambitions of acting as in-
terlocutor for Johnson's roughhewn strength, succeeded
only in making Johnson feel patronized. "Perhaps, as Aunt
Jessie would say," wrote a White House resident, the ne'er-
do-well Sam Houston Johnson, in his book *My Brother
Lyndon*, a useful guide to some visceral Johnsonian reactions,[21] "he [Bundy] was letting his britches ride too
high." On the other hand, such White House innovations
as a reporting system on all telephone calls to the White
House staff were not for the likes of Bundy. When he told

Johnson of an offer of the presidency of the Ford Foundation, the world's richest philanthropic organization—in the hope, some say, of obtaining a counteroffer of a Cabinet post—his exit from the White House may have been faster than he had counted on.

In Bundy's place sat his onetime deputy, Walt Whitman Rostow, the ideologue of the New Frontier, a phrase he was credited with coining. Proudly christened by a Russian immigrant father who named his other son Eugene Victor (for Debs), Professor Rostow had made something of an international reputation with his 1959 "non-Communist manifesto," a theory on the stages of economic growth that undertook to refute Marx, though some economists dismissed it as lightweight. Kennedy, looking for causes for his Presidential campaign, called on him, among others, for ideas, and Rostow, then an economic historian at the Massachusetts Institute of Technology, responded with a fund of them, which remained prolific after he joined the White House staff.

One of his more germinal ideas was contained in a joint report with General Taylor when Kennedy sent the two of them to South Vietnam in 1961 to see what should be done. This was the conclusion that the priority problem in the countryside was not winning over the peasantry, as had been supposed, but providing military security, which could be done by larger commitment of American power— an infusion of military equipment and military advisers (a recommendation Kennedy accepted) and ground combat units initially numbering about 8,000 men (a proposal Kennedy rejected). Rural reforms could come later.[22] Communists, in Rostow's schema, were romantic vandals who interfered with free societies' orderly progression from one Rostovian phase to another, and the U.S. task was to keep them on their side of the line with that "sense of democratic mission which is at the root of our nationhood."[23] The contest in Vietnam was a pivotal one; the

149

bombing and the military operations were certain to succeed; history was on America's side.

Some called Rostow an amiable zealot who was protecting Johnson from unpleasant information on Vietnam, which Bundy never did, and providing optimistic rationales for the President's gut objectives. For Johnson, who had been so indecisive about widening the war, was now embattled as never before in his life. This was his test, as the Cuban missile crisis had been Kennedy's; he would prove himself. The country would prove itself. Americans were not for losing. The ordeal did not bring out the best in him. He railed in private against the press, the "knee-jerk liberals," Fulbright ("Senator Halfbright"), all of whom he felt were only inciting the hawks and giving Hanoi an exaggerated notion of the antiwar sentiment and thus making his policy of neither "surrender" nor further escalation all the more difficult to sustain. He even let fly at his own aides. "I can't trust anybody! What are you trying to do to me? Everybody is trying to cut me down, destroy me!" Angered by an incident in New York in which demonstrators threw eggs to protest Rusk's appearance, he insinuated at a briefing for Congressmen that Communists had been instrumental in directing the march on the Pentagon—encouraging thereby the demands for political repression that were already filling Congressional hoppers.[24] All but dropping his formal news conferences, he appeared less and less in public, confining himself mostly to military bases, were he was spared the eternal sight of the demonstrators with their placards and their awful chant, "Hey, hey, LBJ, how many kids did you kill today?" Johnson sat in the Oval Room with the news at his fingertips—muffled AP and UPI tickers chiming out their bulletins, one of three doors of a special three-screen television console flying open for instantaneous sight and sound when he pressed the appropriate button on his desk—yet he was increasingly out of touch. The news he could not read was that the trust that had been reposed in him by the Gulf of Tonkin Resolution and magnified a thousandfold by his election was being irretrievably withdrawn.

❊

❊ ❊

But Fulbright was not happy either. The impact of the Vietnam hearings exceeded his expectations, and (bringing demands from Goldwater that he resign) his speeches were quoted around the country and around the world.

Power has a way of undermining judgment, of planting delusions of grandeur in the minds of otherwise sensible people and otherwise sensible nations. The idea of being responsible for the whole world seems to have dazzled us, giving rise to what I call the arrogance of power, or what the French, perhaps more aptly, call *le vertige de puissance,* by which they mean a kind of dizziness or giddiness inspired by the possession of great power. . . . If the war goes on and expands, if that fatal process continues to accelerate until America becomes what she is not now and never has been, a seeker after unlimited power and empire, the leader of a global counterrevolution, then Vietnam will have had a mighty and tragic fallout indeed.[25]

But the bombers kept flying closer to the Chinese border, and the "body count" of enemy dead in South Vietnam continued to be the measure of American foreign policy, and no one in the Administration could give assurance that still more troops would not be required.

Sometimes Fulbright seemed to half regret his break with Johnson, wondering whether he had achieved anything more than loss of whatever influence he had had with the President. (His "bleeding," as Morse called it, was an affliction to which the Oregonian was immune. Asked by Johnson how he managed to stay so healthy-looking when a Senate group went to the White House on routine business,

Morse replied equably, "Well, Mr. President, I'll tell you. Every time I read in the papers what you're doing about Vietnam, it makes my blood boil. That purges me, it keeps me fit.")[26] In a troubled colloquy on the Senate floor with Russell, in which Fulbright again repented of his mistake on the Gulf of Tonkin Resolution and Russell assured him that enough mistakes had been made on Vietnam for everyone to claim his share, the Georgian pointed out that the Senator from Arkansas could always have recourse to the repeal mechanism in the resolution's text.[27] The clause, which had been suggested by Russell, a parliamentarian who did not believe in yielding authority without procedural provision for reclaiming it, permitted the two houses of Congress to repeal the resolution by separate votes, without the President's signature being required.

That, however, had been tried. Morse submitted his repeal proposal right after the Rusk testimony, and Russell was on his feet at once, warning his colleagues that they would "hear something from the American people" if they voted to abandon their boys in Vietnam. Saltonstall said such a vote would be "unthinkable," and others joined in to condemn the move in the strongest terms. The war critics were not in favor of the proposal either. The Senate was nowhere near ready to repudiate the President in the middle of a war, and defeat of the repealer by a decisive margin would be exploited by Johnson as a reaffirmation of support. Mansfield moved to table the Morse proposal— in effect, to kill it—and the motion carried by 92 to 5. The dramatic high point came when Fulbright joined Morse, Gruening, McCarthy and Stephen M. Young, Democrat of Ohio, in voting against tabling. But it only made the break with the President more complete.[28]

The dissent Fulbright had rallied in the Senate with his Vietnam hearings had traveled some distance but had run out of steam without affecting the President's policy.

If repeal of the Gulf of Tonkin Resolution was impractical, what else could Fulbright undertake?

✿

✿ ✿

In July, 1967, the mail from Little Rock, Arkansas, brought Fulbright a clipping from *The Arkansas Gazette*. It was a reconstruction of the Gulf of Tonkin incidents of August, 1964, done by a ten-man team of the Associated Press. The AP reporters had spent weeks interviewing members of the crews of the destroyers *Maddox* and *C. Turner Joy*, some of them no longer on active duty. The major dailies, including *The New York Times, The Washington Post, The Washington Star,* and *The Baltimore Sun,* the papers that counted most in official Washington, had not run the article. The piece had been released several days in advance as a Sunday feature, and the news columns that weekend were weighed down by bloody racial rioting in Newark. So this was the first Fulbright knew of it.

His thoughts had been returning to the incidents themselves, as distinct from the resolution they had produced. The theorizing of the Administration's press officers in the aftermath of the incidents—that the North Vietnamese had attacked the destroyers to intensify pressure for an international conference, or to test U.S. reaction before launching a contemplated general offensive, or to draw China and perhaps Russia deeper into the struggle, or (at Chinese behest) to show up the United States as a "paper tiger"—seemed even more strained three years after the event than at the time. What seemed more germane now was the question he had raised on the Senate floor during the debate on Morse's repeal move: "I have often wondered what our ships were doing up there, so close to the seacoast."

His curiosity had been further aroused by one of the

letters he had received after the Vietnam hearings, a letter from a rear admiral, Arnold E. True, living in retirement in La Honda, California. The admiral, who had commanded a destroyer, a destroyer division, and a destroyer squadron during the Second World War and was an authority on destroyer tactics, questioned the official reports of "warning shots" fired by the *Maddox* during the first incident (August 2) to deter the North Vietnamese torpedo boats from their pursuit. "There is no provision in international law," Admiral True wrote,

for "firing a *warning* shot" at another man-of-war on the high seas. As commander of a man-of-war, I would consider any such shot as hostile and would not only be justified but required by Navy regulations to retaliate. It seems to me that if the accounts I read are correct, the U.S. fired the first shot in the war with N. Vietnam and then bombed the torpedo base because they retaliated, and that the resolution was passed on false premises.

Fulbright asked John T. McNaughton, Assistant Secretary of Defense for International Security Affairs, what the Defense Department had to say about True's comment. The best McNaughton could do when he testified before the committee in closed session in May was to confess his inability to say whether "it is correct or incorrect." He was more interested in showing the committee a bullet that, he disclosed, had struck the *Maddox* during the August 2 engagement.

The AP report cast an entirely new light on the question. An interview with Raymond P. Connell, weapons officer aboard the *Maddox,* included the following:

Q. Were these warning shots in the usual sense—intentionally long or short?

A. Oh, no, we were definitely aiming right at them because the speed factor was there. We didn't want to waste too much time in spotting our shots.

Q. So it was shoot to kill?
A. It was shoot to kill.

The American patrol had been described officially as "routine," and Morse's suggestion of provocative aspects was heatedly denied by McNamara when he testified before the Foreign Relations and Armed Services committees. The AP now revealed that the *Maddox* had stopped at Keelung, Taiwan, on its way to the Tonkin Gulf and taken aboard a "mysterious 'black box'" the size of a moving van and a complement of about a dozen men. "They kept pretty much to themselves," a radarman, Andrew M. Adamick, told the AP. "Brought their own special shack aboard and set it up and nobody was allowed in there. All we were told was that it was an ECM electronic countermeasures crew checking on radar and communications stations on shore." That suggested an electronic intelligence mission—hardly a "routine" patrol, in the accepted meaning of the words.

As for the second incident (August 4), McNamara had assured Congressional leaders at the White House that there was no doubt whatever of its having occurred, and the news magazines had given vivid accounts of the battle on the basis of information from press officers at the Pentagon. Thus, *Time*, August 14, 1964:

Through the darkness, from the west and south, the intruders boldly sped. There were at least six of them, Russian-designed "Swatow" gunboats armed with 37-mm. and 28-mm. guns, and P-4s. At 9:52 they opened fire on the destroyers with automatic weapons, this time from as close as 2,000 yards.

The night glowed eerily with the nightmarish glare of air-dropped flares and boats' searchlights. For 3½ hours, the small boats attacked in pass after pass. Ten enemy torpedoes sizzled through the water. Each time the skippers, tracking the fish by radar, maneuvered to evade them. Gunfire and gun smells and shouts stung the air. Two of the enemy boats went down. Then, at 1:30 a.m., the remaining PTs ended the fight, roared off through the black night to the north.

And *Newsweek,* August 17, 1964:

In the mountainous seas and swirling rain, no one knew how many PT boats were involved as they rose and fell in the wave troughs. The U.S. ships blazed out salvo after salvo of shells. Torpedoes whipped by, some only 100 feet from the destroyer's beams. A PT boat burst into flames and sank. More U.S. jets swooped in, diving, strafing, flattening out at 500 feet, climbing, turning 90 degrees at 8,000 feet, and diving again.

For more than three hours the battle continued in the turbulent seas. Another PT boat exploded, sank, and then the others scurried off into the darkness nursing their wounds.

The men interviewed by the AP painted a blurrier picture. The night was "darker than the hubs of hell," according to a *Maddox* radarman, James A. Stankevitz—so dark, said the AP, that the ships' gunners never saw what they were firing at. "The shooting and maneuvering for two and a half hours was strictly by radar." And Connell, the weapons officer aboard the *Maddox,* couldn't even see any targets on his radar screen. "I had nothing to shoot at," he told the AP. "I recall we were hopping around up there, trying to figure out what they were shooting at because we didn't have any targets. We fired a lot of rounds but it was strictly a defensive tactic. We called aircraft and aircraft was there by this time and they couldn't find anything to shoot at."

Ensign Richard Corsette, directing fire from the two forward mounts on the *Maddox,*

said his guns fired only once that night—to clear them of ammunition. "I knew the way our radar was acting, my firm belief was that everything I locked onto was weather," Corsette said.

The AP reporters interviewed one of the pilots, Commander Wesley McDonald.

"I honestly could not see any ships on the surface," he said. He and other flyers concentrated on what they thought were wakes—and once almost shot at the Maddox. The Maddox, still hungry for targets, almost made the same mistake—training her guns on the planes—when their low runs were detected by the ship's radar.

The torpedo reports, it developed, all came from the *Maddox* sonar, a device that can detect torpedoes, under favorable conditions, by listening to their whine or bouncing sound beams off them.

As the sonar reports multiplied, the bridge on the Maddox began to doubt there could be this many torpedoes. The reports seemed to follow whenever the ship made a sharp turn. "What we were doing, we were getting our own screwbeats very loud," said her captain [Commander Herbert L. Ogier]. . . . "Evaluating everything that was going on, I was becoming less and less convinced that somebody was there."

As for evidence of an attack, apart from the radar and sonar detections, it was slim. The *Turner Joy's* skipper, Commander Robert C. Barnhart, claimed seeing a "big black column of smoke" two thousand to three thousand yards away and, "for about fifteen seconds," a searchlight beam, "almost like one of these movie production type things to draw attention." Another man remembered the searchlight, and two claimed seeing several explosions. One man said he had "glimpsed a boat a mile away," and others interviewed "remembered 'a couple of guys who saw one.'" The destroyers couldn't find any debris the following morning, but that "didn't surprise Boatswain's Mate Eusebio B. Estrada of the *Maddox*. 'Those Chinese can clean up anything,' he said."

Fulbright read the report with intense interest. Here was food for thought indeed.

According to Tom Wicker of *The New York Times*, Johnson had not only made the Gulf of Tonkin Resolution part of his wardrobe after it was passed, "he had been carrying it around in his pocket for weeks [before the incidents] waiting for the moment." [29] Fulbright had asked William P. Bundy at a closed meeting of his committee on September 20, 1966 to state when the resolution had been prepared, and Bundy, Assistant Secretary of State for Far Eastern Affairs (and brother of McGeorge Bundy) had given the following account:

BUNDY: We had contingent drafts, which however did not very closely resemble the [final] draft, for some time prior to that . . . prior to August 1964. But this is a matter of normal contingency planning. No serious thought had been given to it, to the best of my knowledge, prior to the Gulf of Tonkin.

FULBRIGHT: Did *you* prepare it?

BUNDY: I did one in my own office, sir.

FULBRIGHT: What was it looking to if it occurred before that [the incidents]?

BUNDY: We had always anticipated and as a matter of common prudence I think should have anticipated the possibility that things might take a more drastic turn at any time and that it would be wise to seek an affirmation of the desires of and intent of the Congress. But that is normal planning. I am not sure that my drafts were even known to others. [30]

So there at least had been a "contingent draft." And suspicions that more than "normal planning" may have been involved were not lessened by the Administration's continuing sensitiveness to parts of McNamara's testimony of August 6, 1964, on the facts of the Gulf of Tonkin incidents. In March, 1966, Fulbright got the committee to agree to release the transcript of the closed-door hearing, subject to the usual censoring of security material by the State and Defense departments. The record, when published in November, contained extensive deletions. Everything to do with the coastal raids carried out by the South Vietnamese just before the *Maddox* began her patrol had been eliminated —not only McNamara's and General Wheeler's answers on the subject but Morse's questions as well. In reply to Morse's protest the State Department explained that the answers were still "classified"—and that publishing the questions alone would "give rise to public speculations as to the possible answers which might not be helpful to the national interest." [31]

And now there was this AP account of a wraithlike engagement, so different from what the Congress and the country had been led to believe had occurred, with a whiff of electronic espionage in the air. All the malignant questions that had been skirted in the committee hearing of August 6, 1964, and had hung back in the shadows of Fulbright's policy hearings, sprang into garish light. Was the mission of the *Maddox* indeed a provocative one, as Morse had charged? Was there actually an attack on the destroyers on August 4? If so, did Johnson seize on inconclusive evidence, because he was waiting for such an incident in order to bomb North Vietnam and rush a resolution through Congress? Or did he act on false or misleading information from the military? How was it that so much military power—an attack carrier group, shoals of fighter bombers, even an antisubmarine force—had been ready to move into Southeast Asia so swiftly after the event?

A new line of inquiry—on the facts of the Tonkin Gulf incidents and on what they revealed of the policy behind them—opened up before Fulbright. A new hearing was indicated. But how to go about it? Whom should Fulbright call to testify? And would they reveal anything damaging to the President? At meetings with the committee staff, Fulbright mused about the difficulty of prying admissions from unwilling witnesses clothed in an expertise conducive to concealment no less than to disclosure, impervious behind the sacrosanctity of any information stamped "classified" in their bureaucratic domain.

Weeks went by without Fulbright making up his mind. Then one of the younger members of the staff, William B. Bader, suggested a novel approach. What the Senator should do, he said, was demand to see copies of all entries in the logs of the *Maddox* and the *Turner Joy* from August 1 through August 4, 1964, and of all communications to and from the two ships during that period. Bader, who had served in the Navy, explained that the Navy's logs, which wind up in Washington for storage, are "inviolate—they simply are not changed." If the Senator wanted to get at the truth, he could do so through the logs.

It was an audacious idea. No Congressional committee during Fulbright's time on the Hill had served such a demand on the military. His constitutional authority for doing so was uncertain. It could be said that the Senate needed the logs and radio traffic in order to find out for itself how the nation had arrived at the predicament in Vietnam and what the Senate should advise or consent to in the months ahead. On the other hand, the material in question could be said to be part of the internal papers of the Executive which the Executive could show Congress at its pleasure but which Congress had no inherent right to see. Yet to convene another generalized hearing, to challenge McNamara and his beribboned admirals on the technicalities of a military action with nothing but a few newspaper clippings in hand, was to court further frustration. After mulling it over for several days, Fulbright told Bader to prepare a letter for his signature.

On August 28, 1967, a secretary in the office of the Senate Foreign Relations Committee telephoned a secretary in the Defense Department's Office of Congressional Liaison with a request that a messenger be sent around to pick up a letter from Senator Fulbright to Secretary of Defense McNamara.

The Investigation 10

Steaming around the South China Sea as air-intelligence officer and part-time bombardier navigator aboard the carrier *Hornet*, Bill Bader had been struck by the depersonalizing effect on him of the electronic system placed at his command. Here he was, a somewhat bookish young man ("the most well-rounded bad athlete Pomona ever had," his college coach had despairingly called him), a Fulbright scholar, a natural for an assistant professorship at one of the better universities: William Banks Bader, twenty-four, B.A., Phi Beta Kappa, Danforth Fellow, turned by his navy stint into an expert at certain mechanical tasks whose first consequence, if the bell for the real thing ever rang, would be the nuclear obliteration of certain Chinese cities —names classified—with a population in the millions. He would target the men who would fly the planes that would drop the bombs. He did it during drills. And he was able to think only of the techniques to be employed. And, therefore, he could sleep well.

Now, twelve years older, going through the newspaper clippings on the Tonkin Gulf incident, Bader was struck again by the capacity of man to blind his perception of the human element by preoccupation with technique. What a denial of the imagination to permit the evidence of radarscopes and hydrophones and teletypes ten thousand miles away to acquire the aspects of infallibility as it pulsed in tightened messages into the decoding room of the Pentagon! What a psychological void between the crisis manager and the crisis to make it possible for a few AP reporters going out with pencils and scratch pads three years after the event to tear such holes in an account so confidently presented by the most vaunted crisis manager of them all! Bader searched through yellowing files stored away in the basement for some sign of admission that blips emerging and receding in the greenish glow of a radar screen are not always the most reliable of informers, that a man with a set of headphones listening for the underwater echo of a sonar beam must sift out with his own mind the many noises of the sea, that all the encrypting machines, scrambler telephones and seamless tie lines of the most magnificent communications system on earth can produce nothing better than the information fed into it by ordinary men whose senses are notoriously deceiving in moments of danger and stress. Nothing: the uncensored transcripts in the basement only amplified the certitudes of the "sanitized" —lovely bureaucratese! as though the truth were faintly soiled—public account.

Bader had been something of a catch for Carl Marcy, the committee's chief of staff, hardheaded veteran of a hundred scrimmages, always on the lookout for young men who would give his team the weight in brains that it lacked in numbers. His B.A. rounded out by an M.A. and Ph.D. from Princeton, Bader had slipped, predictably, into a comfortable berth as lecturer and research associate at Princeton's Center of International Studies, but his taste, he soon discovered, was more for centers of action where one could learn at first hand how government really worked. Trailing ivy he headed for Washington, winding up in the State Department—well-favored and whimsical, the Beau Brummel of the girl secretaries and recipient in 1966 of the department's Meritorious Service Award.

The diplomatic career was to last no longer than the academic one. Marcy offered him a post as one of the Senate Foreign Relations Committee's five professional aides. Congress fascinated Bader as an institution, particularly as it was becoming the center stage of the developing drama over Vietnam; Fulbright intrigued him as an individual. He jumped at the chance.

Almost at once he was up to his ears in altercation. Unknown to Congress, the Pentagon had been engaged in backdoor financing of jet, tank and other arms sales to underdeveloped countries, undermining the very objectives of economic progress and political stability that the United States was supposedly promoting in those areas with economic aid. When Symington got wind of the arrangement he was furious at being kept in the dark and headed up a subcommittee investigation. Fulbright assigned Bader to do the spadework. Bader began asking relevant questions and getting opaque answers. The answers at the subcommittee hearings were even more unsatisfactory, since the Senators, busy men who did not know what to ask, tended to make their questions into little speeches. The practice being investigated was so crassly underhanded that it ended up being fully exposed anyway—and, after bitter floor fights, killed by Congress. But the fray left Bader with a theory.

Though a Congressional committee, with its small staff and limited funds, could not match the Executive pound for pound, it could do something else: go into one particular area with everything it had and learn more about the issue than the Executive. This could be done by having the committee staff investigate the subject in advance of hearings. One aide with the right professional background and the backing of a key Senator could have the State and Defense departments on the ropes by asking for identifiable documents. To reject the request would run the risk of having influential Senators make a public stink about secrecy in government preventing Congress from fulfilling its responsibilities. Executive departments were sensitive to charges of that sort. The aide could thus lay the basis for tightly focused closed hearings at which Senators would know precisely what questions to ask. Illumination of one area would spread light over a broader expanse. There would be a fight each time as to how much of the transcript should be made public. Nevertheless, Bader concluded, if there was a practical way of bringing Congress and the Executive into better balance, leaving aside the fundamental reforms Congress had long been in need of, it was through this technique of capitalizing on the constitutional uncertainty of what Executive material Congress had a right to see.

In asking McNamara on August 28, 1967, for the record of the radio traffic and the ship's logs in the Tonkin Gulf affair, Fulbright was putting his new aide's concepts to the test. A month went by with no reply from McNamara. Fulbright, unsure of his ground, didn't seem to be in a mood to press forward. The project was in danger of dying.

On September 18, Fulbright's office received an anonymous telephone call from a man who said he had information that might be helpful to the Senator in regard to the Tonkin Gulf business. The secretary who took the call put him on to the committee staff member who was handling Asian affairs in general, Norvill Jones. Jones suggested he write the committee a letter. Nothing was heard from the man for ten days. Then the letter arrived. "For three years," the informant wrote,

I have known that the second North Vietnamese PT boat attack almost certainly did not actually occur. In all that time I have never been able to find a way to disclose this information to a responsible person or organization who could and would use it constructively rather than destructively to the embarrassment of the U.S. government.

The informant had read an article in *Newsweek* dealing with Fulbright's regrets on his role in the enactment of the Gulf of Tonkin Resolution, and on Katzenbach's testimony on this issue, and had decided that the Senator was the man he was looking for. "U.S. Navy patrols in the Gulf of Tonkin," he continued,

were undertaken apparently to bait the North Vietnamese. . . . The Navy convinced Defense Secretary McNamara that both [North Vietnamese] attacks actually occurred and McNamara accordingly briefed the press. As a consequence, President Johnson ordered U.S. "air action." . . . [However,] two operations analysts who evaluated the Navy's combat action reports stated to me that there was no evidence that the North Vietnamese actually made the second attack. . . .

Months later the Navy sank two [North Vietnamese] PT boats and captured the crews. . . . During extended military interrogations these crews told all they knew. For example, they revealed the camouflaged locations of all the other PT boats. This information enabled the Navy to successfully attack several more PT boats. These two crews then identified themselves as the two crews which attacked the U.S. Navy destroyer on August 2. However, they said that neither they nor any other PT boat crews made any attack on the night of August 4.

When they said that, the informant wrote, military authorities in Washington, who had been receiving the results of the interrogation in secret messages over a period of several days, ordered the message traffic stopped and arrangements for press interviews with the prisoners canceled. The writer concluded:

I had planned to identify myself, but on the advice of an attorney I have reluctantly decided to remain anonymous. However, I will telephone you to ask if you have further questions.

*
* *

Jack Cowles was not in the navy mold. Very few commanders in the regular Navy took violin lessons when they were seven, for one thing. His parents (his father was an ordained Baptist minister) encouraged the boy's aptitude for music, and Jack majored in music at San Diego State College. Deciding he wasn't talented enough to be a successful musician, he graduated from the University of California at Los Angeles with a B.S. in business administration. It was the eve of the Second World War, and Cowles volunteered for navy flight training. After Pearl Harbor he was co-pilot and then pilot on bombing runs out of the Aleutians. Japanese antiaircraft fire damaged his plane in 1944 and he crash-landed in Siberia. The Russians flew him and his crew across Siberia to Tashkent, to join a hundred or so other American flyers who had headed for Russian territory when their planes were hit. After about six months, the Russians, who were allies in the European war but careful to maintain their neutrality in the Pacific war, arranged for their "escape" across the border into Iran. Cowles liked flying and went regular Navy. In between duties as air intelligence officer in Far Eastern waters during the Korean war and as air officer and navigator in the Persian Gulf and the Mediterranean, he took various naval courses in the next ten years. But the courses weren't enough to move him up to flag rank, and when he found himself in a "contingency-planning" desk job in London and passed over for promotion, he knew that his career had peaked.

On August 4, 1964, Commander Cowles, forty-six, was on station in Flag Plot, the Navy's "war room" in the Pentagon, and saw the messages from the Gulf of Tonkin. It seemed to him that none of it added up to anything solid, and when the President announced retaliation he felt the country had rushed into it on the basis of unsubstantiated evidence. Talking to the two specialists who were sent over a day or two later to evaluate the messages confirmed his belief that a very regrettable thing had occurred. As the country became more deeply involved in Vietnam, the significance of what he knew began to build in his mind. The telephone call to Fulbright's office was not the first time he tried to communicate with someone in authority. When the possibility of a halt to the bombing became an issue at the United Nations, he had had an interview with an aide of Arthur Goldberg, the new UN Ambassador; the aide had failed to see what bearing Cowles' information had on the bombing question. When he phoned Norvill Jones of the Fulbright committee staff the second time—to ask if Jones had any further questions—he inadvertently mentioned the UN interview and realized, an instant too late, that Jones could easily find out his identity by a call to Goldberg's office. So he identified himself and, at Jones' urging, agreed to see Fulbright.

He came soon afterward—a tall man in full uniform, with his Distinguished Flying Cross, Bronze Star and Purple Heart ribbons, "clearly a responsible person," Jones recalls, "but without what is called a military bearing." Jones and Bader took him into Fulbright's office. The commander said he had carried this burden on his conscience for years and was glad to be able to transfer it to the Senator's shoulders. He spoke of the national interest and said he wanted to help see to it that this kind of thing did not happen again. He had no new information to impart, but Fulbright was impressed by him. The interview had the effect of showing Fulbright and the committee staff that they were on the right track. There was no question after that of dropping the Bader experiment.

Feeling he had done his citizen's duty, Cowles told a colleague of his visit when he returned to his new station in New York City—and found himself volunteered for psychiatric examination in a naval hospital. It was true that he had been upset because of marital problems. His kicking over the navy traces with his visit to Fulbright convinced his superior officer that he was in need of psychiatric help. Throughout a month-long examination it was suggested to him that he retire voluntarily, for his own good, on "physical disability." Cowles refused to submit to what he regarded as a form of intimidation, and in the end the navy psychiatrist cleared him for duty and all navy review levels gave him a clean bill of health. But he was left with a do-nothing job until mandatory retirement (speeded up after ten years without a promotion) washed him out of the Navy's hair in 1969.

*

* *

In October, Fulbright repeated his request to McNamara, a shade more tartly. Still no response. He tried a little public pressure. On a visit home in Arkansas he tossed off the remark that, in voting for the Gulf of Tonkin Resolution in 1964, "I had not the slightest suspicion that the [North Vietnamese] gunboats had [not] fired on U.S. ships. Now I have reservations about it. In spite of my many inquiries to the Pentagon, I cannot be sure it was [not] a provoked incident." United Press International picked it up, and it was featured in *The Washington Post*. A few days later a navy enlisted man arrived at the committee offices with a foot-high package wrapped in brown paper and tied with a string.

The experiment was beginning to work. Perhaps it had been decided that the best way to handle the problem was to bemuse the committee with a jumble of messages in navy jargon that they would find unintelligible. Seeing the many references to torpedoes in the water and destroyers under attack, Fulbright could say, Oh, hell, sure there was an attack, and drop the matter.

If that was the plan, it had reckoned without Bader. Looking over the collection with the eye of a former naval intelligence officer, Bader could see that it was highly selective. "It made exciting reading," he said. "You'd think we were dealing with the sinking of the *Bismarck*." Many of the messages were not Xeroxed but typed out, as though excerpted from longer messages containing information the Pentagon preferred not to divulge.

Each message was preceded by a "date-time" code and

cryptic references to earlier messages. "They used funny words and all that," Fulbright recalled later. "They didn't mean anything to me." They did to Bader, and he wrote out a new request for the missing messages, identified in the Navy's own communications lingo.

Again there was no response. Weeks passed in silence. The investigation was stalled.

Fulbright was becoming peeved. When things got sticky, Defense officials had a way of claiming they were responsible only to the Armed Services Committee. Fulbright went to see Russell. He told him what he was doing and asked for his help in getting at the truth. Russell agreed.

Just then Russell received another request for help on the same subject—from the number-two man at the Pentagon.

* * *

There seemed to be hardly a time in the postwar era when the name of Paul H. Nitze was not associated importantly with whatever administration was in office. A college professor's son who made his pile on Wall Street as a young man before World War II and dedicated himself thereafter to the strategic aspects of foreign policy, Nitze had one of the most durable reputations in Washington for tough-mindedness, intelligence and a sense of proportion. As head of the State Department's Policy Planning Staff under Acheson, he joined with Acheson in the winter of 1949–1950 in producing the arcane (and still classified) National Security Council paper NSC-68, the charter for a policy of strenuous American effort to strengthen the Free World economically and militarily against the Communist menace. He served Eisenhower as consultant on strategic problems, Kennedy as an Assistant Secretary of Defense, and Johnson as Secretary of the Navy and now, with Cyrus Vance having just retired, as Deputy Secretary of Defense.

With Fulbright's inquiry threatening to precipitate a row

between his committee and the Executive branch, Nitze went to William Bundy at the State Department to give him a fill-in. He said, in effect, I don't blame Fulbright for having his doubts on the basis of the other evidence, but look, here's proof that the North Vietnamese did attack on August 4. The evidence he laid out consisted of special intelligence intercepts of North Vietnamese naval messages.

Nitze also called Russell. The President and the Secretary of Defense, he said, were unhappy about Fulbright's latest tangent; it would reflect on the Administration's credibility if it became public, even though there was no substance to Fulbright's apparent suspicions. Nitze had some material to show Fulbright that would dispose of those suspicions, but the White House felt that this disclosure should be made within the purview of the Armed Services Committee, so if Russell could arrange a meeting in his office—

The meeting took place on December 14. Fulbright thought its purpose was to persuade the Defense Department to be more forthcoming with the Gulf of Tonkin messages. Nitze was there with the object of persuading Fulbright to call off his inquiry. Russell was the arbiter.

Nitze came in with a collection of documents and the Secretary of the Navy, Paul R. Ignatius. He dug into his papers and said to Fulbright, "Here, read these."

"It was a very short message," Fulbright was to recall later. "I think it was only about a paragraph, and I read it very rapidly."

Nitze explained that he was showing the two Senators a series of North Vietnamese naval messages intercepted just before, during, and just after the August 4 engagement. They were the Administration's "conclusive" evidence that an attack had occurred. Since special intelligence activity was involved, the intercepts were beyond top secret. If their existence became known, it would reveal to the North Vietnamese that we had broken their code. There were only something like six other people who had seen the messages.

They were for the Senators' eyes only. He could not give them copies.

The messages were brief. One of them gave the co-ordinates that would fix the location of two "enemy" vessels. Another was an order to certain naval units to make ready for operations. A third message reported that the enemy was under attack, that an enemy vessel had been "wounded," and that an enemy aircraft was seen falling. The final message was that two enemy planes had been shot down and two boats had been "sacrificed," and that a certain North Vietnamese naval commander, identified by name, had met the enemy.

Fulbright was not impressed. How can you consider this conclusive evidence, he asked, when it is wrong on its face? You know they didn't knock down any of our planes or touch our ships.

Nitze could not understand Fulbright's reasoning. The enemy is often wrong in some of his messages during a battle, but that doesn't make all of the messages wrong. The North Vietnamese were wrong in saying they had damaged a vessel and shot down two planes, but it showed they were there and attacking. The final message, in which they admitted the loss of two boats, was particularly significant. The destroyers, it should be remembered, had claimed sinking two boats. He rested his case primarily on that intercept.

The matter was left there, and they proceeded to Fulbright's request for the radio traffic and the logs. Though Russell had been brought in ostensibly because his committee had jurisdiction over military matters, there could be little doubt that Johnson hoped Russell would prevail on Fulbright to drop his inquiry. And the two Senators did have a discussion at this point as to how far a committee's right to Executive information extended. But the outcome was different from what Nitze had apparently expected. Russell turned to him. The Foreign Relations Committee is interested in this, he said. The meeting on the Tonkin Gulf Resolution took place under their aegis. They are entitled to all the relevant documents. I think it is your duty to make them available.

Nitze had made it quite clear that Fulbright's investigation, which was bound to become known if it was pressed much further, would be harmful to the national interest in the Administration's view, as it would lend credence to Communist propaganda and undermine public confidence in the President's Vietnam policy. But with Russell cutting the ground from under him, he could only agree to make the "relevant" information available and leave. Can you give me these now? Fulbright asked, indicating the stack of papers. No, said Nitze, he preferred to send them by messenger.

Fulbright did not know it, but Nitze's own confidence in the President's Vietnam policy was very much in question. Nitze was a member of a highly secret discussion group initiated by Katzenbach in the spring of 1967 after he became Under Secretary of State. Katzenbach, who didn't think bombing would force North Vietnam to the negotiating table, sounded Johnson out on the notion of weekly bull sessions among second-level officials—men like himself, Averell Harriman, Vance and McNaughton from Defense, Rostow from the White House, General Wheeler, Richard Helms, the former newspaperman who had taken over from McCone at CIA—as a way of germinating fresh ideas on Vietnam. Johnson's encouraging response convinced Katzenbach that deep down the President had his own reservations as to whether he was getting anywhere. The members of the "nongroup," as Katzenbach called it (if it didn't have a name it was less likely to become known), sat over drinks in Katzenbach's office at the end of the day. Each man was to speak freely and not "departmentally," there were to be no substitutes and no notes were taken. It was, at bottom, a bureaucratic plot to flush out doubts about the President's policy and induce him to alter his course, an approach Katzenbach regarded as more promising than the head-on opposition of his predecessor, George Ball. Ball, an advocate of Atlantic Community who called Vietnam a "gluepot," had argued strongly against escalation within the President's councils—and, in the view of some, had ended up in the ineffective role of official Devil's Advocate. Others would later contend that the Katzenbach way of influencing policy by putting up a bland front only led to the "effectiveness trap" that produced even less results than Ball's one-man opposition. Be that as it may, Nitze, who joined the "nongroup" when he took over from Vance, revealed himself to be vehemently opposed to the bombing and critical of the entire Vietnam involvement as a diversion from the contest with Russia. Yet the meeting with Fulbright cast him in the role of supporter of that policy. Such was the code of loyalty to the President, superseding loyalty to conviction, that kept internal opposition to Johnson's intractable course hidden from the public for so long.

*
* *

Another bundle arrived. It contained the messages Bader had requested, or some of them. The new messages contained new cross-references. Bader wrote out a new request. There was another hiatus, a shorter one. A third bundle arrived. Bader repeated the process. The Pentagon found itself on a downward slide it could not arrest without admitting, in effect, to holding back evidence.

As Johnson feared, the inquiry became known.

It started with a letter that appeared in the New Haven, Connecticut, *Register.* The letter might have passed unnoticed, but the AP picked it up and put it on its national news wire. Written by a young Connecticut high school teacher, John White, it said:

In August 1964 I was serving as a commissioned Naval officer aboard USS Pine Island (AV-12) in the Pacific. Pine Island was the first U.S. ship to enter the war zone in response to the "attack" upon the destroyers Maddox and Turner Joy. I recall clearly the confusing radio messages sent at that time by the destroyers—confusing because the destroyers themselves were not certain they were being attacked. Granted that some North Vietnamese motor torpedo boats were in the area and used harassing maneuvers, the question is this: did they actually fire shells or torpedoes at U.S. warships? The answer is no.

I learned this by speaking with the chief sonarman of the Maddox who was in the sonar room during the "attack." He told me that his evaluation of the sonarscope picture was negative, meaning that no torpedoes were fired through the water, at the ship or otherwise. . . . Yet the Pentagon reported to the President that North Vietnam had attacked us, and the President reported it to Congress. Why? . . . in a moment of panic, based on false information, the President was given unprecedented powers, which today enable him to conduct an undeclared war involving over a half a million men and costing billions of dollars. That is a pretty high price to pay for a bad radio report. Let's hope our warships aren't attacked by Chinese sampans next.[1]

White sent Fulbright a copy of his letter and came down to Washington, at the Senator's request, for an interview. He explained that he had encountered the "chief sonarman" at a naval shipyard in Long Beach, California, and could not remember his name. The man's identity remained unclear, since there were no chief petty officers listed among the *Maddox* crew, but Fulbright's interest in the details of the Gulf of Tonkin incidents was revealed when White was interviewed on CBS, and that put a *New York Times* reporter named John W. Finney on the scent.

Finney, assigned to the Hill that fall after specializing in science and technology news, was back on his old beat; he had covered Congress for the United Press before joining the *Times* in 1956. Moseying around the Senate Foreign Relations Committee offices, he came upon Bader with naval hydrographic charts of the Gulf of Tonkin spread out on the floor. Bader was discreet. So was Marcy. But Finney on a story was a genial Bulldog Drummond, and in a few days the *Times* ran a dispatch that began:

WASHINGTON, Dec. 20—Some members of the Senate Foreign Relations Committee, skeptical of Administration accounts, are quietly inquiring into the details of the Gulf of Tonkin incidents in 1964 . . . and these members question whether the destroyers were actually attacked by torpedoes and automatic weapons [on August 4], as stated by Defense Secretary Robert S. McNamara in testimony before Congressional committees.

Assailed by inquiries, Fulbright had to issue a statement. He said the committee had been receiving information and letters on the Gulf of Tonkin incidents from what it believed to be responsible individuals, and this had raised a number of questions. In order to clear up these uncertainties, he had asked the Defense Department for certain information bearing on the episodes, and the department had been "very cooperative." When the examination was concluded, its results would be presented to the committee.[2]

Whatever hopes for the success of the Nitze mission may have lingered in the Pentagon and the White House were blasted. Worse, the implication that North Vietnam had been attacked and the 1964 resolution passed on the basis of possibly erroneous information was now in the open. The Defense Department was out with a rebuttal within a few hours:

Any suggestion that the August, 1964, attacks on U.S. destroyers in the Tonkin Gulf did not occur is contrary to the known facts. . . . The attacks were seen, heard and detected electronically by the crews of the ships. . . . The evidence that the destroyers were attacked is conclusive.

In the case of the August 4 incident, there were seven items of "conclusive" evidence:

1. Radar tracks of fast small craft paralleling and then closing in on the destroyers *Maddox* and *Turner Joy*.
2. Numerous sonar detections of torpedoes fired at the de-

stroyers, reported by the sonarman who manned the *Maddox*'s equipment throughout the attack.

3. Visual sighting by an officer and several crewmen of the wake of a torpedo passing near the *Turner Joy*.

4. Visual sighting of the attacking craft lit by aircraft flares and by shells fired during the engagement.

5. Visual sighting of a searchlight beam from one of the attacking craft.

6. Visual sighting of antiaircraft fire directed at American planes overhead.

7. Visual sighting from aircraft of the wake of a small, fast craft near the destroyers.

Persons who have examined all of the evidence can have no doubt that the *Maddox* twice and the *Turner Joy* once were attacked by North Vietnamese small naval craft well in international waters without provocation.[3]

The statement, as will be seen, did not reveal anything that was not contained in the AP story of the previous summer, other than the sighting of antiaircraft fire by a pilot or pilots more sharp-eyed than the flyer interviewed by the AP. But to anyone who had not read the AP report the Pentagon's terse announcement of December 22 would be news, and it was displayed prominently in *The Washington Post*, dressed up by pictures of the torpedo boats involved in the August 2 incident that were just then released, for the first time, by the Pentagon press office, little as they had to do with the point at issue. Bader called it the Pentagon's pre-emptive strike.

But someone in the Pentagon was on Fulbright's side, for a week later he received another anonymous letter. The writer, obviously privy to the Fulbright-McNamara correspondence, suggested that he ask for a top secret study by the Weapons Systems Evaluation Group (WSEG) entitled "Command and Control of the Tonkin Gulf Incident, 4–5 August 1964," based on communications that passed through the Pentagon's National Military Command Center during that period, including tape recordings of telephone conversations between the President, the Secretary of Defense and Admiral Sharp in Honolulu. This study "will disclose several embarrassing things," he said.

One is that the first attack, that on the *Maddox*, was very probably made because the NVN confused the *Maddox* [with] operations which were covering SVN hit-and-run attacks against NVN coastal areas. . . .

Another point will be that the attack on the *Turner Joy* the following day [sic] was indeed probably imaginary.

After the first report of the attack there was a report there probably had not been an attack at all. But the President was to go on the air to address the nation about the retaliatory attacks that had already been planned, and after another flurry of confusion Admiral Sharp said there had been a real attack after all.

At this point the Secretary of Defense decided to advise the President that the attack on the *Turner Joy* was real and to order the retaliatory attacks and go ahead with the speech because it was getting very late for the address to the nation and, moreover, the retaliatory attack planes had been kept in a state of takeoff readiness for the maximum time.

It was clearly a case of making a definite decision when operational circumstances dictated haste but the facts suggested caution.

One may wonder how much the Secretary of Defense, who is a man of honor and conscience, has worried about this since. Because later events all indicate that the second attack was at best a trick of false radar images.

The writer said he was sure that if he signed the letter he would lose his job, but if Senator Fulbright proceeded wisely he should be able "for the good of the country" to ascertain the truth of what the informant had written. The letter concluded:

The Gulf of Tonkin incident was not a put-up job. But it was not the inexcusable and flagrant attack upon U.S. ships that it seemed to be. . . . It was a confused bungle which was used by the President to justify a general course of action and policy that he had been advised by the military to follow. He, like the Secretary of Defense, was a prisoner. He got from them all the critical and decisive information and misinformation and he simply put his trust in the wrong people.

Since Nitze had agreed to supply the committee with all relevant documents, Fulbright addressed McNamara a request for the WSEG study. But that apparently was carrying the agreement too far. A reply from Jack Stempler, McNamara's personal assistant, said the study was an internal staff paper of the Joint Chiefs of Staff and was currently under review by the chairman.

*

* *

Finney ambled into Marcy's office and said, "What about that black-box information?"

Marcy said, "What do you mean?"

Finney said, "Well, they are saying over in the Pentagon building—"

"Who are 'they'?"

"The press officers. They are saying they have positive proof that the incident occurred because of a black box, and so I keep asking them about the black box, and they say they can't tell me anything about the black box."

Presumably they were referring to the "black box" in the AP report; that appeared to signify that the messages Nitze had shown Fulbright had been intercepted by the special communications unit placed aboard the *Maddox.* Marcy, of course, could not tell Finney anything about *that,* but it was interesting that the Pentagon should be throwing out these hints to the press after Nitze had made such a point of the need for secrecy. Bader thought it was interesting too. One of the items in his now-voluminous collection, a message radioed from the *Turner Joy* to the carrier *Ticonderoga* just before the August 4 incident, read, "Received info indicating attack by PGM [patrol gunboat] P-4 imminent." This "info" appeared to refer to something other than radar contacts. It seemed to be a guarded reference to one of Nitze's intercepts, relayed to the *Turner Joy* from the "black box" aboard the *Maddox*. Here was a thread which, pulled adroitly, might even bring those mysterious intercepts skidding down. Fulbright agreed to try. Off went a letter to Secretary of the Navy Ignatius, citing this message and adding, "If the information comes from a communication intercept, I would appreciate having the text of that intercept as well as any other intelligence interceptions relating to the second incident in the Gulf of Tonkin."

That was going *much* too far. Ignatius, in a frosty two-sentence reply, said it was his "understanding" that the matter in question had been discussed at length at a meeting of Nitze, Russell and the Senator; "There is nothing further I can add to those discussions."

Their anonymous informant in the Pentagon, however, did have something to add. Urging them to "keep up the good work," he wrote:

You certainly have us here in DOD scurrying around trying to cover up the incident and inundate you with facts to circumvent the main point. That is, that the so-called second attack of August 4 never took place.

Before Mr. Nitze signed out the last letter to you he conferred with Mr. Bundy of State and Walt Rostow and the three of them even went so far as to confer with the President. Do you think this would have happened if there was nothing to hide?

There were a couple of other messages he thought Fulbright should ask for, and he gave the date-time groups by which they could be identified. One of them was from the Naval Communications Station in the Philippines to the Joint Chiefs of Staff and the Chief of Naval Operations. Bader wrote out the request for Fulbright's signature.

＊

＊　＊

The Finney problem was assuming a double aspect. Committee members would not appreciate it if Bader's findings came out in dribs and drabs in *The New York Times*. On the other hand, this indefatigable newsman, with his background in technology and the sea—he was a PT-boat officer in the Pacific during the Second World War and roamed around the world as a deckhand on a tramp steamer before settling down—had become almost as engrossed in the Tonkin puzzle as Bader himself. Willy-nilly, the two of them began bouncing questions off each other, and Finney would shoot them into the Pentagon press office. A typical Finney questionnaire:

John Finney/NY Times/ January 10, 1968.
Re Tonkin—August 4, 1964, incident.
What were the sea and weather conditions during the incident?
What were the atmospheric conditions for radar operations? Were there ducting conditions?
What were the sonar detection conditions? Were there inversion layers?
Prior to the incident, when had a BT [Bathythermograph] reading been taken by the DDs?
What types of sonar were carried by the *Maddox* and *Turner Joy*? What was their state of repair? Were the DDs on active or passive sonar at the time of torpedo detection?

The naval savvy of these questions created the feeling at the Pentagon that that fellow of Fulbright's (who they could see now was no landlubber) had a great deal more than Bader in fact had, and the bout between them took the form of the Pentagon trying to anticipate committee disclosures with an overkill of official denials, succeeding only in heightening public and Congressional interest in the subject. What disposition would be made of Bader's report to the committee would depend to a large degree on how hot the issue was politically, so Finney's persistence was helpful in keeping Bader's labors from ending up in the file-and-forget cabinet. In addition, while some of Finney's questions could be disposed of with the all-purpose Pentagon answer, "This information is classified," the press office across the Potomac was under institutional compulsion to provide some replies to queries from the media, and Finney's dispatches proceeded to move from the bra ads to the front page with a series that placed the Tonkin Gulf inquiry into the center of attention in political Washington.

Thus, on January 7, 1968, he raised the question of whether all seven items of "conclusive" evidence of the August 4 attack adduced by the Defense Department were available in Washington when the decision to retaliate was made. Citing indications that the evidence was sketchy and contradictory, he asked:

Was contradictory information interpreted in the light of an initial conclusion that an attack was taking place or in the light of a growing belief within the Administration that the time had come to carry the war to North Vietnam? [4]

Certainly not, replied the Pentagon the next day:

All the basic facts, verified, about the [August 4 attack] were before Department of Defense officials in the Pentagon prior to the United States decision to make a retaliatory strike.

But a day later Finney came out with two more reports: that the most direct piece of evidence, the sighting of a torpedo track passing near the *Turner Joy*, was not obtained until after the retaliatory strike, and that the Weapons Systems Evaluation Group (WSEG) had found it necessary to make a study of the command-and-control procedures followed during the incident, a study the Pentagon officials "declined to discuss." [5] Then Finney smoked out the Nitze episode—enough of it to report that the Deputy Secretary of Defense had been sent on a "mission of persuading Senator Fulbright to call off the inquiry," that Nitze had cited special-intelligence information consisting of North Vietnamese radio messages as part of the conclusive evidence, and that "Senator Fulbright did not find the intelligence information persuasive." The Defense Department, he said, refused to confirm or deny the existence of such messages, possibly because confirmation would raise a question "as to whether the *Maddox* may have been on an electronic 'spoofing' mission, undertaking maneuvers to raise North Vietnamese radio and radar circuits and then monitoring their signals." [6] Finney even found out about trouble with the sonar aboard the *Maddox* just before August 4, a significant factor, he explained, since the conclusion that an attack had occurred appeared to have been based in large measure on reports from the *Maddox* that her sonar had detected numerous torpedoes. The Defense Department, he said, refused to discuss this problem either.[7] Disturbed by Finney's dispatches, *The New York Times* said editorially on January 25, 1968, that

the facts unearthed so far . . . clearly warrant investigation. . . . The United States will never extricate itself with honor from its Vietnam involvement unless it achieves a better comprehension of how it became entrapped.

By this time Bader's work was done. His report, covering twenty pages, was locked in a safe in Marcy's office. Any committee member who wished to do so could come by and read it—and there was a parade. Then the committee met behind closed doors to be briefed by Marcy and Bader and decide what to do next. There were plaudits such as "magnificent staff effort" and "wonderful job," but there was also an undercurrent of bewilderment. The reality Bader had stripped of its technocratic mystique was more than most of the committee members had counted on.

The *Maddox* was not engaged in a "routine" sea patrol, as McNamara had testified, but in a special electronic espionage mission that took the ships well within North Vietnamese territorial waters and was of such sensitivity that it had to be approved by the Joint Chiefs of Staff. There was considerable evidence that one objective of the patrol was to provoke the North Vietnamese and then bloody them if they responded.

Not only was the *Maddox* running in and out of territorial waters while the North Vietnamese were smarting from the South Vietnamese coastal attack of the night of July 30–31, but a second South Vietnamese raid took place on the night of August 3–4, twenty-four hours after the *Maddox* was joined by the *Turner Joy* and nine hours before the second incident. There was every reason to believe that the North Vietnamese could have concluded that the patrol was part of the South Vietnamese operations. McNamara had misled the committee in saying the Navy was unaware of the South Vietnamese attacks.

The second incident, which McNamara had described in such positive terms, was actually a highly confused event. There were ample grounds to question whether North Vietnamese boats were there at all. If they were, the evidence that the *Maddox* and the *Turner Joy* were attacked was circumstantial. Bader's best belief was that while North Vietnamese patrol boats may have been shadowing the destroyers, there was no attack on the night of August 4.

In any case, the evidence of attack that had been received in Washington at the time of the decision to retaliate was not only skimpy but of questionable quality. From the communications traffic it would seem that the facts increasingly demanded caution, but the operational demands of striking North Vietnam within a few hours were so overwhelming that there was not time for amplifying information to come in.

There had been enough residue of doubt after the event for steps to be taken to buttress the official case. Two Defense officials, Jack Stempler (McNamara's personal assistant) and Alvin Friedman, Deputy Assistant Secretary of Defense for Far Eastern Affairs, were sent to Subic Bay, the Philippines, to interview crew members of the *Maddox* and the *Turner Joy* and gather evidence of an attack for presentation to the Security Council. With Hanoi refusing to recognize UN jurisdiction over the Vietnam problem, the material gathered was never made public, but it did not affect the conclusions of the Bader report.

General Burchinal, the Director of the Joint Staff, went over the radio traffic and, on August 6, gave McNamara his personal evaluation: "The actuality of the attack is confirmed."

Vice Admiral Roy L. Johnson, commander of the Seventh Fleet, to which the *Maddox* and the *Turner Joy* belonged, went over the message traffic too and stated on August 14 that he was "convinced beyond any doubt that *Maddox* and *Turner Joy* were subjected to an unprovoked surface torpedo attack on the night of August 4, 1964." His immediate superior, Admiral Thomas H. Moorer, commander of the Pacific Fleet, added his imprimatur to this finding.

Yet the Navy's normal method of clearing up serious doubts about the facts of a naval engagement, a Board of Inquiry, was never employed.

A Board of Inquiry *was* convened at Subic Bay after the September 18 incident in the Gulf of Tonkin, which took place under a half-full moon and scattered clouds, with visibility up to four miles, and was strikingly similar to the incident of August 4. The commander of the destroyers *Edwards* and *Morton,* Captain Hollyfield, radioed that he had been "attacked" by boats contacted by radar. The two ships then had a running battle with numerous radar contacts, firing 170 rounds of five-inch shells and 129 rounds of three-inch shells. Crew members testified before the board that they had seen tracer bullets, flashes of light and shell bursts. Yet the board found that no attack had occurred.

A Board of Inquiry is the Navy's most serious form of investigation. It involves reputations; it transcends the chain of command and calls in civilian technical experts. Was that why the Navy did not convene a Board of Inquiry after the August 4 incident, preferring to sweep the matter under the rug with cursory "evaluations" of the radio traffic and collection of ammunition for debate at the UN?

Bader had one caveat. At a meeting with Senator Fulbright, Mr. Nitze presented for the chairman's eyes messages from special intelligence purporting to be conclusive evidence of an attack. Not having seen this information, the committee staff had no way of judging how conclusive it was.

There were a dozen committee members at the meeting, and no one knew quite how to react. They had been badly misled. Had McNamara been misled himself before he misled them? Had he really not known that the Navy knew about the South Vietnamese raids? Had the President been misled? Was the whole thing contrived by the military to trick the President and the country into war?

What was the committee to do now? Call in naval officers? Put them, in effect, on the stand?

What, the more conservative members wanted to know, was the committee after?

A good look at the vaunted new command-and-control system at the Pentagon, Fulbright suggested. Suppose the next incident involved Russia?

But the doubts on the left were just as strong as on the right. The implications, it was argued by some of the liberals, went far beyond broken codes and other narrow national-security considerations that had been cited by conservative opponents of a full-scale investigation. The committee had a case here that was potentially comparable to the Dreyfus case, in that proof that the country was taken into war on the basis of falsified testimony could discredit the military and could discredit and quite possibly destroy the President.

It was highly doubtful that the committee could obtain such proof. There were a hundred ways in which the Navy could cover up. The staff report itself expressed doubt that it could ever be conclusively proven that the attack did occur or that it did not occur. It would be the committee's judgment against that of commanders on the scene and Defense officials in Washington.

The committee should be very careful before taking this into the open. This would be by far the most serious inquiry it had ever launched. If it did not have enough evidence to back up the charge that the Congress and the country were the victims of a giant hoax—and the staff report provided only a basis for an investigation—the committee could end up by discrediting itself.

At the end of three hours they decided that Fulbright would show the staff study to Russell and consult with him, since his committee was involved as well, and they would meet again. To Finney and other reporters waiting outside the hearing-room door, Fulbright said the committee had considered the staff report and postponed a decision on what to do next. The whole thing was "very complicated," he said, "very sensitive." Mundt, a molting hawk, said he had been skeptical about the study but now was "shocked at the mass of material and new evidence."

Mundt, and others, had even more reason for astonishment by the time they reconvened January 30. The message from the Naval Communications Station, Philippines, that had been identified by the anonymous tipster had been pried loose. It turned out to have been sent to the Joint Chiefs at 1:25 P.M. August 4, Washington time, or 1:25 A.M. August 5, Tonkin Gulf time—just after the second incident ended. The message read:

> Review of action makes many recorded contacts and torpedoes fired appear doubtful. Freak weather effects and overeager sonarman may have accounted for many reports. No actual visual sightings by *Maddox*. Suggest complete evaluation before any further action.

Here, apparently, was a naval facility in the Pacific that

186

had monitored the flow of radio traffic back and forth during the second incident and was raising serious reservations in a message that presumably was communicated immediately to the Secretary of Defense. Yet less than six hours later the President was informing the leaders of Congress that he had ordered retaliation against North Vietnam, and neither he nor McNamara gave any hint as to the doubts that had been raised within the Navy itself. Quite the contrary. Replying to Hickenlooper, McNamara, it will be remembered, assured the legislators that there was no doubt whatsoever that the destroyers had been attacked.

Still the committee hesitated. Lausche, who had been absent at the previous meeting, was present this time, and he seemed to regard the committee discussion as virtually treasonous. A new complication was the January 23 seizure by the North Koreans of the USS *Pueblo*, a vessel identified immediately as having been engaged in electronic intelligence. The similarities between the *Pueblo* case and the Gulf of Tonkin incidents made some committee members, such as Mundt, favor an investigation of the procedures for approving potentially explosive missions of this nature. Others argued for postponing action while the Administration was seeking to negotiate the release of the *Pueblo* crew. The trouble with waiting, however, was that McNamara, the man the committee wanted most to reinterrogate, had been appointed by Johnson to the presidency of the World Bank and would be beyond the committee's reach, as an international servant, in another month.

Fulbright, who had been saying little while he gauged the sentiment among his colleagues, now made his own feelings clear. He was no longer sure, he said, what the committee's function was. He used to think it was to participate in examination of policy with the Executive branch of government. If it was simply to say amen to everything the Executive did, the committee had a very minor function and shouldn't kid itself about having any influence. His own view was that it was very dangerous to let the Executive continue with present procedures for making decisions that could—and had—led to war without indicating that this committee, at least, was deeply concerned.

He had been greatly at fault as chairman in August, 1964. He had believed the Administration's story; he had been carried away, influenced by other things of a domestic political nature. If he knew then what he knew now he would certainly not have advised the committee to recommend the resolution to the Senate. On that score he could speak for Senator Russell as well. When he showed him the staff study and said he felt at fault, Russell had said, "I do too. I don't know why I did not ask for some further consideration. I sat with you, my committee sat with you, and we all just accepted it without question."

If the committee decided to forget the whole thing, he, Fulbright, was not going to make any big howl. But he thought an attempt to find out what happened was well worth making, if the committee was to amount to anything. If the members were discreet enough to keep their mouths shut, national security would not be endangered. He did not want a big furor. It was really up to them.

The effect of his homily was told in front-page headlines of the following day.[8] The Senate Foreign Relations Committee had decided by "consensus" (actually, only Lausche and one or two others were still opposed) to invite Secretary of Defense Robert S. McNamara to appear before it in secret session as part of the committee's review of the Gulf of Tonkin incidents of August, 1964. Subsequent news stories—McNamara would be happy to accede but in view of other commitments in his few remaining weeks in office . . . ; McNamara would be happy to appear but his other scheduled appearances on Capitol Hill—reflected the difficulty Marcy was having in pinning McNamara's office down to a date.

At one point Jack Stempler called Marcy, saying Mc-

Namara was asking when he was going to get a look at that staff study. Stempler was a big-league lawyer with his role to play in the Executive branch, just as Marcy had his role in the Legislative branch. The two understood each other perfectly and always got along well. Marcy could not resist replying that the study was an internal working paper of the Senate Foreign Relations Committee and currently under review by the chairman—the phraseology employed by Stempler in refusing to let Marcy have the command-and-control study on the Tonkin Gulf incidents done by WSEG. Stempler laughed.

Marcy was candid with him. The staff study was based exclusively on official material supplied by the Defense Department, and the department could easily put a task force of sixty people to work tearing it apart. No doubt holes could be picked in the study; McNamara, in appearing before the committee, would have to pick out no more than two or three to discredit the study in many members' eyes and then snow the committee with a hundred affidavits from the destroyers' crew.

Stempler agreed that these were valid points from Marcy's point of view, but the Secretary did need to know what was bothering the committee and what points he should address himself to when he appeared (the date having finally been set for February 20). It was agreed that this was an issue that could be resolved only between the Secretary and Senator Fulbright, and that the Secretary ought to telephone the chairman to make the request himself.

The Secretary did—to no avail. A letter from Fulbright to McNamara the next day made it formal. The chairman expressed appreciation of the Secretary's concern that his testimony be fully responsive to the wishes of the committee, but the committee did not wish to release the study at this time. The interest of the committee was not in a discussion of the staff study but in the Secretary's testimony before the committee on August 6, 1964. Therefore, in the interest of a thorough discussion, the committee was making available to the Secretary's office a copy of the transcript of the 1964 testimony. The chairman hoped that the Secretary would be able to review this transcript and bring the committee up to date.

The chairman looked forward to seeing him on the morning of February 20.

Return Engagement **11**

His limousine drew up at the Senate entrance at
five minutes of the appointed hour, as always, but this time
he came not as he had three and a half years before, the
distinguished Secretary of Defense accompanied by the distinguished Secretary of State and the Chairman of the
Joint Chiefs of Staff, all three of them happy to accommodate the distinguished Senators in the performance of a
necessary chore. This time Robert S. McNamara came as
adversary, striding, almost charging, through the tranquil
corridors into the glowing room of historic memories, brush-
ing past the assembled reporters, with General Wheeler
and half a dozen aides in tow, files to flip open for any
detail that might escape his mind, and two hundred copies
of a twenty-page statement that, Marcy was quick to notice,
was not preceded by the usual embargo against release to
the press.

Fulbright, as always, drew him aside for a chat in Marcy's
adjoining office, inquiring after his wife Marge, who was
feeling poorly, and, as to the business ahead, expressing a
preference for no statement for the press, at least not until
they could issue a joint statement or simultaneous statements. And when the eighteen Senators and their taciturn
witness were seated around the great oval table, Wheeler

next to McNamara across the table from Fulbright, their aides (including two navy captains) perched on a row of chairs behind them, and Marcy and Bader at the vacated secretaries' desks behind the chairman, Fulbright began with a graceful little tribute to the Secretary's talents and energy and his long and arduous service to his country, saying it wasn't the purpose of the hearing to apportion blame but to evaluate past decisions in the light of later developments so as to help future Senators and Secretaries and Presidents develop wiser procedures in foreign crises. He knew the Secretary was fond of T. S. Eliot, and "you will therefore appreciate the thought behind Eliot's words, 'History may be servitude, History may be freedom.'"

Fulbright's reconciliatory attitude had a reason. He had been surprised by McNamara's performance on a "Meet the Press" television program a week before. In contrast to Rusk, who appeared on the same program and sat like a wooden Buddha admitting to no lapse of wisdom in his past, present or future, McNamara was discursive, open-minded on the problems of being Secretary, quoting Eliot instead of figures—the private after-sundown McNamara permitted to push the public daytime McNamara aside a bit, and in full view. Perhaps, Fulbright mused aloud, in a meeting with his staff, McNamara had softened; perhaps he was ready to be more relaxed about the Tonkin affair and have a frank talk with the committee, if approached the right way.

McNamara, everyone knew, had had a bad year. The metallic efficiency of his F-111 project, the all-purpose fighter bomber for the three services, was unraveling like tin foil. The navy version was too heavy to meet its height and range requirements, just as the admirals with their seat-of-the-pants approach to these problems had told him it would be. The air force model was still having wing-breakage problems in its final tests. Russell suggested that McNamara lose an F-111 in Russia so the Russians would copy it and "put their air force out of business." Other Congressional friends of the military who had long waited for their revenge joined in the mockery. Johnson took it all in. His awe of his Secretary of Defense was on the wane.

Then there was the missile controversy. McNamara had completed the gigantic buildup of offensive missiles begun in 1961. But the Russians were closing the gap, there was a beating of drums for a new jump in American production, and somewhere in the depths of his projection charts McNamara was stricken by an enormous truth. In the kingdom of megadeath, nuclear "superiority" was a mirage, the think-tank calculations of controlled response against missile sites but not against cities one huge absurdity. The nuclear race had to be wound down; "parity" was enough. But the weapons he had created were generating their own constituencies, another Presidential campaign was in the offing, and in the fall of 1967 McNamara made an extraordinary speech. First he demolished all the reasons being given for deploying an antimissile defense system (ABM). Then he announced a decision to deploy an ABM, a "thin" one, he explained, for defense against China. It was a bit of flummery that fooled no one. The mini-ABM was aimed not against the Chinese but against the Republicans, who were planning to use against Johnson the same phony "missile-gap" charge that had been used against them by Kennedy. Once in place, the thin ABM would thicken. McNamara, overruled by Johnson, contributed to the "mad momentum" he had tried so hard to stop.

But it was Vietnam that brought him down. The quantifier of the war had failed to quantify something, for while his measurements kept recording steady progress, his common sense told him that his master equation—x amount of power applied against y amount of resistance will bring z results—was off on a cybernetic kick of its own with no relation to reality. The numerical magic that had worked so well, give or take an F-111 now and then, had produced a disastrous, immeasurable flop, and the reason why was a question that was driving him, some of his friends intimated, to a crisis of personal identity. He began trying to write off the war as he wrote off the Edsel, but the war's constituency now included the Joint Chiefs of Staff and the President. If he could glean any satisfaction from the experience, it was in the way it ended, in a dramatic public split with the Chiefs before the Stennis subcommittee in which he opposed expanding the bombing of North Vietnam as militarily ineffective, except if taken to a point likely to bring China into the war. He won on points and lost with Johnson, for Russell and Stennis told the President they wouldn't support him on the war if he didn't support the Chiefs on the bombing, and the bombing was expanded. And in November of 1967, to McNamara's and Washington's confoundment alike, Johnson announced his regretful decision to accede to his Defense Secretary's wishes to be transferred to the presidency of the World Bank (a job they had discussed glancingly as something that might be looked into after the 1968 election).

For Johnson, after the election was too late. A Secretary of Defense who was putting the Chiefs in a rebellious mood and making dovelike sounds at parties with Bobby Kennedy and not standing one hundred percent behind him on Vietnam was not a man he wanted on his campaign team. And Johnson, as McGeorge Bundy perhaps had learned, was a master of the fast shuffle. And yet a question remained. Did Johnson, seeing McNamara's discomposure over Vietnam, also mean it as an act of kindness, and did McNamara practically connive, if only subconsciously, at his own banishment, accepting failure at the end with a kind of relief?

At any rate, there he was, Robert Strange McNamara, reshaper of the American military establishment, in his final fortnight in the Pentagon—a good guy suddenly to the liberals, who saw in his abrupt exit the removal of the last moderating influence from the inner councils of an obsessed President; a humanist, as he saw himself, worried, guilt-ridden perhaps, over a war he had made possible by providing the General Purpose Forces with which to fight it; wondering perhaps if he had really brought the Pentagon under civilian control or whether, in expanding the generals' budget and schooling them against their will in the techniques of modern management, he had made them all the more powerful and harder to resist. Might not McNamara in such humor be willing to admit that the Gulf of Tonkin incidents had not been handled in the best possible manner; that it had been a difficult moment, with many men under great strain; that some mistakes had undoubtedly been made; that even though he still stood by his decisions as the best he could have reached in the circumstances, it might be good for him and the committee to go over the record together and see what lessons for the future could be drawn?

It was along these lines that Fulbright appeared to have reasoned after seeing McNamara on television. Bader found him the T. S. Eliot quotation from "Little Gidding" that he read to McNamara in his opening statement, paraphrasing it as embodying, in the context of the hearing, "your own desire that the United States profit from its mistakes, not repeat them."

McNamara thanked Fulbright for his "personal kind wishes and compliments." He acknowledged the felicity of the quotation. And he came on roughshod—McNamara in combat, as deaf to compromise as the McNamara of yore.[1]

First, about his statement. He doubted that the Pentagon would be able to withstand "pressures of the press" for release of the statement before the day was out. Fulbright objected that this would present a "one-sided picture," since it would be impossible for the committee to release anything comprehensive that soon. Gore pointed out that statements presented at secret hearings were normally released only with committee permission. McNamara was unresponsive. He complained about the staff study. The committee's refusal to let him see the study placed him under "very serious handicap." Fulbright pointed out that the study was based exclusively on material from the Secretary's office. McNamara picked up his statement, racing through it until Case requested him to read slower, so the members could follow.

Over three and a half years had passed, McNamara read, since he appeared before this committee to testify concerning the attacks on the *Maddox* and the *Turner Joy*, but "even with the advantage of hindsight, I find that the essential facts of the two attacks appear today as they did then."

Was the patrol for legitimate purposes? Certainly. These patrols, code-named DeSoto, had the "primary purpose" of observing infiltration by sea from North to South Vietnam, and the "secondary purpose" of "area familiarization" and visual and electronic observation of any other activity of military interest. There was nothing sinister about the extra equipment brought aboard the *Maddox*. It consisted "in essence" of standard shipboard radio receivers to give the ship "an added capability for detecting indications of a possible hostile attack on the patrol."

Were the attacks unprovoked? Of course. Prior to the August 2 incident, the *Maddox* was under orders to go no closer to the coastline than eight miles and no closer to any offshore island than four miles. After the August 2 incident, the *Maddox* and the *Turner Joy* were under orders to go no closer than eleven miles to the coast. The orders were followed. That meant that the ships stayed well outside North Vietnamese territorial waters—

(Surprised looks around the table: Didn't North Vietnam claim a limit of *twelve* miles?)

—which the United States had to assume extended three miles from shore, since Hanoi had proclaimed no change in the three-mile rule of the French colonial administration, announcing a twelve-mile claim only on September 1, 1964. The patrol was in no way connected with the South Vietnamese coastal raids, being 130 miles away from the scene of the bombardment at the time of the first foray on the night of July 30–31 and at least 70 miles away at the time of the second raid on the night of August 3–4. As to why he had not told the committee of the second raid when he testified on August 6, "I learned [about it] subsequent to my testimony."

Did the August 4 attack on the destroyers really take place? Unquestionably. Although the radio messages from the destroyers contained some "apparent ambiguities and contradictions" which we "reconciled to our satisfaction," the evidence of an attack was conclusive: radar contacts of high-speed craft shadowing the destroyers and closing in; a report that two torpedoes had passed close to the *Turner Joy* and that gunfire against the patrol had been observed; visual sightings by various crewmen of a torpedo wake, a boat silhouetted by flares and another boat silhouetted by a shell burst, a column of black smoke rising after a radar-registered hit, a searchlight beam, and lights that appeared to be the cockpit lights of a patrol craft; and visual sightings by two American flyers of gun flashes and a "snaky" high-speed wake on the surface of the water and light antiaircraft bursts in the air.

Was all this evidence in before the President ordered "our limited, measured response"? Not all, but enough "to establish beyond any doubt then or now that an attack had taken place," particularly when taken together with "intelligence reports received from a highly classified and unimpeachable source" revealing that the North Vietnamese intended to attack the patrol, then that they had reported being involved in an engagement, and finally that they had reported losing two boats.

"No one within the Department of Defense has reviewed

all of this information without arriving at the unqualified conclusion that a determined attack was made on the *Maddox* and the *Turner Joy* in the Tonkin Gulf on the night of August 4, 1964." That included Admirals Johnson and Moorer and General Burchinal, the Director of the Joint Staff.

Why then, in the face of all this evidence, were there still "persistent questions as to whether or not an attack took place"? He could only conclude that many of the questioners were confusing the August 4 incident with the incident of September 18, 1964, in which, of course, the destroyers' reports of an attack proved to be erroneous.

A "final point." There had been a

suggestion that in some way the Government of the United States induced the incident on August 4 with the intent of providing an excuse to take retaliatory action which we in fact took. I can only characterize such insinuations as monstrous. . . . I find it inconceivable that anyone even remotely familiar with our society and system of Government could suspect the existence of a conspiracy which would include almost, if not at all, the entire chain of military command in the Pacific, the Chairman of the Joint Chiefs of Staff, the Joint Chiefs, the Secretary of Defense and his chief civilian assistants, the Secretary of State, and the President of the United States.

He would now be happy to answer questions.

＊

＊　＊

To a number of the Senators the last paragraph was the tip-off. McNamara was addressing himself not to the committee, primarily, but to the public. He was determined to win a propaganda victory over the committee, and the vehicle for his victory was his opening statement, a model of selectivity in which everything that helped his case marched in serried measures and anything that weakened his case was camouflaged or hidden or left out, and come hell or high water he was going to release his statement and appropriate the headlines in the next morning's papers and bury whatever Fulbright or other committee critics might have to say.

Fulbright had figured that to be his strategy when he saw his mimeographed stack, but hoped he would change his mind. The insinuation that the committee was alleging the existence of a conspiracy was deeply offensive to Fulbright. The appeal to the "new" McNamara had been a waste of time. However troubled his spirit over Vietnam in general, his guard on the Gulf of Tonkin affair was as impenetrable as ever. There was nothing for it but to go down the list of questions suggested by Bader on the basis of the radio traffic and the ships' logs, and this Fulbright proceeded to do.

Did the U.S. military, in the seven or eight months prior to the Gulf of Tonkin incidents, recommend extension of the war to North Vietnam by bombing or any other means?

McNamara seemed to suffer a loss of memory. "Mr. Chairman, I would have to check the record on that. . . . I can't recall. . . ."

Did General Wheeler remember?

General Wheeler wasn't sure either, but "to the best of my knowledge and belief during that period there was no thought of extending the war into the North. . . . I will check for the record."

The written answer supplied during the subsequent forty-eight hours seemed oddly indefinite:

We have identified no such recommendation. A check of the records of the Joint Chiefs of Staff is continuing.

The most immediate result of the Gulf of Tonkin incidents was the deployment of fighter bombers into South Vietnam and Thailand, Fulbright continued. "Is that not so?"

McNamara could not recall that either, even though he

had announced it himself and Morse read his 1964 testimony on the deployments back to him. He said he would check.

"Were these units alerted to impending movement prior to the Tonkin incidents?" Fulbright asked.

Wheeler said he'd check. The written answer to that was positively elliptical:

We have not identified any air unit which had been alerted for movement into South Vietnam or Thailand prior to the Tonkin Gulf incidents. A check of the records is continuing.

On August 6, 1964, Fulbright went on, the Secretary testified before this committee that the destroyers were "engaged in a routine patrol." Was the *Maddox* in fact engaged in an electronic spy mission similar to the *Pueblo*'s?

The questions, as cutting in tone as in substance, were getting under McNamara's skin. "I haven't compared, myself, item by item, the equipment on the *Pueblo* and the *Maddox*." But, yes, electronic surveillance was one of the *Maddox*'s missions. Such missions were, of course, routine. They had been going on along the coastlines of Communist countries in the western Pacific since 1962. Electronic surveillance was not, of course, the *Maddox*'s primary mission. The primary mission, as he had already explained, was to observe coastal infiltration.

Fulbright went down his list. "The *Maddox* was authorized, and I quote from the orders, 'to stimulate Chicom–North Vietnamese electronic reaction.' What does that language mean?"

"It means that they turn on certain kind of equipment on board the *Maddox* which, in turn, leads the Chicoms or the North Vietnamese to turn on the radars so that we can measure the radar frequencies."

And what was the purpose of that—"to be better able to

attack North Vietnam by air from our aircraft carriers offshore?"

"I rather doubt that the people who were gathering the information had any basis for believing there would or would not be attacks on North Vietnam."

"Mr. Secretary, why was the *Maddox* ordered to go within what the North Vietnamese believed to be their territorial waters?"

"Mr. Chairman, as I explained earlier, the North Vietnamese had not claimed waters beyond three miles, so I do not think the question is pertinent."

But it was. McNamara's statement that the United States had assumed that Hanoi regarded its territorial waters as extending only three miles to sea was a startling shift of official position. The general assumption had been that North Vietnam claimed a twelve-mile limit. The Hanoi radio all but confirmed that assumption in an English-language news broadcast of July 28, 1964, in which it accused South Vietnamese naval vessels of having "intruded into the territorial waters of the DRV" three days previously to kidnap North Vietnamese fishermen; the coordinates given by Hanoi placed the incident at nine miles offshore.[2]

Fulbright referred to the twelve-mile limit on three separate occasions when he was acting as floor manager for the Gulf of Tonkin Resolution, and the Administration, which was supplying him with arguments, did not correct him. Cyrus Vance, who was then Deputy Secretary of Defense, had this to say in a Voice of America radio interview on August 8, 1964:

FRYKLUND (*Washington Star*): Do . . . Communist China and North Vietnam claim the gulf as their territorial waters?

VANCE: Not to my knowledge. I think that they do claim a twelve-mile limit as opposed to a three-mile limit.[3]

And John McNaughton, the Assistant Secretary of Defense

for International Security Affairs (who had since been killed in a plane crash), had testified as follows in his May, 1966, secret appearance before the Foreign Relations Committee:

FULBRIGHT: Had your ships within days before the incident gone within territorial limits recognized by North Vietnam?

McNAUGHTON: Within the twelve-mile limit, Mr. Chairman.

FULBRIGHT: This is the territorial limit.

McNAUGHTON: I think that it is. If that is the case, the answer is "Yes." . . .

FULBRIGHT: . . . they claimed twelve miles. But our ships had gone into it.

McNAUGHTON: Yes, sir; that is correct.[4]

Morse read the transcript of that testimony to McNamara. All McNamara could say was that McNaughton was wrong.

Fulbright turned to the South Vietnamese coastal raids. The attacks, the material supplied by the Secretary's office had made clear, had been conducted by American-trained crews aboard American-supplied vessels and had been assigned an American code name: Operations 34-A. Under Morse's questioning at the August, 1964, hearing, the Secretary had stated that: "our Navy played absolutely no part in, was not associated with, was not aware of, any South Vietnamese actions, if there were any." Did he still think that was an accurate statement?

Yes, McNamara replied, if you read the whole statement, in which he had also said, "The *Maddox* . . . was not informed of, was not aware of, had no evidence of, and so far as I know today has no knowledge of any South Vietnamese actions."

In saying "our Navy" had not known, he meant the *Maddox* and the *Turner Joy* had not known. Higher echelons had known, of course.

Another surprise twist. Cooper intervened. He wanted to be sure he understood. Was the Secretary "stating as a fact," as he had known it then and as he knew it now, "that the commanders of the [two] ships did not know that the South Vietnamese vessels had attacked the two islands?"

"Yes, exactly so." He had asked one of his aides, just prior to this hearing, to recheck that with the commander of the patrol, Captain Herrick, "and he [Herrick] certifies that was true."

Whereupon Fulbright produced one of the messages in the flow of traffic right after the August 2 incident. Sent by Admiral Moorer in Hawaii and received, among others, by Herrick aboard the *Maddox*, the message, dealing with the decision to resume the patrol with two ships, said:

The above patrol will:

(A) Clearly demonstrate our determination to continue these operations.

(B) Possibly draw NVN PGMS [North Vietnamese naval patrol boats] to northward away from area of 34-A ops.

(C) Eliminate DeSoto patrol interference with 34-A ops.

Fulbright looked fixedly at McNamara. "It is unusual that, having received that cable, that the *Maddox* did not know what 34-A was."

Flustered, McNamara shifted ground. "The *Maddox* did know what 34-A was, no question about that. But the *Maddox* was not associated with 34-A, was not playing a part in it, was not planning to draw forces away from it."

"I thought you said they did not know anything about it," Morse said.

"Now wait a minute, I did not say they did not know anything about it!"

"You said, 'were not aware of.' "

"They were not aware of the *details* is what I said, of the attacks, as to location, or as to time, and unless one is aware of that, you cannot properly plan a diversionary effort."

Morse said, "I think we were using them [the destroyers] as a decoy."

The emotionalism that so often underlay McNamara's cold denials was coming to the surface. "No, because the North Vietnamese boats *knew* that our boats had no hostile intent and played no hostile role. They knew that from having tracked them the previous nights, and they knew that from previous patrols, so there was no basis for this assertion by the author of that cable . . . . it was not possible and it was not a plan, and it was not the purpose of the DeSoto patrol, and the Joint Chiefs had never considered that and would never have approved that purpose, nor was the patrol carried out in such a way as to permit such a purpose to be achieved!"

Fulbright produced another message, this one from Captain Herrick aboard the *Maddox*:

Evaluation of info from various sources indicates DRV [Democratic Republic of Vietnam] considers patrol directly involved with 34-A ops. DRV considers U.S. ships present as enemies because of these ops and have already indicated their readiness to treat us in that category.

What now of McNamara's assertion that the North Vietnamese "knew" that the American vessels were not hostile? The commander of the patrol had informed higher command of quite the opposite. Why wasn't the patrol broken off?

"Because," McNamara said, "we were on the high seas and operating legally and entirely within our rights." Because Captain Herrick had "no basis" for reporting that North Vietnamese considered his patrol involved in 34-A. It was "unfounded speculation" and "Herrick himself now states he can recall no basis" for saying it. "Frankly, I have in my own mind an explanation of why he sent it, but I do not think it bears on the issue at hand, and I am not going to repeat it to you."

Lausche, who had been exercising, for him, iron self-control, finally exploded. "I would more clearly be able to see what is sought to be proved if I knew the objective of this meeting. It looks to me as if it is trying to put the United States in a bad light and the North Vietnamese in a good light, and I cannot subscribe to that!"

Gore said the objective was to "develop as fully as possible the true facts relating to the incidents in the Gulf of Tonkin."

All right, Lausche steamed, but the questions all seemed to be directed toward proving that "the Communists had the right to shoot at us."

✳
✳ ✳

"I want to read a cable sent to Washington in the immediate aftermath of the second incident by the Naval Communications Center in the Philippines."

Fulbright turned to the message that had been identified for Bader by the anonymous informant in the Pentagon. "I want to note, as background, that this naval facility had monitored all of the messages coming from the *Maddox* and the *Turner Joy* during the incident."

He read the cable out loud:

Review of action makes many recorded contacts and torpedoes fired appear doubtful. Freak weather effects and overeager sonarman may have accounted for many reports. No actual visual sightings by *Maddox*. Suggest complete evaluation before any further action.

With a cable like that from the Philippines, why was there not "at least some reasonable investigation or delay" before retaliation was ordered? "I think, Mr. Secretary, you will have to admit that this was a pretty clear warning that there were some uncertainties about the situation."

McNamara was on the qui vive. "Mr. Chairman, let me make sure we have the right cable."

"Mr. Bader, bring the document."

There was a rustling of papers. Bader was trying to find

his copy. The two captains behind McNamara were fumbling in their briefcases. McNamara was saying, "Give me the date-time. . . ." One of the captains found what he was looking for and handed it to McNamara.

"Yes," McNamara said. "You say it is from the Philippines?" He had a way of turning punctilious when catching someone in error. "My message in front of me indicates it is from the commander of the task force."

Bader was nonplussed. In his copy the sender of the message was clearly identified. "It is from the communications Center, Philippines, to CINCPAC Fleet."

A schoolteacher dedicated to a somewhat retarded class could not have been more patient. "I think I am correct in saying this is a message from the task force commander. It is of some importance, as you will see later, who it came from. The underlying message is here. I will be happy to give it to you. It is exactly the same words."

Bader still couldn't understand. "Mr. Secretary, it is marked as NCS Phil."

"Yes. *But that is the relay point.* The message from the task force commander goes to the Philippines and then is relayed in here."

There was silence as the information sank in. Then Fulbright observed, "I am not sure it makes it any weaker."

The same thought appeared to have struck everyone around the table—McNamara included. It was indeed of "some importance" that the copy sent to the committee bore only the relay point's identification and not the patrol commander's, but not in a way that did McNamara's case any good. A message like that from the Philippines was admonition enough. From Herrick aboard the *Maddox* it was a klaxon call for scrapping all the preparations then being made for reprisal. Yet twelve hours later the planes were on their way.

This, Bader and Marcy agreed later, was the turning point of the hearing. Up to then the committee had sat back watching Fulbright in his almost personal showdown with the Executive, the first confrontation over a complex technical dispute of his long career, taking on the capital's most formidable technician without the help of Special Counsel that investigations of this kind usually demand, and being as rough on his witness as they had seen any chairman be on a Secretary of Defense—sat back fascinated, repressing intrusion, withholding judgment. But the revelation that the commander of the patrol himself had cast doubt on his own earlier reports of an attack swung the committee bodily into distrust of McNamara's whole position.

Why did McNamara rush in to correct the staff study? Because he wanted to get the facts straight? In a dramatist of the managerial art who had spent seven years volunteering only those facts that propped up his production, such purity of motive would be refreshing indeed. More in keeping with what the Hill knew of him was that he had been tripped up by his own determination to have the last word and discredit the competence of the committee staff.

* * *

Shortly before the hearing was recessed for lunch, the Pentagon press office called James Reston of *The New York Times*, alerting him to the imminent release of a statement by the Secretary of Defense on the Gulf of Tonkin controversy.

Just before leaving the hearing room, McNamara told Fulbright, "It will be my intention to walk out there and say nothing [to the reporters]." Fulbright said that was his intention too.

Leaving after the Chairman and the Secretary, Eugene McCarthy told the reporters that McNamara had admitted penetration of North Vietnamese territorial waters by the *Maddox* and the *Turner Joy*. A news item quoting McCarthy to that effect came over the UPI news tickers.

Shortly afterward, copies of McNamara's statement were released to reporters at the Pentagon.

The hearing reconvened, and Fulbright's first words were, "The press says the Pentagon has released it."

McNamara said, "We have, Mr. Chairman." He wanted to explain why. UPI 109, timed at 1:22 P.M., quoted a member of the committee as reporting that he, McNamara, had admitted penetration of territorial waters. He handed the UPI item to Fulbright.

Fulbright glanced at it. "It says Senator McCarthy said it."

McNamara was aggrieved. "But that is just contrary to what I said this morning." So, he explained, he had ordered his statement released to let the public know what he did say.

The explanation had a hollow ring. For one thing, it is doubtful whether anyone present, with the possible exception of Lausche, took seriously his allegation that the United States had assumed in August, 1964, that Hanoi claimed only a three-mile limit. Had he been able to produce some document of the time, even of a confidential nature, showing the Administration to have been proceeding on such an assumption, he obviously would have done so. But the only document on this issue which subsequently came to light pointed the other way. It was a memorandum from the Director of Naval Intelligence to the American diplomatic mission in Saigon, dated May 1, 1963, and stating:

According to best information, DRV has not publicly proclaimed limits of territorial seas. . . . However, there is good possibility DRV will subscribe to the twelve-mile limit claimed by other Communist nations if issue were raised.[5]

To any Senator who read the Bader report, McNamara's casuistry about Hanoi announcing a twelve-mile limit only after the Tonkin incidents covered a deliberate decision in early 1964 to permit the DeSoto patrols to violate North

Vietnamese waters while keeping a healthy fifteen-mile distance off the gulf's Chinese coast.

But even if McCarthy could be said to have misquoted McNamara in failing to explain the shift in official position as to where "territorial waters" began, McNamara could have easily set the record straight with a denial clarifying what he did say on that one point. He did not have to release his entire twenty-page statement. He had used McCarthy's comment as an excuse for doing what he had intended doing all along, to wrest the headlines away from Fulbright.

Fulbright did not dwell on this. He returned to the Herrick message. McNamara, having had two hours to ponder his pre-lunch *gaffe*, plunged into an account of the "complete evaluation" recommended by Herrick—"because, needless to say, we were concerned about the question raised." He, McNamara, had called Admiral Sharp in Honolulu, "and I have a transcript of that telephone conversation in which the specific words were, 'We obviously don't want to carry out the retaliatory strike unless we are damned sure what happened.'" There was a meeting with the Joint Chiefs, more messages from Herrick, consultations with the President ("I was just checking my diary last night as to the number of calls and meetings I had with him and it exceeded eleven during the day"), and finally, all doubts resolved, the conclusion both in Washington and in Admiral Sharp's headquarters that the ships had indeed been attacked.

The chronicle did not have the desired effect. Nothing was having the desired effect. A glaze of disbelief seemed to have come over the hearing. And though the Secretary's pique was drawn by any suggestion, as others joined in the questioning, that he was hiding anything ("I don't have anything to hide. . . . For seven years I have tried not to hide the actions of the Department. . . . I believe in disclosure, and I believe that the truth will support itself"), he backtracked when Fulbright asked for the transcript of his telephone conversation with Sharp ("I do not know all of the records that are available in the Department on such matters") and for a copy of the WSEG study, which turned out to be the work of one John Ponturo, an employee of the Institute for Defense Analyses, a private group under contract to the Joint Staff to make critical studies of command-and-control procedures during specific international crises ("I am not familiar with the man, and I don't know the degree to which he had access to all of the information that is required to obtain a proper understanding of the incident. . . . I am not willing to release a report until I know more about it").

*
* *

Fulbright read out the message from the *Turner Joy* that seemed to refer to an intercept of a North Vietnamese message. He read his letter to Ignatius asking for the text of this and other intercepts, and the Navy Secretary's rejection of his request. What could the Secretary of Defense tell the committee about these intercepts?

McNamara said, "We have some problems." He had the intercepts with him. He would be happy to show them to the Senators. But the committee staff would have to leave the room. "The staff has not been cleared for certain intelligence, and we are under specific written instructions from the President not to furnish such intelligence to uncleared personnel."

It took the committee a while to recover its wits.

LAUSCHE (dumfounded): The members of our staff are not cleared? . . . May I ask the chairman, are all the members of our staff cleared?

FULBRIGHT: All of those who have worked on this matter, but he is talking of a special classification of intelligence communications.

GORE: Mr. Chairman, could we know what particular classification that is? I had not heard of this particular classification.

FULBRIGHT: The staff are cleared for top secret information. This is something I never heard of before either.

MCNAMARA: Clearance is above top secret for the particular information involved in this situation.

GORE: I thought top secret was top secret.

McNamara was happy to elucidate. There were many kinds of clearance, rising in pyramidal structure from official to confidential to secret to top secret, to name just some. There was Q clearance. And there was the special-intelligence clearance that related to intercept information.

It was not really a question of degree of clearance. Persons were cleared on the basis of a "need to know."

Fulbright did not press the point, preferring to develop this new phase of the questioning.

According to the Secretary's opening statement, one of the North Vietnamese messages, intercepted just before the August 4 incident, stated "that North Vietnam was making preparations to attack our destroyers with two Swatow boats and with one PT boat if the PT could be made ready in time." The Defense Department's original report of six or so attacking boats was in a fair way to be scaled down to two or three. But the more significant aspect of the message was another one: there were two distinct types of patrol boats involved.

North Vietnam's sixteen or so PT boats—this prior to the American air strike—were torpedo craft of Soviet design, aluminum-hulled, most of them, equipped with 25-mm. guns, and fast (45 knots). Yet as a London dispatch to *The Christian Science Monitor* of August 8, 1964, pointed out, sending torpedo boats against destroyers in a night action was extraordinarily brash. The British, who had had considerable experience with torpedo boats protecting their sea-lanes during the Second World War, were portrayed in the dispatch as puzzled. They had thought that use of PT boats against destroyers had gone out of fashion in 1943, when a night-long skirmish in the North Sea demonstrated the extreme vulnerability of PT boats to the new technique of radar-controlled gunnery. Torpedo boats remained valuable, the dispatch said, for such work as mine-laying, security patrols, commando raids and shore screening.

Working in conjunction with their own destroyers, and under radar control, they were also used by the Royal Navy for torpedo attacks on enemy shipping. But PT boats alone to take on destroyers? No, sir.

What added to the puzzlement, in the committee's view, was the professed disclosure by the intercept that in preparing for their attack the North Vietnamese had relied principally not even on PT boats but on Swatows. Given that designation by the U.S. military because they were first observed from the air in the Chinese harbor of Swatow, these were wooden-hulled coastal patrol craft equipped with 37-mm. guns but no torpedoes, fairly slow (24 knots) and in no way designed for action against destroyers. Some twenty-five to thirty Swatows built in China from Soviet blueprints were transferred to North Vietnam in 1961.

Wasn't it unusual, Fulbright asked, for a boat of this type to attack a destroyer under any circumstances?

"Well, Mr. Chairman," McNamara replied, "I am prepared today to show you the order to Swatows to do that." But the committee staff would have to leave the room.

Fulbright still preferred to continue.

Both Swatows and PTs have radar. When a vessel such as a destroyer is contacted by a radar beam, it is told so by its electronic countermeasures (ECM) equipment. One of the *Turner Joy*'s messages after the August 4 incident noted that there had been "no ECM" immediately preceding or during the action; "must admit," the message said, that this "lack of radar signals" was a factor to be weighed.

How could the North Vietnamese vessels have located the destroyers sixty-five miles out to sea, on a black and stormy night, without use of radar?

McNamara was stumped.

Wheeler and the two captains huddled for about thirty seconds. They obviously weren't prepared for the question either.

"I have been given three answers," Wheeler said. "They could track on the wakes of the destroyers, they could have been vectored by radars on shore, or they could have been vectored from Swatows over the horizon."

Constrained as he was by protocol, there was no way for Bader to communicate to the committee his professional disdain for these answers. "Vectored" meant nothing more than steered. A shore station or a boat at sea could steer an attacking vessel to its target by voice broadcast or Morse signal, but to do so it would have to locate the target by radar. And the target would know it was being contacted by radar. And there was no radar contact in this case.

As for tracking the destroyers' wakes, finding wakes on a night like that would have been as difficult as finding the ships themselves.

Judging from the expressions on some of the Senators' faces, the committee did not need Bader's help to find the explanation contrived.

Wasn't it "extraordinarily stupid" of the North Vietnamese, Fulbright plowed on, to leave their patrol boats tied at the dock in broad daylight, vulnerable to the American air strike, if they had attacked American ships the previous night?

"I suppose they presumed since we had not retaliated against them after the first attack on *Maddox* that we would not retaliate when they had a second attack, Mr. Chairman," Wheeler ventured. Or maybe they "did not anticipate that we would be quite as prompt."

FULBRIGHT: Mr. Secretary, how do you account for the fact that the North Vietnamese boasted of their attack on the *Maddox* on August 2 and yet vehemently denied that there had been an incident on August 4?

McNAMARA: I cannot answer the question, Mr. Chairman. Their damage may have been greater on the 4th than it was on the 2nd, I just do not know.

FULBRIGHT: Do you have any idea, General Wheeler?

WHEELER: I have no idea, Mr. Chairman.

Fulbright, however, had a clue—the testimony of a senior commander of the North Vietnamese navy who was captured, along with nineteen other naval personnel, when three PT boats were sunk in an engagement with U.S. naval forces in the Gulf of Tonkin in 1966.

Acting on the tip in Commander Cowles' letter, Bader had obtained a copy of the interrogation record. The senior officer had been interrogated for more than a hundred hours. He was described as cooperative and reliable—not particularly unusual qualities among prisoners undergoing interrogation. When the question of the August, 1964, incidents came up, the officer proved to know all about the action against the *Maddox* on August 2. He said he had written the subsequent action report. He also gave the Navy information that enabled it to destroy a number of North Vietnamese patrol boats in their bases.

Fulbright read McNamara an excerpt from the interrogation report. The prisoner "obviously has traveled in higher circles and has proved himself exceptionally knowledgeable on almost every naval subject and event of interest. *Yet he specifically and strongly denies that any attack took place" on August 4* [italics added].

How account for this denial from a man who had proved so credible in all other respects, Fulbright asked, particularly since the other captured crewmen, according to the same report, also "disclaim any knowledge of such an attack" and "state definitely and emphatically that no PTs could have been involved"?

True, the report did say that North Vietnamese torpedo-boat crews apparently had little contact with other types of ships, and that "When pressed further on this issue he [the commander] states that if such an attack did take place it could only have been committed by Swatows." But Swatows have no torpedoes, and where would that leave the Navy's evidence of a torpedo attack?

This time McNamara had an answer ready.

The testimony of the prisoner captured in 1966 was not nearly as "comprehensive" and "illuminating" as that of another man, an individual of some rank in the North Vietnamese navy, who was captured a year later, in July, 1967. This prisoner "gave us the name of the squadron commander in charge of the PT boats participating in the August 2 attack." And in one of the North Vietnamese messages intercepted on August 4, *this same PT-boat squadron leader was identified by name and boat number as participating in the August 4 attack.*

So—McNamara drove the point home—there *were* PT boats attacking on August 4, and the 1966 prisoner who said there weren't any was wrong.

All this "came to light only within the past few days," and it bore on the information in the intercepts, "and I am afraid that the record will be distorted unless we introduce it at this point." But those not cleared for special intelligence, other than the Senators, would have to leave the room.

This time Fulbright acquiesced.

What followed was remembered by Bader as curiously theatrical. "There was a certain numbness to it all. The unexpected became the acceptable. Somehow I didn't even question the idea of leaving the room, which seemed peculiar to me even as I did it. What surprised me more than anything else was that so experienced and astute a personage as Marcy, the Great Gray Owl, didn't react to it any more than I did. We were all Kabukilike, with stylized roles to play in the last act of the McNamara saga."

Triple-cleared for security, the chief of staff of the Senate Foreign Relations Committee and his naval-intelligence-trained consultant got up from behind their piles of top-secret naval documents and retreated into Marcy's office like a pair of faintly suspicious interlopers, closing the door behind them—an awkward and embarrassing moment, some of the others thought, quite new to the committee's experience. The number of persons who had been cleared to see the intercepts must have increased since the day when Nitze told Fulbright that only half a dozen others had seen them, for McNamara's aides remained in their seats. The official reporter joined the outcasts in the back room. What followed was not recorded by anyone, not even for the committee's own private files.

McNamara said he had known when he released his opening statement, which contained the gist of the intercepts, that he would thereby be revealing to the North Vietnamese that the United States had broken one of their codes. But after McCarthy violated their agreement that nothing was to be said to the press, he, McNamara, decided that it was more important to preserve the Administration's credibility with the public than to keep the existence of the intercepts secret from Hanoi.

He then read the intercepts to the committee, saying he was sure the Senators would agree that the messages provided conclusive proof of an August 4 attack. As to the need for such secrecy, he read a communication from General Joseph F. Carroll, head of the Defense Intelligence Agency (an overall intelligence clearing house for the Joint Chiefs and the Secretary of Defense), saying the United States would face serious penalties if the source of the information were disclosed.

Fulbright moved the hearing back to normal. The door to Marcy's office was opened, and Marcy and Bader—sitting far back, as though to obviate any suspicion of having had their ears to the keyhole—went back to their desks. The official reporter resumed taking down the proceedings for the record. The interlude had lasted ten to fifteen minutes.

*

* *

Winter evening darkened the windows. In seven hours of testimony, McNamara had done nothing to clear up the doubts raised by the Bader report. In fact, Gore told him, "there is more question now than when you came."

Fulbright concluded with an indictment. It had been "very unfair" of the Secretary to ask the committee to vote for a resolution on evidence "as uncertain as I think it now is, even if your intercepts are correct." The Herrick message alone, if he had known of it, would have stayed him from steering the resolution to adoption—"a great disservice to the Senate," something he regretted "more than anything I have ever done in my life." And was the Pentagon now resorting to intimidation to keep its people from talking to the committee? Was the Secretary aware that a navy commander who was in the Flag Plot at the time of the incidents and who recently had come to see him, Fulbright, to relieve himself of a burden on his conscience was picked up the next day and sent to a psychiatric ward?

Fulbright's anger over the sequel to Commander Cowles' visit spilled out in the release of resentment against the Secretary of Defense he had trusted so completely. McNamara said he was "not aware of that incident" but would look into it. He could not believe that anyone in the Defense Department would be subjected to psychiatric examination for speaking to the committee. Besides, the man in question "was *not* assigned to Flag Plot at the time of the incidents." *

* This was a technicality that was to be repeated by Pentagon officials in an obvious attempt to discredit Cowles. The commander was not assigned to Flag Plot formally until August 20, 1964, but he was on "training station" there—to learn the job—beginning July 23.

Gore felt he had "been misled and the American people have been misled." Morse said he had heard nothing the whole day to make him change one word of his Tonkin Gulf speeches of August, 1964. Of the hitherto hawkish members, only Lausche had come to McNamara's defense, and that so incoherently as to be more of an embarrassment than a help. Symington, who had come to Rusk's aid during the Vietnam hearings, was no longer to be counted on. Having concluded that the military would not get from the civilians what they needed in the way of manpower and freedom of action in Indochina to achieve their objectives, and having just about given up on effective support from the peoples of the area for resistance to Communist expansion, Symington had turned against the whole enterprise. In the months to come, as head of the Subcommittee on United States Security Agreements and Commitments Abroad, he was to be Fulbright's principal investigator into the ancillary roots of involvement in Thailand, Laos and Cambodia.

McNamara was unchastened. To the last he retracted nothing, amended nothing, admitted nothing (except that he may have stumbled into "ambiguity" in saying "our Navy" did not know about 34-A Ops when he meant "the patrol"), repeating whole chunks of his opening statement ("I worked until 8:30 last night trying to be certain this statement was accurate, I had some of the best lawyers in the Department work on it, and I submit to you it is *not* misleading"); insisting that the Administration was "absolutely not" in any doubt about the August 4 attack when it retaliated; denying that the reprisal was excessive considering that no damage had been done to the American ships ("The crime was not measured by the amount of damage done, it was measured by the violation of our right to navigate freely on the high seas"); maintaining that the electronic and eyewitness evidence had been solid enough for the Administration to have reached the conclusion it did even without the intelligence intercepts, though committee members who had looked into the matter knew that his evidence added little to the AP report while omitting the AP's disclosures of doubt and confusion; even fishing into his pocket for the bullet of August 2 that he seemed determined to get triumphantly into the record: "Here it is, right here!"

Gore, who had a low tolerance for that particular exhibit ever since McNaughton "kept waving it in our faces" in the May, 1966, hearing, complained, "You hold one bullet and we sent sixty-four [sorties]," and Fulbright observed that with the Secretary's statement in the hands of the news media there was pressure on the committee to right the balance by releasing the entire hearing transcript.

McNamara was unfazed. "I would be delighted to see it released," he said, obviously confident that he had not only bested the committee with his statement but had swept the decks with his answers.

Fulbright just as obviously thought the transcript would show up the weakness of the Administration's case, and there he was content to rest—to stop short of an assault on the enigma that remained embedded in the hearing record and rendered his investigation inconclusive in the end. For if the most reasonable deduction to be drawn from the physical evidence was that the attacking force on August 4 had been a phantom of electronic tricks and fevered imaginations, how reconcile that with intercepted North Vietnamese radio messages attesting to the actuality of the attack?

Fulbright might have got at the riddle. When McNamara showed himself eager to bring out the intercepts, his ace in the hole, but dead set against letting Marcy and Bader remain in the room, Fulbright might have asked himself, Why? Was there something about those messages he did not wish to expose to questioning by the committee staff after the technical competence it had shown in its study of the radio traffic to and from the destroyers? Fulbright might have said, All right, Mr. Secretary, we will accept this material in evidence; we will ask the staff to leave the room. But that will not dispose of the matter. As Senators without expertise in this field, we may not be able to ask the right questions. I would like your Department to give Mr. Marcy and Mr. Bader the proper clearance as soon as possible, so that the committee may evaluate this crucial material for itself.

It would have been difficult for McNamara to refuse: the criterion for clearing otherwise "cleared" personnel for special intelligence information—their "need to know"—would certainly have been operative. Clearance would have been accomplished by a car ride by a Pentagon security officer to Capitol Hill.

Fulbright did not make the request. He chose instead to indicate by his demeanor what he had expressed at his meeting with Nitze: his scorn for messages that included claims the Americans knew to be false. Gore sought to denigrate the messages on the same general ground after Marcy and Bader resumed their places—first, by forcing McNamara to concede that the so-called "attack" message directed the North Vietnamese boats not to "attack" but merely to "make ready for military operations," and second, by arguing that the other messages, with their claims of bringing down enemy planes and damaging an enemy vessel, could have been the exaggerations of a North Vietnamese commander. But that only begged the question. As Nitze said, the North Vietnamese crews may have been boasting, but their messages showed they were there and attacking. If Fulbright wanted to prove or disprove his now-apparent belief that there was no attack at all, he could do so not by discounting the contents of the messages but by digging into their origin, their nature, their timing, the technical background in which the answer to the mystery lay. Why he did not pursue the investigation to this bitter end is a question to which some speculative answers may be offered.

He was emotionally drained by his daylong contest, feeling he had been outmaneuvered by McNamara on the publicity level, concerned with the difficulties of making public the material he had—the Executive took its time about "sanitizing" transcripts even if the committee would agree to release it—rather than with going after new information. At the same time, the hearing had lifted from him a tremendous psychological burden. No longer could anyone—no longer could he—wonder whether in some part of his being he had acted in August, 1964, in complicity with the White House. He had proved to the Senate, to the American people, to himself, that he had been deceived.

He had made a political dead letter of the Gulf of Tonkin Resolution, Johnson's engine for the Vietnam war, by establishing that it had been passed by Congress on the basis of misleading testimony, and he had thereby thrown the validity and legality of the whole Vietnam venture into sharpest question—or he would, as soon as the transcript was out. He had forced a confrontation that was nudging the Senate into a reassertion of its war-making power. The atmosphere in the committee room after McNamara left was heady. The Senators had ventured into unknown territory and had prevailed.

Why push things further? To call in admirals in a Pearl Harbor type of investigation, pit their word against that of other witnesses, dig into the supersecret workings of the National Security Agency, the code-breaking arm of U.S. intelligence, would have placed him outside the limits of political reasonableness as understood in the Senate, tearing the delicate nexus of relationships with colleagues and constituents on which a moderate like Fulbright depended and bringing rightist charges of treason on his head, and all this in a year in which he was up for re-election. What public good would come of it? Fulbright was a gentle man, a profound believer in the American process who was appalled at the very thought of a conspiracy, rather like a husband with complete faith in his young wife's virtue who would still shy from inquiring too closely into her comings and goings.

He had carried the investigation as far as he cared to. He would have preferred to have carried it further at the hearing itself—to have arrived with McNamara's cooperation at a balanced verdict on the Gulf of Tonkin incidents, a verdict of comprehension and hence forgiveness of whatever sins of commission or omission were present on both sides, marking the start of a healthier Congressional–Executive relationship, a re-examination of the way a great nation goes to war, even a "limited" one, and he had been prepared to drop the role of prosecutor to obtain that magnanimous accord. But the hope had been illusory from the outset, for it required of Robert McNamara that he submit to what for him would have been a terrible judgment—not that he had been wrong, for he had always been able, if with difficulty, to admit a mistake, but that he had been unsure, and in the confusion had lost control, expertly mismanaging the whole thing.

Backstage 12

Even if Fulbright had wanted to carry the investigation further, he would not have had a majority of the committee behind him. The zest of battle in a righteous cause was quick to evaporate as the encounter moved into the open, and Fulbright's charge that the nation was being deceived by its Secretary of Defense raised the combat to a raging dispute between the committee and the Executive. Morse, Gore and McCarthy were game for it (Church would have been too if not for a difficult election ahead), but Mansfield pleaded for a truce in these "most troublous days in the entire history of the Republic," and members who had been bluntly critical behind closed doors offered mild comment in public, while Lausche and Thomas Dodd of Connecticut accused the committee of "giving aid and comfort to the enemy." Release of the hearing transcript was the most the committee would agree to, and when its revelations were spread across the front pages the next Sunday morning—the Pentagon having "sanitized" the document within twenty-four hours, deleting only 250 of its 620,000 words, and Marcy having worked until 4 A.M. putting it in shape for the Government Printing Office—Fulbright was satisfied. He had not been able to influence the President's policy, but he had succeeded in obtaining a good portion of the truth and bringing it to the people, who could not be expected to exercise their judgment if the truth were concealed from them but who could, with their votes, change both Presidents and policies once the truth was made known. Or so he hoped.

In a final act of political courage, Morse stood in an almost empty Senate, Bader's report in hand, and read the bulk of the radio messages to and from the destroyers into the *Congressional Record*, flaunting the restrictions on revealing classified material.[1] And at the end of 1968, a year that saw Lyndon Johnson fall and Martin Luther King and Robert Kennedy assassinated and the capital burn and a Democratic party convention turn into a rehearsal for civil war, there was a little item in the papers that had, it could be argued, some bearing on the origins of the darkness coming over the land. It recorded the appearance of a new Senate Foreign Relations Committee pamphlet, a fourteen-page document rounding off some of the unanswered questions of the McNamara hearing of the previous February.[2]

Little wonder that the new answers were hardly noticed. Who, in a year like that, still remembered the controversy over North Vietnam's territorial sea limit (the new release uncovered the 1963 memo of the Director of Naval Intelligence saying Hanoi probably placed it at twelve miles); or McNamara's and Wheeler's testimony that they knew of no plans pre-dating Tonkin Gulf to extend the war to North Vietnam (the committee now had a letter from Assistant Secretary of Defense Paul C. Warnke conceding that the Joint Chiefs in early 1964 had done contingency planning for "several types of military action which might be brought against North Vietnam," although "no definitive recommendations for extending the war to the north had in fact been made"); or the fact that the Defense Department, in disregard of Nitze's agreement with Fulbright that all "relevant" documents would be made available to the committee, was still refusing to turn over the study of the Tonkin Gulf incidents done by John Ponturo of the Institute for Defense Analyses (the release included a letter from Warnke reiterating that "the study is not considered appropriate for dissemination outside the Department" since the author "did not have access to sources of information that would be essential to an overall evaluation"); or various similar points over which McNamara and his questioners had sparred?

"These documents," Fulbright wrote, "are not offered with the view to revive the controversy over the incidents in the Gulf of Tonkin but to complete, to the best of the committee's ability, the public record." And so the Fulbright inquiry was formally over. But the public record was far from complete. Just as the Vietnam hearings of 1966 had broken the spell of silence on the war for the general public, so the McNamara hearing of 1968 had made "Tonkin Gulf" into a code word in the public mind for some kind of trickery easing Johnson's slide into the war—without, however, establishing whether trickery had indeed been practiced and, if so, what precisely it had consisted of. In Congress and in the media, obscured by the stress on more immediate national concerns, the questions that had bedeviled Bader's inquiry still festered.

Were the Gulf of Tonkin incidents deliberately provoked? If so, why? So the United States could retaliate against North Vietnam? And Johnson get his war mandate from Congress? Was there an attack on August 4? Did the President and the Secretary of Defense retaliate knowing there was no attack? Or were they misled by the military? Where did those intercepts come from? Were they misread or doctored or fabricated? By whom? "Monstrous" as McNamara held the thought to be, indignantly as Fulbright denied that anyone on his committee had ever entertained the idea, was there a conspiracy?

* * *

It would have been difficult for even the most assiduous

reader of the major dailies in the winter and spring of 1964 to have formed a very clear notion of how the Johnson Administration was viewing the fortunes of the Saigon government and its 16,000 American advisers in the post-Diem phase of the Vietnamese civil war. There were occasional veiled warnings of possible unspecified punishment for the North Vietnamese for helping the Vietcong with infiltrators, supplies and direction, and South Vietnam's air force commander, Commodore Nguyen Cao Ky, distressed the American military in Saigon by revealing that his men had been flying commando teams north of the seventeenth parallel, but Washington officials played down this activity as sporadic, small-scale and ineffective and reiterated that the contest was one that had to be fought and won in the South. The net impression was that the President and his advisers, while watching the Vietnam situation closely, were fairly sanguine about it. Cultivated at Johnson's behest as part of his effort to keep everything sunny until the November election, this impression was wholly false. In the long history of violent swings between the high and low points of Washington's expectations in Vietnam, the plunge to pessimism in the flow of operational and intelligence estimates to the White House had never been more marked.

Unknown to anyone outside a small circle of high-level officials, bold plans for reversing the trend were afoot. The plans were to remain one of the best-kept secrets of modern history. Their gist began to have underground currency in some political and academic circles only in late 1970, when the contents of a highly classified and richly documented 7,000-page Defense Department study of the Indochina involvement—ordered by McNamara in June, 1967, to clarify the whole enterprise for the government and (he later said) for future historians (and, one suspects, for himself)—began to leak out. Then *The New York Times* obtained a copy of the so-called "McNamara Papers" and published a partial account of the study—an admirably candid if fragmented history of government decision making, on the whole—in a series of reports starting June 13, 1971.*

The Joint Chiefs of Staff made their proposal in January, 1964. Unimpressed by the counterinsurgency, pacification, land-reform and other schemes of the civilian dabblers for wresting the initiative from the Vietcong, the military concluded that the war could not be won by measures confined to South Vietnam, short of the introduction of hundreds of thousands of American combat troops. But it could be called off. By the other side, naturally. The problem was how to make the other side do it.[3]

What the Joint Chiefs proposed was all-out bombing of North Vietnam, starting with a big B-52 night raid on the Phuc Yen airfield with its cluster of MIGs just outside Hanoi and continuing with the systematic obliteration of the country's industry, communications network and, though this was left delicately vague, population centers. Only such a "sharp and sudden shock," the Chiefs argued, could destroy Hanoi's will and ability to prosecute the war and make Hanoi order the Vietcong to put down their arms.

The premise behind this brutal simplicity—that the Vietcong, for all their southern coloration, were under Hanoi's effective control—was shared with varying degrees of sophistication by all policy-planning centers within the government, and the bombing proposal was examined in March and April at meetings at the highest level. While agreeing that sustained, unrestricted bombing of the North would probably have the desired effect in the South, the CIA thought the Vietcong would lie low only temporarily, prepared to resume the struggle when conditions permitted; also, there was a chance that the bombing would provoke a real North Vietnamese invasion. Some of the civilian

* This chapter, however, is the product of the author's independent research and interviews completed before the *Times'* coup, which came as the manuscript of the book was on its way to the printers. Therefore, while some of the documents published by the *Times* have been cited, the account here is the author's own.

analysts in the Defense and State departments and the White House saw other disadvantages. Bombing MIGs and the ground-to-air missiles the Russians were beginning to emplace in North Vietnam could kill Russians and lead to confrontation with the Soviet Union. Using B-52s for "precision bombing" of air defenses, factories, rail depots, bridges and similar objectives concentrated in heavily populated areas would ensure the realization of some of the civilians' worst nightmares, since conventional bombs released at great heights by planes designed for nuclear weapons would tend to miss their targets by wide margins. People would be butchered without seeing the aircraft overhead (something that the Joint Chiefs realized, of course, without admitting it, any more than the United States ever admitted going for population centers in World War II).

The civilians had their own plan. They favored a program of "low-level pressures" that would make it clear to the North Vietnamese that the United States was going to impose a cost on their support of the guerrillas in the South. The pressures would rise, slowly but inexorably, to a "crescendo," whose exact nature was left undefined, since the hope was that the North Vietnamese, realizing what they were up against, would disengage from the struggle before it became necessary for the United States to decide how far to go in punishing Hanoi. Abandoned by the North, the Vietcong would be reduced to a manageable problem for the American-supported Saigon regime, whose mettle and morale would be vastly enhanced in consequence. (Bombing the North as a means of stiffening the regime in the South was a concept that seemed to appeal particularly strongly to McGeorge Bundy.) While regarding this plan as hopelessly inadequate, the Joint Chiefs were prepared to accept it as a first step. Late in 1963, the Commander in Chief, Pacific (CINCPAC), then Admiral Harry D. Felt, translated the initial phase of the "crescendo" concept into a plan for covert military pressure, called OPLAN 34–63. Soon afterward, MAC/V (Military Advisory Command, Vietnam) and CAS (the CIA's cover name overseas, standing, some say, for Controlled American Source) refined CINCPAC's program in an annex, called OPLAN 34-A.

OPLAN 34-A comprised a variety of things. It would incorporate the ineffectual Saigon program of infiltration and sabotage, improving the training of South Vietnamese agents and commando teams air-dropped north of the seventeenth parallel and sending them across in greater numbers. There would be leaflet raids designed to create a sense of foreboding in North Vietnamese cities and villages. Taking psychological warfare a step further, unmarked planes would fly in singly now and then to drop a few bombs. And there would be maritime operations (MAROPS) in the form of clandestine coastal raids.

The plan went in January to the hush-hush 303 Committee, known by that name, some said, because it met once in Room 303 of the Executive Office Building, and composed at that point of McGeorge Bundy, CIA chief McCone, and the number-two men at State and Defense, among others. The committee, whose job was to scrutinize all plans for "black operations" as well as for the lily-white variety, approved 34-A except for the bombing part, which was left to the future. The President directed that an initial four-month phase of the program be implemented by February 1, and the CIA went to work.

February 1, 1964, must therefore go down as one of the key dates of the American involvement. On that day, without the nation knowing anything about it, the Johnson Administration embarked on a new course in Vietnam, a covert military operation against the North. The airdrop activities had to be built up, but the maritime operations had to start from scratch. The CIA bought eight patrol boats from Norway, aluminum-hulled craft armed with machine guns and 40-mm. cannon and capable of speeds above

50 knots. To man these boats it proceeded to collect and, with the help of borrowed naval personnel, train crews of Vietnamese and foreign mercenaries, including two dozen or so Chinese Nationalists, a somewhat larger number of European adventurers and possibly some Thais.

McNamara was to tell the Senate Foreign Relations Committee three years later that the operation was "under the command of the South Vietnamese," but that was simply the cover story—and protecting a mission's cover is a form of lying the national-security managers employ without notable discomfort, even against Congress. The Saigon government participated in planning the missions for these Swift boats, as they were called, but was not otherwise involved. The boats did not bear South Vietnamese navy markings. The crews did not wear South Vietnamese uniforms. They did not include South Vietnamese naval personnel. It was a covert, "nonattributable," "deniable" MAC/V-CIA operation under the operational control of MAC/V. Plans included seizing junks in northern waters for interrogation of those on board, landing teams on the North Vietnamese coast for kidnaping raids and demolition missions, and shelling radar stations and other coastal targets. The primary motive of all this was to create enough harassment to convey a message to Hanoi: "We are changing the rules. You no longer have a sanctuary. The war is entering a new phase." Also, to the degree that the raids became known—through protests by Hanoi to the International Control Commission, for instance—they could be acknowledged and defended as South Vietnamese navy operations aimed at stopping coastal infiltration from the North. (McNamara was to make a start in this direction after the August 2 and 4 Tonkin Gulf incidents by intimating to Congress that the raids on the North Vietnamese offshore islands of Hon Me and Hon Ngu were the work of South Vietnam's anti-infiltration force of paramilitary junks.) In the course of time, 34-A would establish the legitimacy of a pattern of pressure which the Americans could then join. Finally, the raids could provoke the North Vietnamese into an attack on the Swift boats or some other act of retaliation —to which the United States could "respond" by attacking North Vietnam or escalating in South Vietnam or both without damaging Johnson's "restraint" image in the election campaign.

But would 34-A be enough of a signal? Some of the crisis managers thought not. Some form of additional pressure would not be amiss.

*
* *

The United States Navy had long wanted to get in on the Vietnam war. The Army and Air Force both had missions in the South, the former with its fighting "advisers" in the field, the latter with its bomb-dropping, weapon-firing "trainers" in the South Vietnamese air force. All that the Navy could boast of were two brief "elint" (electronic intelligence) patrols in the Gulf of Tonkin, one carried out in 1962 and the other in 1963—spillovers from the program, code-named DeSoto, being conducted off the coasts of China, North Korea and the Soviet Union to ferret out the "military and civil activity of the Asiatic Communist bloc." The "low-level pressure" campaign initiated in January, 1964, gave the Navy an opening for a more respectable role.

Let the "elinting" be extended, the admirals proposed, by scheduling regular one-ship patrols, several a month, off the North Vietnamese coast. The ships could pinpoint and analyze coastal radar to set the stage for naval bombardment, blockade or seaborne invasion, should any of these measures prove necessary as the scale of pressures ascended (although for a bombing offensive the preparation would, admittedly, have to be done by spy planes able to measure radar attached to missile sites farther inland). The ships could eavesdrop on radio conversations among command posts and thus plot troop locations and movements —always a useful endeavor, and of particular interest now in view of some hazy intelligence of Chinese troop movements near the Vietnamese border that could be checked on by letting the patrols skirt the Chinese coast before leaving the gulf. They could take depth soundings, make "visual observations," photograph landmarks—all worthwhile tasks for a military establishment always on guard against being caught with obsolete information in an area in which action may erupt.

Even more to the point—although this did not have to be spelled out in the formal instructions to the ships' commanders—the parade of destroyers off the North Vietnamese coast would be menacing, and intentionally so. It would tie in with 34-A as one more aspect of the program of pressures on Hanoi. In fact, the photographing would be helpful in picking out targets for the 34-A raids. Taken altogether —the destroyers, 34-A and the bombing option—it was really a revival in modern dress of the gunboat policy of the nineteenth century under which men-of-war would appear in coastal waters to overawe and, if necessary, apply measured and limited force (such as the one-gun bombardment of the viceregal yamen in Canton at ten-minute intervals by a British warship in October, 1856) [4] in order to compel the local authorities to cease obstructing the beneficent spread of free trade, Christianity and the white man's civilizing mission, although the Washington planners would probably have rejected the parallel if it had been pointed out to them.

The Navy's proposal went to the 303 Committee. The committee approved. The President authorized. The Joint Chiefs issued the basic instructions to CINCPAC:

CPA [closest point of approach] to the ChiCom coast is 15 NM [nautical miles]. CPA to the North Vietnamese coast is 8 NM. CPA to North Vietnamese islands is 4 NM.

The "crescendo" plan had a diminuendo beginning. The first DeSoto patrol, conducted in March by the destroyer *Craig,* was a washout due to bad weather; the North Vietnamese may not even have known about it. The first 34-A raid in April was abortive. The commando teams airdropped in the North were rounded up before accomplishing their missions. The Joint Chiefs in Washington could be forgiven if they smiled to see their skepticism of these dilettante schemes borne out. Still, the Chiefs supported them as a foot in the door, particularly since their own chairman, General Taylor, was adopting a position at variance with theirs.

Disagreeing with the CIA estimate that only all-out bombing on the scale proposed by the four service Chiefs had any hope of getting Hanoi to liquidate the war, Taylor thought he could achieve the same result with something in between the civilians' "low-level" approach to North Vietnam and the Chiefs' prescription for wiping out the country. Taylor favored bombing the infiltration routes on an ever-widening scale—not in the hope of cutting off supplies, not with any real thought that supplies were the critical factor, but to demonstrate to Hanoi that things would get progressively worse for the North until it called off the Vietcong. Even if it called them off only temporarily —the best the CIA could hope for—a temporary peace could last for years and give the Administration a chance to ease off gradually while telling the American people that they had won. The idea looked good to many of the civilians, McNamara included. And Taylor and Rostow thought that with luck the peace would prove permanent.*

In May, "pressure planning," as it was known, was brought to a head by a crisis in Laos.

The Joint Chiefs had already recommended air and

* This was the plan Johnson finally adopted a year later. The CIA and the Joint Chiefs were proved right about the inadequacy of the "middle position," though not about their own preferred plan, which was never tried.

ground strikes by the South Vietnamese against Communist supply lines in Laos, combined with hot pursuit of the Vietcong into their Laotian and Cambodian border sanctuaries, all this complementary to bombing of North Vietnam. But now a political event in Vientiane, the Laotian capital, threatened the whole non-Communist half of Laos with collapse. As a result of another rightist coup that toppled Prince Souvanna Phouma yet again from his precarious premiership and delivered the final deathblow to tripartite government in Vientiane, neutralist troops in the Plain of Jars began deserting in droves and the Pathet Lao took the opportunity to send the remainder fleeing in disorganized retreat. Washington panicked, and the Joint Chiefs pressed anew for unrestricted bombing of North Vietnam, arguing that the Pathet Lao were as firmly under Hanoi's control as the Vietcong, if not more so, and that in Laos, no less than in South Vietnam, victory could be had only by destroying Hanoi's will and ability to stay in the fight.

Another critical development in May was the buildup of international pressure for reconvening the 1954 conference in Indochina. The British and the French were proposing a new meeting, and the Russians and the Chinese were distinctly favorable to the idea. In their own minds, the policy planners in Washington were by now willing to accept any substitute for victory that would enable them to say they had not lost, yet their terms for not losing would look to the other side very much like terms for the Vietcong's surrender, and the last thing the Administration wanted was to be drawn into negotiating from its current "position of weakness" in Vietnam. Military action that would smother these diplomatic initiatives was one way out.

May, then, was the month in which the action plans were brought into focus. Out of urgent meetings just below the Presidential level there emerged a "thirty-day program" for launching air attacks against North Vietnam in the politically acceptable guise of a response to Northern pressures. A planning team headed by William Bundy drew up a timetable that included the following:

D-Day minus 30 days—The President makes a speech on the Vietnamese situation reporting on Hanoi's mounting aggressiveness and requesting a Joint Congressional Resolution.

D-Day minus 20—The President obtains a Joint Resolution approving past actions in Indochina and authorizing him to take whatever action he considers necessary in that area.

D-Day minus 16—CINCPAC is directed to take all preparatory logistic action for D-Day that can be taken quietly.

D-Day minus 15—U.S. obtains General Khanh's agreement to start overt South Vietnamese air attacks on the North, with a guarantee of American protection in case of North Vietnamese or Chinese retaliation.

D-Day minus 14—Washington consults with Bangkok and Manila on deployment of additional units to the American air bases in Thailand and the Philippines. Britain, Australia, New Zealand and Pakistan are asked to give their open political support for the bombing when it begins and to join in military preparations against possible North Vietnamese or Chinese retaliation.

D-Day minus 13—The Administration releases a detailed report on infiltration from North Vietnam into South Vietnam.

D-Day minus 12—CINCPAC is directed to begin preparations for air strikes against North Vietnam.

D-Day minus 10—General Khanh makes a speech demanding a stop to North Vietnamese aggression and threatening unspecified military action if the demand is not met.

D-Day minus 3—The President, referring to Khanh's speech and declaring support for South Vietnam, informs the American people, and thereby Hanoi, that action against North Vietnam cannot be excluded.

D-Day minus 1—Khanh announces that all efforts at a peaceful settlement have failed and that an attack on North Vietnam is imminent. He stresses the limited goal of the operation and, possibly, offers food imports to alleviate food shortages in the North if Hanoi calls off its aggression.

D-Day—U.S. dependents in South Vietnam are removed. Air

strikes against North Vietnam are launched by the South Vietnamese air force, with U.S. aircraft joining in as the bombing campaign expands. Selected air and naval units are deployed to the western Pacific, including South Vietnam and Thailand. Washington calls for a conference on Vietnam and reports its action to the U.N., explaining that its aim is not to overthrow the Hanoi regime but to stop North Vietnamese direction of Vietcong terror, and making clear that the air action will continue until terrorism, armed attacks and armed resistance to pacification efforts cease in South Vietnam.

Rusk, McNamara, McGeorge Bundy and McCone went over the program at a meeting of the Executive Committee of the National Security Council May 24 and 25. They abandoned the timetable aspect of the program as containing too dangerous an element of escalatory momentum, but retained many of the scenario's elements—including the request for a joint resolution.

The need for such a resolution had been propounded by Rostow to Rusk as early as February and had been accepted by all concerned. Without a Congressional resolution the President's action would be almost certain to draw strong criticism from the Capitol and lose its intended effect of impressing Hanoi with the depth and sincerity of the American commitment. It would also impair the appearance of "moderation" the President had to preserve in the domestic political campaign. Then, though the planners didn't really expect it, bombing could lead to Chinese or Soviet reaction, either in Southeast Asia or in North Korea or elsewhere, and Johnson wanted Congress aboard if things got tough. Finally, although there was almost no discussion of it, American ground forces might have to be employed if Hanoi responded to the bombing by moving its own troops south of the seventeenth parallel.

So William Bundy sat down on May 25 and drafted a Congressional resolution which said that whereas North Vietnamese support of the Vietcong and the Pathet Lao constituted violation of the Geneva accords of 1954 and 1962, and whereas it was essential that the world fully understood that the American people were united in their determination to take all necessary steps to help the people of South Vietnam and Laos to maintain their independence and political integrity, the United States was prepared—if the President determined the necessity thereof—to use all measures, including commitment of the armed forces, to assist those countries in defending themselves against aggression and subversion supported, controlled and directed from any Communist country. To this end, the resolution authorized the President to use certain specified funds in the 1964–1965 fiscal-year budget.

With such a resolution as a political foundation—and a legal one as well, given the likelihood that some in Congress would claim that the powers of Commander in Chief alone were not sufficient for attacking a foreign country— the President could wait for the opportune moment to strike. He would not have to wait long. Some action by the Vietcong would provide a pretext. The President would order "retaliatory" bombing of North Vietnam, explaining that he was attacking the source of the aggression against South Vietnam in line with his Congressional mandate. The retaliation would develop into a sustained bombing program on a somewhat higher level than that envisaged by General Taylor but well short of the all-out aerial offensive proposed by the Joint Chiefs.

By the end of May everything was ready. A list of ninety-four bombing targets in North Vietnam photographed by the high-flying U-2 spy planes had been developed and forwarded to the Secretary of Defense. The tactical problems of attack routes, flak suppression, protection against MIGs, search and rescue had been solved. McNamara had ordered the military to be geared to "reprisal" at 72 hours' notice. The Congressional resolution was in satisfactory form.

Four years later McNamara was to testify before the

Senate Foreign Relations Committee that he could not recall any recommendation prior to the Tonkin Gulf incidents
for extending the war to North Vietnam; General Wheeler's
answer at the same hearing was that "to the best of my
knowledge and belief during that period there was no
thought of extending the war into the North"; the Defense
Department's reply after a "check of the records" was,
"We have identified no such recommendation." * William
Bundy was to testify before the same committee in 1966
that he was "not sure" that his drafts of the Congressional
resolution "were even known to others." † The fact is that
three months before the Tonkin Gulf incidents President
Johnson's principal foreign-policy advisers were agreed on a
plan for going to war, and not a "contingency" plan either
but one meant to put into effect. All that was missing was
the choice of the specific targets and the specific date and
a formal recommendation to the President.

And then, at the last minute, they drew back.

The military crisis in Laos had eased. The Pathet Lao
had not advanced beyond the Plain of Jars, the neutralist
troops had rallied, and Souvanna Phouma was back as
premier, with Washington's support. The Laotian scare had
yielded one tangible benefit to the Navy: Johnson authorized the Seventh Fleet to provide fighter escorts for the
unarmed Air Force and Navy jets that had been flying
reconnaissance missions over Laos since 1962, gathering
photographic intelligence for bombing raids by a fleet of
propeller-driven fighter bombers that bore Laotian Air Force
markings but were piloted mostly by Thai mercenaries or
employees of Air America, a supposedly private airline run
by the CIA—all this in secret. When two of the reconnaissance planes were shot down on June 6 and 7, Johnson
authorized retaliatory strikes, the first direct act of war by
the United States against the Communists in Indochina. To

* See page 199.
† See page 158.

238

carry out the escort-*cum*-retaliation mission, the Navy stationed a carrier at the mouth of the Gulf of Tonkin. But as an argument for bombing North Vietnam, the Laotian situation was no longer compelling. And that placed primary importance back on the domestic political factor: Johnson's unwillingness to up the ante in Vietnam, unless he absolutely had to, before the November election.

It would be unlike Johnson not to know the substance of the recommendation his advisers were considering placing on his desk, and it does not seem improbable that he made known to them his strong preference for avoiding a decision of this kind until after November and that this was what finally ended the argument. At any rate, in the last days of May it was decided to postpone recommending the "30-day program" to the President until the end of the year. The top advisers—McNamara, Rusk, McGeorge Bundy, Taylor and Lodge (soon to relinquish his ambassadorial post in Saigon)—held their scheduled Honolulu conference June 1 and 2, but merely to ratify the postponement decision. The rationale at Honolulu was that, the Laos crisis having receded, a postponement would give more time to strengthen the Saigon regime against the North Vietnamese counterpressures the bombing might produce, and more time to plan for deployment of U.S. troops to South Vietnam in case of necessity. The real reason was the domestic political one.

What, though, of the Congressional resolution: Should the President go ahead with his request for that? What worried the crisis managers was that they did not have good answers to the questions Congress was bound to pose, such as: "Why are you asking for this resolution now?" If they were to give an honest answer it would be: "We want to plaster North Vietnam the way the Republican front runner, Barry Goldwater, says it should be plastered, even though we have called his proposal insane, and the reason we want to do it is that we know of no other way of stopping the serious deterioration in South Vietnam." The next question would be: "Is South Vietnam that important to us, worth the risks of a clash with Red China and Soviet Russia?" The answer would have to be: "It is tremendously important, and we don't think the risks are that great," but neither assertion would be easy to prove.

Then, on the question of how much aid was really going from the North to the South, they had little hard information to offer. Publicly they justified American aid to Saigon by giving an exaggerated impression of the flow of men and weapons to the Vietcong, but within their own councils they admitted that infiltration did not amount to much, perhaps four to five thousand men a year and small amounts of matériel, most of the Vietcong's weapons being bought or captured within South Vietnam. The key element, in their opinion, was Hanoi's direction of the war, and it would be even more difficult to prove that conclusively enough to establish it as a basis for Congressional authority to bomb the North. McNamara, Rusk, McGeorge Bundy and their top advisers held an all-day meeting June 15; Bundy made it quite clear that the President saw no need to ask Congress for a joint resolution at that juncture, and it was decided to postpone that as well.

What remained, then, after all the plans and conferences of March and April and May? The smaller programs of January: 34-A and the DeSoto patrols. These could now go forward at a stepped-up pace. The Honolulu conference extended the 34-A operations for another twelve months, the President gave his approval, and word that the government was considering certain cross-border actions by the South Vietnamese was duly leaked to the press. As for DeSoto, the Joint Chiefs approved a series of five-day one-destroyer missions in the Tonkin Gulf, the timing to be determined by the Pacific command.

If anyone in Washington had noticed that the first destroyer patrol and the first 34-A bombardment were scheduled so close together at the end of July that the North Vietnamese would in all likelihood regard the two as part of the same operation, he would not have been unduly disturbed. The destroyer's presence alone would be enough to activate the North Vietnamese radar units and radio traffic, but the 34-A assault would activate them even more, and that wouldn't hurt. The planners knew that the destroyer would not participate in the 34-A raid—that it would be going in just to make a show of force and do an intelligence job in the process—but if Hanoi got the idea that the Americans were behind the coastal forays, that wouldn't hurt either; it would make the combined pressure all the more effective. The planners did not imagine that the North Vietnamese would do anything so foolish as to attack an American destroyer. In the middle of the night some feisty admiral aching for a scrap may have dreamed of a scenario in which the Navy, bloodied, gave the little bastards hell, but in the light of day who would expect them to present the Americans with such a golden opportunity?

The Captain   13

John Jerome Herrick's father was a railroad man. Telegraphy was the primary means of communication in the railroads in those days, and Mr. Herrick would tap out the messages that flew ahead of the steam engines across Minnesota and beyond, when John Jerome was a child. As the father rose up the ladder—depot agent, yardmaster—the family moved to Wisconsin. John's brother, eleven years his senior, had made West Point, and when he came home on a visit the younger boy observed that his brother seemed to be having a pretty good life in the military. He decided to make that his life too.

He applied himself during his two years of college at Superior and was selected—no, not for West Point, but for Annapolis, which was just as good. They called him "Jigjig" at Annapolis. That was just navy for J. J. Most everybody who didn't have an individual trait meriting a special nickname went by his initials.

World War II was on, and Ensign Herrick served on board the battleship *New York* in the Iwo Jima and Okinawa campaigns. A suicide plane hit the ship but went right on overboard; the ship was hardly scratched. The *New York* was a very lucky ship. Herrick, now lieutenant, junior grade, was below decks with a damage-control party. That was the closest he came to danger during the war.

He put in for flight training and they sent him to the Naval Air School in Dallas, but the war was over and they were being tough on trainees: two downs for young Herrick and it was back to the sea. He didn't fret; a line officer's life would be just as good as an aviator's. Besides, he met Geraldine Kane. She was the daughter of a retired navy dentist, and he asked her to dance at a tea social at Coronado, California, where navy bachelors could meet the town's "recommended" young damsels. Herrick had come from the China Sea and had to go out to China again, but he wrote her every day, making up his mind to marry her, which he did as soon as he got back eleven months later. The Herricks settled down in Annapolis, he as "steam prof" at the academy, teaching marine engineering. Two sons were born to them, John Jerome, Jr., and Patrick Kane, and Herrick built a folding car crib in the academy's woodwork room.

Then to the Far East again; the Korean war was on, and he was given a gunnery ship, his first command. Then back to Annapolis as ordnance and gunnery instructor. Then more commands (Herrick still wrote at least twice a week), more shore duty, more promotions in rank. The Herricks had another son, Dennis Martin, and a daughter, Maureen Teresa. On April 1, 1964, he was made captain. He was then commanding officer of the destroyer *Edson*, plying the Taiwan Strait, and in all the United States Navy it would have been difficult to find a more contented captain than he. He had been right in going navy. It *had* been a pretty good life. And it promised to continue that unruffled way.

Next month he was made commodore of Destroyer Division 192, also a part of the Taiwan patrol, and moved aboard the division flagship, the *Berkeley*. There were two other ships under his command. One was called the *Picking*. The other was called the *Maddox*.

* * *

The man who gets up from behind his desk is stocky in his blue service uniform, with his service ribbons on his chest, careful and measured of speech, his most pronounced feature his earnest, reticent eyes under heavy black eyebrows in a face just beginning to go soft. Captain Herrick is fifty now. It is 1970.

The standard printed "Officer Biography Sheet" supplied by the Navy Public Information Office contains the line, "(b) Newsworthy data on personal life, such as 'Wife was former Wave,' 'Son at Naval Academy,' 'Escaped from Corregidor,' etc." Underneath are the typewritten words, "Task Group Commander on board USS *Maddox* (DD-731) during Gulf of Tonkin incident, August 1964." It was an experience, he says, he would just as soon have missed.

There is a hint of wariness about his eyes, in his pauses. He has been used, wheeled into the thick of the wrangle between the Fulbright committee and the Pentagon to help rebut the critics, then picked over by the critics; some of his statements, some of his old messages from the Gulf of Tonkin, twisted he feels by people intent on suiting them to their own preconceptions. Then relays of interviewers. He still doesn't know what some of them will write.

Why doesn't *he* write his story? "I've thought about it. One newspaper editor who talked to me suggested I write a book. But suppose I sit down and write everything I know. That will take twenty pages. What do I do for the rest of the book?" He has written one speech, expressing amazement that there should still be people who wonder if his ships were really attacked, and has delivered it half a dozen times before Rotary and Kiwanis clubs around the country.

The intercepts? No mystery about that. It's all straightforward. All part of the job. All within the rules of the game. The North Vietnamese simply broke the rules.

Why was *he* picked for the job? Any special experience, qualities they were looking for?

He shakes his head. "They just picked Destroyer Division 192 because it was on the Taiwan patrol and was the closest to the Gulf of Tonkin. That I happened to be the commander of it at the time was pure chance."

It was in June, 1964, during a stopover at Yokosuka, Japan, headquarters of the Seventh Fleet, that Captain Herrick was informed that he'd be heading a patrol into the Gulf of Tonkin. His ships were back in Japan in July for Rest and Recreation, and he was briefed on his mission—"by the people," as he puts it, "who are in charge of such missions." Herrick is properly tight-lipped on classified information, even when it is public knowledge. The "people who are in charge of such missions" may be the National Security Agency (NSA), but he isn't going to go into that with an uncleared civilian. "I don't know that," he says. He straightens in his chair; the Navy's starchy side shows. He relaxes, and his next remark has a more persuasive ring. "What you're not supposed to know you don't ask yourself about." *

Nonetheless, wasn't he apprehensive about such a sensitive mission?

"We had no idea it was a sensitive mission. I knew we were going into an unfriendly body of water, but they assured me at the briefing that there'd be no trouble. Our ships had been doing this off China for years. To us it was routine. We suspected we might get one of their 'serious warnings,' but nothing more."

After all, his ship would be in international waters at all times, outside the three-mile limit. Oh, yes, eight miles from shore would put the vessel in waters the North Vietnamese might technically regard as their own, but "that didn't bother me; eight miles seemed plenty of leeway."

* The description of the August, 1964, Tonkin Gulf patrol contained in this and the following chapter was gathered from various sources. Only those statements and opinions directly attributed to Captain Herrick should be taken as coming from him.

The day the United States accepted the twelve-mile limit, the Navy would find some of the world's most important straits closed to it. "The three-mile limit was ingrained into my thinking in my entire naval career, so twelve miles don't indicate a barrier to me."

The Navy assigned the *Picking*, an old World War II model, for the patrol, but Herrick saw that the special-intelligence comvan (communications van), of which he had been told, wouldn't fit on the *Picking* except on the fantail, where it would get wet and mask the afterguns. He couldn't have the *Berkeley*, a fairly modern ship; the *Berkeley* had been assigned to a carrier. So he got permission to take the *Maddox*, which was a little larger than the *Picking*.

The third destroyer to bear the name of William Alfred Truman Maddox, a captain of the Marine Corps who hoisted the American flag in San Diego at the outset of the Mexican war of 1846–48, the *Maddox* (DD-731) was launched in Bath, Maine, in 1944 and took part in the naval offensives against the Philippines and Taiwan as escort for the *Ticonderoga*—the carrier that, as it happened, was stationed in May, 1964, at the mouth of the Tonkin Gulf. In 1945 both vessels were put out of action by Japanese kamikaze attacks in a battle off Taiwan, with the loss of 42 men killed or wounded aboard the *Maddox* and 345 aboard the *Ticonderoga*. In the Korean war the *Maddox* was splattered by shore batteries while making runs into Wonsan harbor to shell the port. By now she was one of the oldest destroyers in the Seventh Fleet.[1]

The skipper of the *Maddox*, Commander Herbert L. Ogier, forty-one, was a friend of Herrick's. The two had been fellow instructors when both were "steam profs" at Annapolis. In the patrol ahead of them Ogier would still be captain of the *Maddox*, but Herrick, as commodore of Task Force 72.1 (consisting in this case, of only one vessel), would be in overall command.

Their conferences aboard the *Maddox* started rumors flying. "We knew that we were going on a special exercise," says James A. Stankevitz, radarman aboard the *Maddox*, "but we didn't know what was coming up." [2]

Herrick's specific instructions came July 17 in a message from Admiral Moorer's headquarters in Hawaii: "The primary purpose of this patrol is to determine DRV coastal activity along the full extent of the patrol track." [3]

"DRV coastal activity"—infiltration into South Vietnam by sea—was negligible in the spring and summer of 1964; most of what little infiltration there was came overland. This directive provided the patrol with its cover. Crisis managing calls for covers to be included in official instructions: if the mission blows up, the message can be cited to lend authenticity to the public version of the event. As a good crisis manager, McNamara was able to quote this message in 1968 to the Fulbright committee to back up his testimony that the "primary purpose of the *Maddox* was to observe North Vietnamese naval activity in these waters, in view of the evidence we had of infiltration by sea by North Vietnam into South Vietnam."

The message also said:

Other specific intelligence requirements are as follows:

Location and identification of all radar transmitters, and estimate of range capabilities;

Navigational and hydro information along the routes traversed and particular navigational lights, characteristics, landmarks, buoys, currents and tidal information, river mouths and channel accessibility;

Monitoring junk force with density of surface traffic pattern;

Sampling electronic environment radars and navigation aids;

Photography of opportunities in support of above. In addition, include photography as best detail track would permit of all prominent landmarks and islands, particularly in vicinity of river and built-up areas; conduct coastal radarscope photography by ship which is transmitting from point A, which is the end of the mission.

From the Joint Chiefs of Staff came a note of caution: "Activity in 34-A operations has increased." And on the same subject, a copy of an order from Admiral Sharp to fleet units involved in planning for Tonkin Gulf patrol: Contact MAC/V "for any additional intelligence required for prevention of mutual interference with 34-A operations and such communications arrangements as may be desired." [4]

What did "34-A" mean to Herrick? "Only that there was some clandestine operation up the coast," he says. "I didn't know by whom." It may have been mentioned at the briefing but only "very vaguely." (And, of course, what you're not supposed to know you don't ask yourself about.) Admiral Sharp had given orders to keep 34-A, whatever it was, separated from his patrol. That was all he had to know.

The *Maddox* left Yokosuka July 23. The men were not told of their destinations, which made for more rumors. They pulled into port at Keelung, Taiwan, an important NSA listening post, and the crew had their cameras taken away. (Stankevitz, on an impulse, hid his.) The instructions had said:

Embark comvan with personnel, MAC/V rep and mobile photo unit photographer in Keelung, Taiwan. Offload personnel and equipment Keelung upon completion patrol.

But the MAC/V representative did not show up, Herrick says. Why? He does not know. McNamara, in his 1968 testimony, explained that

the MAC/V representative was, in effect, invited to participate in the patrol, assuming that he might find it useful to obtain at first hand the intelligence information the patrol collected, because of MAC/V's concern about sea infiltration. . . . In any case MAC/V did not accept the invitation. He did not feel he would benefit from it, and there was no MAC/V representative on board.

The comvan was hoisted aboard by a crane and placed

between the smokestacks. Crew members who caught a glimpse of its insides saw it was jammed with equipment. They were to describe it later as black or slate gray, but Herrick says it was khaki.

"An ex-Army van," he says, "a mobile van. You could put it on wheels or you could put it on a ship. They used the van on earlier DeSoto missions.

"What they had in there was listening equipment for intercepting radio transmissions. It augmented our own equipment. They could listen in on circuits we couldn't get. There were certain frequencies we couldn't handle. The comvan was designed to read intercepts."

And to measure radar?

"No. The comvan did not have dual capacity."

Herrick won't talk about it, but that part of the mission was performed by the destroyer's own equipment, its ECM (electronic countermeasures) gear.

Wasn't the *Maddox* a bit old for special surveillance?

Herrick is laconic. "She could handle the job."

In that connection, McNamara's 1968 testimony that the *Maddox* stimulated North Vietnamese radar by so-called "active" electronic measures—"they turn on certain kind of equipment on board the *Maddox* which, in turn, leads the Chicoms or the North Vietnamese to turn on the radars so that we can measure the radar frequencies"—was denied by Herrick right after the hearing. Herrick said the ship had "passive" gear only and could stimulate the radar stations only by its presence; the Defense Department press office said the Secretary had been "mistaken."

Herrick chuckles, recalling the incident. "A newspaper reporter told me I was the second person to tell McNamara he was wrong and get away with it. The first was his wife."

Fifteen enlisted men (nine navy, six marines) came aboard with the van. They were under the command of a lieutenant in the Naval Reserve, Gerrell Dean Moore, who is identified in the Fulbright committee's December, 1968, pamphlet as having been attached to "Naval (deleted) Activity, Taipei, Taiwan." Herrick describes him as "a nice young man in his late twenties, typical of the intelligence type. He didn't say too much voluntarily. Pretty closed-mouthed individual." Moore and half of his team were on loan to NSA and other cover installations in Taiwan, Japan and Hawaii, and the other half were from the naval communications relay station in San Miguel, the Philippines, but all that the ship knew was that they were CTs, communications technicians, who shared quarters with the crew, said nothing about their work and kept to themselves. Some of them were Vietnamese-language specialists, and it was then, as Stankevitz recalls, that the rumors narrowed down to one: "that we were going into the gulf." [5]

The people who briefed Herrick in Yokosuka flew down to give him another briefing. They didn't have much more to add. "One of the briefing officers," Herrick recalls, "said we'd have a 'Sunday cruise.'"

The cruise had a sticky beginning, though. They reached the mouth of the Tonkin Gulf on July 31, and, as the Navy Department's official "History of Ships named Maddox" tells it, "As she [the *Maddox*] refueled from the oiler *Ashtabula* (AO 51) that morning, two Russian-built PT boats of Communist North Viet Nam hovered on the horizon."

The boats—there were actually four of them—came down from the north, and "to our inexperienced eye," Herrick says, "they looked like Soviet craft," and that's what the *Maddox* reported by radio. Later, he says, "We assured ourselves that these were South Vietnamese patrol boats and they were just exercising. We took a deep breath and relaxed again." Actually, of course, they were the CIA's Norwegian-made Swift boats returning from their attacks the previous midnight on the offshore islands of Hon Me and Hon Ngu.

250

The tanker had mail for the *Maddox* crew (thoughtfully flown down from Yokosuka) and picked up a bagful of hastily written letters from the men, and at noon on July 31 the *Maddox* slipped into the Gulf of Tonkin, its ECM gear cocked, the comvan with its whip antennas ungainly between the smokestacks, cooling units humming to keep the van's cramped interior at a bearable temperature for the CTs at their electronic cabinets. The *Ticonderoga*, a slab of congealed power in the gentle shallows off Danang, fell behind. The curving tropic shore with its silent watching hills drew them deeper into the gulf. Commander Ogier spoke to the men over the public-address system. He explained that they were going into the Tonkin Gulf to "observe the coast" by radio and study water conditions. They'd be staying in international waters, he said, and it shouldn't be dangerous.

*
* *

The 34-A mission of the previous night had not been successful. Two of the Swift boats were to have landed a party on Hon Me and blown up the island's radar station; the other two boats were to have done the same at Hon Ngu, two and a half miles from the port city of Vinh. At both places the raiders ran into heavy defensive fire—it was later rumored that there had been a security leak—and had to throw their sensitive demolition charges overboard in view of the danger of blowing themselves up. This created a series of explosions along the beaches, however, and the boats took some targets under fire with heavy weapons, so all in all there was enough commotion to produce the intended psychological effect. A babble of radio messages flowed into the *Maddox*'s communications van as the destroyer "orbited" its way up the coast the following morning, doubling on its tracks, looping in and out of the twelve-mile limit. The North Vietnamese, the messages made clear, were alarmed—and the *Maddox* was adding to their alarm. "They were tracking us by radar," Herrick says, "from the minute we went in. We had an idea something was stirring them up."

In fact, as revealed by a White Paper issued in Hanoi in September, 1964, the "signal" that Washington was sending the North Vietnamese with its "pressures program" was getting across strongly as the *Maddox* began its patrol. The 34-A bombardment and the destroyer's appearance were recognized by the North Vietnamese, according to the White Paper, as part of "a new and most serious step forward" in a program under which "the U.S. imperialists and their henchmen" had for some time been seizing fishing boats in North Vietnamese waters and infiltrating "spy commandos" along the coast and by parachute—all this an outgrowth of rumored "U.S. plans to extend the war to North Viet Nam." The American warships placed at the mouth of the Tonkin Gulf and sent into the gulf were deployed, the White Paper said, "to try to intimidate the Democratic Republic of Viet Nam" and to provide cover for the "henchmen's" raids. And the White Paper linked all this with the intensified American fighter-bomber activities over Laos, charging that on August 1 and 2 four of these planes strafed a North Vietnamese frontier post and village just over the border.[6] (A State Department memorandum of November 7, 1964, contained in the "McNamara Papers" indicated that these points were probably bombed inadvertently by the Thai-piloted propeller-driven aircraft; officially the department denied knowledge of the raids.)

Hanoi, in short, was getting the message. Was Herrick?

In line with the tradition that keeps the captain away from the SOD-Hut, the Special Operations Department space aboard his ship where the CTs work, Herrick did not go into the communications van, but Lieutenant Moore, the head of the comvan team, showed him whatever intercepts pertained to his command. And there was quite a bit to show. If the Swift boats did not put Herrick on his guard, the radio traffic did. The *Maddox* had been close enough to shore on the afternoon of July 31 (five miles, Hanoi's White Paper claims) for its number, DD-731, to have been seen through binoculars, and it did not make Herrick any easier to see his ship identified by number in some of the messages. He had been told in Tokyo and Keelung that some of the junks in the Gulf might be paramilitary, and the searchlights he threw on a covey of junks farther out to sea that night were the product more of cautiousness than— as the White Paper charged—"provocation." On August 1, in keeping with his schedule, he meandered back and forth in the area of Hon Ngu, and, thirty miles to the north, Hon Me. Whoever was cleaning up on the islands after the destruction of thirty-six hours before had a new and more formidable warship to worry about.

Shortly after midnight, while in the vicinity of Hon Ngu and a neighboring island, Hon Mat, the *Maddox* ran into a swarm of junks, "hundreds of them." Hanoi's White Paper charges that the *Maddox* "repeatedly directed its headlights at, or gave chase to, [these] Vietnamese boats fishing in Vietnamese waters." But Herrick remembers the incident quite differently.

"There were a great number of small craft," he recalls, "and they seemed to be approaching us rather closely, blocking our path. We could see antennas on some of them. We knew if we got into the middle of these junks, they could come up to us, and they could have been used to mine us or bring explosives alongside. It was a dark night, and we had been using a lighthouse on Hon Mat as a navigation point. And just then the lighthouse was turned off."

Any competent commander would have realized by then that he was in a hazardous situation. His was only the third

United States ship to appear in the gulf since 1963—perhaps only the second observed by the North Vietnamese, if the March, 1964, patrol by the destroyer *Craig* had indeed been hidden from them by foul weather. (The line that was to be put out in Washington after the August 2 incident— that units of the Seventh Fleet had been patrolling the gulf for a long time and that the North Vietnamese "knew" the *Maddox*—was misleading.) His ship had appeared while the North Vietnamese were still smarting from a coastal bombardment, the first such action of the civil war. It had come from the same direction as the raiders, and it had spent two days running in and out of North Vietnamese territorial waters in the very sector of the coastal attack. One didn't need intercepts to deduce that the North Vietnamese could well regard the *Maddox* as part of the same military operation. The radio traffic left little doubt that they did. Patrol boats were being ordered to bolster the defense of Hon Me and Hon Ngu. Now there was this concentration of junks, already beginning to envelop the *Maddox,* and the lighthouse being turned off.

Was it an ambush? Herrick sounded the alarm. Crewmen sleeping on the deck in the sweltering heat scrambled to their posts. It was the first of several sleepless nights they were to experience. The *Maddox* turned seaward and gave the flotilla a wide berth.

The van picked up another message. The orders to the patrol boats were becoming more disquieting. At 3:50 A.M. August 2, Herrick placed a message of his own into the destroyer's communication channel to the naval relay station at San Miguel, the Philippines, with copies to Admiral Johnson, commander of the Seventh Fleet, Admiral Moorer, commander of the Pacific Fleet, Admiral Sharp, Commander in Chief, Pacific, and the Joint Chiefs of Staff: Intelligence information indicates "possible hostile action" by the North Vietnamese. Three hours later, approaching Hon Me again, he followed up with another cable: "Consider continuance of patrol presents an unacceptable risk." Abandoning his appointed route, he made for the open sea.

＊

＊ ＊

For a man with so blazingly martial a record (Annapolis, naval aviator in 1932, carrier-based fighter-squadron leader in the Pacific war, medal after medal for courage and feats of efficiency and ingenuity in higher commands), Vice Admiral Roy Lee Johnson was attractively soft-spoken, but that was only his overlay of Southern manners. His staff at Seventh Fleet headquarters had soon learned that his quietness at meetings, his calm strong face and observant blue eyes, were the surface below which a passion for performance—navy performance, getting the job done—ruled R. L. Johnson's life. His favorite expression, one of his officers recalls, was a drawn-out, exasperated "Jee-zus Kee-rist," a preface to his very succinct remarks when he felt that somebody had loused up.

It is safe to assume that "Jee-zus Kee-rist" was among the expressions used by Admiral Johnson when Captain Herrick's cables were relayed from San Miguel to the guided-missile cruiser *Oklahoma City* at Yokosuka, which rotated with her sister vessel, the *Providence,* as his flagship. His answer was brief:

Ref. to Alpha, Bravo and Charlie noted. [The patrol route was marked by a series of checkpoints; these three were in the area the *Maddox* had been covering before putting out to sea.] When consider prudent, resume itinerary. . . . You are authorized to deviate from itinerary at any time you consider unacceptable risk to exist.

In other words, Take care of yourself, Herrick, but resume the patrol.

＊ ＊

＊

The *Maddox* was ten miles from land, on the edge of the Red River delta, the northernmost point she had yet reached. It was 11 A.M. Sunday, August 2, a clear calm day. Some of the men were sunbathing on deck.

Herrick says he didn't feel too bad about Admiral Johnson's orders to stay in there. "You expect that of an old sea dog. Freedom of the seas is pretty basic in the Navy. You can't back down on it, especially with a little outfit like the DRV."

Didn't he feel, though, that his warning had been disregarded?

"We thought they'd have cooler heads up there on the beach than we could have on the spot. Besides, permission to deviate from the itinerary gave us more leeway. We relaxed after that."

But not for long: events proved his warning well-founded, wouldn't he say?

Herrick clearly doesn't want to say, Yes, I was right and the old sea dog was wrong. He says, "You do what you can and carry out your orders whatever they turn out to be. We visualized that there could be a tremendous incident, and I wanted to make sure that this was their decision, that this is what they wanted to do after I told them what I thought. I didn't want to take the responsibility for starting a war, you might say."

"Their decision" appears to have been confined to the Pacific command. Herrick's warning and his recommendation that the patrol be broken off did not reach McNamara before the August 2 incident, and a high former Defense Department official is sure that if they had reached Wheeler the Chairman of the Joint Chiefs would have passed them on to the Secretary of Defense. A member of Bundy's White House staff says they did not reach the White House. "The President should have known about it," he says. "Clearly. We should have had a better control mechanism."

Would Washington have ordered the *Maddox* pulled out

of the gulf if Herrick's messages had reached the top echelon?

"Retrospectively," the former White House official says, "it would have been wiser to have withdrawn the patrol." The former Defense Department official says he feels Mc-Namara "would have said get out" had he known of Herrick's message; "it was not worth accepting the risk for that kind of patrol." Both former officials saw it as a problem of command and control: An admiral's whole training disposes him not to relay a subordinate's warning if he disagrees with it but to make a decision himself, and how to identify situations calling for specific orders to commanders to report on any unforeseen alarms is a puzzler.

Whatever Herrick's own worries as his ship approached the Red River delta just before noon of August 2, the patrol didn't have too many days left. Farther north, the checkpoints would take the *Maddox* up past the delta, past Haiphong, to where North Vietnam ended and China began, then around the little Chinese island of Weichow Tao and down the coast of North Vietnam again: three more days and out, back to the Taiwan patrol, the letters from home, the next assignment. But first, the *Maddox* had to dip south again and look in on Hon Me another time, as called for by the itinerary.

Three small craft came out of one of the rivers of the Red River delta and sped south, followed by a tanker. They were close enough to see: Soviet-made P-4s or P-6s, torpedo boats. "We were not too excited," Herrick says. "We knew the North Vietnamese had PT boats. We knew some of them were kept in that area."

The *Maddox*, bearing south in leisurely circles, observed the patrol boats reaching Hon Me and disappearing in what Herrick thought was a bay or cove behind the island. The tanker followed them in.

The *Maddox* nosed into another mass of junks, about seventy-five of them, and was changing course to avoid

257

them when there was another intercepted message from the van. "We heard the orders to the PT boats directing them to attack us after they had fueled," Herrick says. "And the next thing we knew they came out at us from behind Hon Me."

Stankevitz, manning the surface-search radar—the kind used by ships to seek out other ships—in the Combat Information Center (CIC), remembers that Ogier "stuck his head in Combat and told us to keep a tight watch on the scope for PT boats." [7] The *Maddox* altered course to southeast, toward the mouth of the gulf, and put on speed.

It was about 2 P.M., and the destroyer was about sixteen miles from Hon Me. Out of the spray of fishing junks on his radarscope Stankevitz picked out the ones that moved like patrol boats. They were moving at 45, then 50 knots, on a course that would lead them to intercept the *Maddox*. The *Maddox* increased her speed to 25 knots, then 30. That was all she could do.

Herrick apprised the Pacific command of the situation: "Being approached by high-speed craft with apparent intent to conduct torpedo attack. Intend to open fire in self-defense if necessary." [8]

He also requested air support from the *Ticonderoga*. And he watched the patrol boats gaining on the radar scope in CIC. "I think I said, 'Why did it have to happen to us?'"

It was, in fact, an ironic reversal of the roles assigned by the "pressures planners" in Washington. The captain who was supposed to spread an air of menace along the North Vietnamese coast felt menaced himself and was in flight. As he recalls that incident in his speech:

We were taking no chances, so we went to general quarters, in which the entire ship is put into battle condition. This was the first time I had to order this, other than a drill, since the Korean war, but it seemed to me it was going to be the real thing.

The Captain of the *Maddox* [Ogier] and I held a conference. We decided that if the PT boats approached to within 10,000 yards [5.8 miles] we would fire warning shots across their bow.

On the bridge, Ogier saw the radar contacts become dots on the horizon, the dots become boats in column formation, closing to five miles west of the *Maddox* as the *Maddox* steamed southeast.

It was at this juncture, Herrick continues, that "we fired the warning salvos. The PT boats kept coming, didn't veer one way or the other."

But the log of the *Maddox* gives a somewhat different version. The entries are:

1430 [2:30 P.M.]—Went to general quarters. . . . This ship is being closed by three patrol craft.

1442 [2:42 P.M.]—CS [Changed speed] to 25 knots. . . .

1508 [3:08 P.M.]—MT [mount] 52 and MT 53 open fire with one round apiece on patrol craft bearing 270, range 9800 yards.

Nothing here about "warning shots," just that the *Maddox* opened fire with two of her five-inch guns. And what of the 1967 statement to the AP by Lieutenant Connell, the officer of the deck, that "we were definitely aiming right at them. . . . It was shoot to kill"?

Captain Herrick straightens himself in his chair again. "I ordered warning shots," he says, "and the message came to me in the CIC from the bridge or gunnery control, 'Warning shots completed.' I thought if we fired some warning shots, they would stop the pursuit. If we were trying to hit, we would have both barrels loaded. But we fired only one shot from each of the three mounts."

And what of Admiral True's opinion that "There is no provision in international law for 'firing a *warning* shot' at another man-of-war on the high seas"?

"I don't know Admiral True," Herrick says. "I don't know how much of an expert he is. What we fired were warning shots. Whether they were within the rules of war, I don't know. It was a chance for them to cease and desist, which they did not take."

Ogier appears to be less certain of his rights in firing the "warning shots," judging from what he told the AP:

Of course, you know, if they had just turned and run away after we'd started firing at them, then we could have been in trouble. Because they could have said, "Here we were in international waters, too, and you went and fired at us." But they came on in and fired torpedoes at us, which was good.

They kept closing at an angle from starboard, 500 or 600 yards apart, creeping up to a position in line with the destroyer's bow that would be advantageous for a torpedo attack. After consulting with Ogier, Herrick says, "I gave the order to open fire."

Didn't that mean he fired the first shots, even if the earlier salvos could be considered warning shots?

"We were estimating what the range would be before they could fire their torpedoes, so we weren't going to wait too long to fire ourselves. I don't know of any doctrine on this. This was based on our own judgment. Also, we had those messages directing them to attack us. So we had a pretty good assumption they were going to fire at us."

Could they have just been chasing the destroyer out of what they considered to be their territorial waters?

"They chased us well out into the gulf. If they were trying to chase us away they had already accomplished that. No, they were on an attack course. There was no doubt in my mind that we were being attacked."

The *Maddox* opened up with her six five-inch guns, as well as with shells timed to explode over the target and scatter shrapnel over it and shells with proximity fuzes that explode seventy-five feet from the target.

It was just after 3:00 P.M. when the second and third boats wheeled to commence their torpedo runs. The first torpedo was sighted when the boats were 2,700 yards away. "You see a little wake going by and a sort of spray or smoke coming up behind it," Herrick says. The *Maddox* swung to port, and the wake passed 100 to 200 yards to starboard. Then there was a second torpedo to evade. The two boats fired one torpedo each, passing down the destroyer's starboard beam at a distance of about 1,700 yards (one mile) and firing their automatic weapons. They moved to the stern of the *Maddox* and passed across the destroyer's wake.

Now the lead boat turned to make her run against the *Maddox*, pumping away with her guns—and was hit by one of the destroyer's five-inch shells. A torpedo was either launched or dislodged by the destroyer's fire; it did not run in the water, and the boat stopped dead, out of action. On the *Maddox*, a great cheer went up.

Astern of the *Maddox*, a second boat appeared to have been hit. It slowed down, and the third boat approached it, as though to help. This was Herrick's chance to finish them off. He was turning around to do so when the aircraft from the *Ticonderoga* arrived—three needle-nosed Crusader jets that emptied their 20-mm. guns and Zuni rocket launchers in several passes at the second and third boats. Six of the rockets appeared to have missed—the early-model Zunis were designed for use against fixed targets—but two hit. The aircraft broke off the engagement after about eight minutes and the *Maddox* began closing in, but one of the pilots reported that his plane had been damaged by machine-gun fire and that he might have to bail out. The *Maddox* followed him down the gulf for fifteen or twenty minutes until he decided he was in good enough control of his aircraft to make it back to the carrier. (Whether the pilot had mistakenly thought he had been hit Herrick doesn't know; there were no reports of any damage to the navy planes during the engagement.)

And then Admiral Johnson took matters in hand. The

admiral, who had been following the action from the war room of the *Oklahoma City*, ordered the *Maddox* to retire from the area. The order was transmitted through Rear Admiral Robert B. Moore on board the *Ticonderoga* (not to be confused with Admiral Thomas H. Moorer, commander of the Pacific Fleet). As the flag officer closest to the scene, Rear Admiral Moore had automatically become Herrick's immediate commander when the action began. Herrick was turning around again when he received a message from Moore: "Do not pursue and proceed to the southeast and await further instructions."

It was a clear victory for the United States. The comvan intercepted a message admitting damage to the torpedo boats, including the sinking of one of them. Reconnaissance planes from the *Ticonderoga* located the boats in the early evening and obtained photographs of two damaged vessels. The third boat, hit by the destroyer's five-inch guns, was last seen burning and was presumed to have sunk.

This was the boat that was believed to have scored the only hit for its side—a bullet that pierced the pedestal of the three-inch aftergun mount and splintered into three pieces, ricocheting around the magazine below but missing the men working there. Stankevitz brought out his hidden camera and took a picture of the bullet hole. Herrick had the bullet pieced together and sent it in a little cardboard box to the Joint Chiefs of Staff.

*
* *

Hanoi's version of the August 2 incident was somewhat different. It appeared in a domestic broadcast of August 12, 1964—printed the next day by the FBIS Daily Report, a foreign-broadcast monitoring service for circulation within the government in Washington, but unnoticed by the Western press. With garbled words in brackets, as they appear in the FBIS text, this is how the broadcast described the day's action:

At noon on 2 August a group of boats called Group X went to sea on patrol. It was rather foggy. The sea was calm. Then the group was informed that a U.S. destroyer was heading toward the south of Hon Me. At times it was only four or five miles from San Son Beach. Group X immediately turned around and headed toward the enemy. Having [a high sense of duty?] the members of Group X could not help being excited at the prospect of their first encounter with an enemy greatly superior in terms of equipment, total strength and armament. Indeed, the pirate destroyer is 132 meters long, has a tonnage of 2,000 tons, and carried some 2,000 sailors. It is equipped with scores of large caliber guns and carries much ammunition. Our side was but a unit of small boats with [scant] equipment, including [two words indistinct] machine guns and torpedoes.

But the enemy had brazenly violated our territorial waters. We had to show him the brave [words indistinct]. Because the U.S. navy destroyer has the strength of long-range firepower, we had to move in close to it. Lively, mobile, witty and courageous, we were determined to fulfill our duty to protect the tranquil waters of our fatherland.

Raising high this determination, the small boats of our combatants increased their speed, gliding over the water as though in flight, and waved signal banners and wished one another success. At 1500 hours [3 P.M.] the U.S. destroyer, which was identified as the Maddox [was observed]. It was zigzagging north of Hon Me Island near the mouth of the Day River. Immediately, Boat Group X, going full speed, sped over the waves toward the destroyer. Upon seeing our boats, the enemy destroyer immediately attacked.

Like thunder its guns fired one after another, causing high columns of water to spout around our boats. But our boats kept silent and continued to speed swiftly against the enemy ship. The nearer we came, the more bewildered the enemy became, scurrying about the deck in disorder. Continuously they fired [rounds?] of every caliber they had. Our boats kept advancing, dodging enemy shells. They waited until they were very near the enemy ship before returning the fire.

The enemy was confused. The U.S. warship changed its course, and when it reached [Vinh] it departed from our territorial waters at full speed. While fleeing, the U.S. warship sent a message for help.

Five jet aircraft from a U.S. aircraft carrier rushed to the spot to give aid. Our naval units once more resisted an enemy having superior speed. The U.S. aircraft swiftly attacked our boats from all directions. Our combatants closely observed the paths of the enemy, maneuvering the boats to avoid the enemy, and fired back violently.

The first jet aircraft was hit. It tried to climb, but it was too late. The U.S. jet burst into flames in the skies. Then the second U.S. jet was hit. It hurriedly fled, leaving behind a stream of black smoke. When the third jet was hit, the two others were panic-stricken, fired innumerable bullets into the sea [several words indistinct] and finally flew away.

At 1530 hours the sea was calm, the wind mild, and the group of boats named X returned to shore with flags of victory flying high in the air. Within a mere half an hour of heroic and active fighting, our young naval combatants succeeded in chasing away the U.S. pirates, who fled breathlessly—both the pirates on the sea and in the air—in order to protect the inviolable territory of the heroic fatherland.

*

* *

With McNamara weekending in Rhode Island and Rusk about to leave for a speaking engagement in New York, the crisis managers were completely unprepared for the messages from the Tonkin Gulf that enkindled the Flag Plot at the Pentagon before dawn on Sunday, August 2. The President's midday conclave with his top advisers was a bemused affair. Didn't these North Vietnamese *know* we were itching to hit them? And they sent three PT boats thirty miles out to attack our destroyer?

Here was a peg on which to hang the whole war package so carefully put together and, at the last minute, so discreetly put on the shelf. A navy ship deliberately attacked in international waters while on routine patrol to observe the coastal infiltration that feeds the forces of Communist aggression in South Vietnam! A test of American resolve by Hanoi, Peking and Moscow that had to be met with an immediate response lest the Communists decide that they have only to press harder for Washington to retreat and South Vietnam to fall! The "30-day program," with its bombing and its Congressional resolution, waited on some action by the Vietcong that could be used as a pretext some time after the November election; this incident in the Gulf of Tonkin gave the planners a vision of how the program could be triggered by a DeSoto patrol instead.

But the vision had appeared too abruptly; neither Johnson nor his top civilian aides were ready for it. Having decided in June to keep the lid on until after the elections, they had taken the public stance that bombing North Vietnam wasn't necessary, at least for the present, and the impression conveyed by Johnson's speeches was that he wasn't planning on doing it ever. His "resolute but restrained" campaign image was now weighted more toward restraint. Oh, yes— he would demonstrate his resolution. He would order that ship back into the Tonkin Gulf, he told McNamara and Rusk, and he would warn Hanoi against any further interference with the American patrol (motions pungently seconded by Rusk). But retaliating, popping off right away after the first torpedo, a minor skirmish in which they may have lost two boats while we weren't even scratched—that would not look so good. It wouldn't seem very restrained. It would seem more like a concession to Goldwater's "recklessness" and "irresponsibility," and that was the last impression Johnson wanted to create. The decision was to play down the incident as unwelcome but not especially serious.

Of course, if it happened again. . . . But it was a fluke, the bravado of some crazy PT-boat commander who would now be firmly sat on. It really *couldn't* happen again.

The Event   14

Both Vice Admiral Johnson and Admiral Moorer were products of the Deep South: Johnson was born in Big Bend, Louisiana, in 1906, Moorer in Mount Willing, Alabama, in 1912. Both were World War II fighter pilots. Both had just taken over their Pacific commands. But if pride in performance was Johnson's most noticeable characteristic, his superior in Hawaii was governed by a larger pride, pride in America. Six years later, when the Tonkin Gulf incident was only a dimly remembered episode in a career even more vivid, valorous, bemedaled and brilliant than Johnson's, Thomas Hinman Moorer wrote a farewell message to the men and women of the Navy upon assuming the chairmanship of the Joint Chiefs of Staff, and the words he used then to evoke the values of his young manhood—"before what is phrased these days as 'doing your own thing,'" when "belief in God and Country [was] the binding cement"— were, to those who knew him, an expression of the man. "Somewhere along the line something has been forgotten by a great number of our people," he said in his farewell, but, he thought, something had been learned too: "that when any nation's freedom is denied, ours is threatened." "We as a people face our problems more squarely than others," he

266

was sure, "and keeping the armed forces positioned to dissuade the forces of aggression" was a problem that Americans had unflinchingly to face.[1]

The problem created by the *Maddox* incident was one he was prepared to face without waiting for instructions from Washington. Five and a half hours before the President, McNamara, Rusk and Bundy met to decide what to do about the news from the Tonkin Gulf, a message "from CINCPACFLT [Commander in Chief, Pacific Fleet] to his units" radiated through the navy communications system from Moorer's headquarters at Makalapa near Pearl Harbor:

In view Maddox incident consider it in our best interest that we assert right of freedom of the seas and resume Gulf of Tonkin patrol earliest.

For COMSEVENTHFLT [Commander, Seventh Fleet]. UNODIR [unless otherwise directed] conduct patrol with two destroyers, resuming ASAP [as soon as possible]. When ready, proceed to Point Charlie, arriving first day, thence patrol northward toward Point Delta during daylight hours. Retire to the east during hours of darkness. On second day proceed to Point Delta, thence patrol south toward Point Charlie, retiring at night as before. On third day proceed to Point Lima and patrol toward Point Mike, retiring to east at night. On fourth day proceed to Point Mike and patrol toward Point November, retiring at night. On fifth day return to November and retire to south through Points Oscar and Papa and terminate patrol. CPA to North Vietnamese coast 8 NM. CPA to North Vietnamese islands 4 NM.

Moorer was laying out an entirely new schedule for Herrick, scrapping the one that was to have brought the patrol to an end on August 5. With two ships to his task force, Herrick would now spend two more days in the Hon Me–Hon Ngu area; then, orbiting north, with little time for the Chinese phase of the exercise, the ships would be out of the gulf August 7, "Unless otherwise directed." Meaning, presumably, unless the Moorer plan was rejected. Which it wasn't. Twenty-four hours after the *Maddox,* having re-fueled, re-entered the gulf, with the *Turner Joy* 1,000 yards astern, the Joint Chiefs of Staff formally approved resumption of the patrol, with only one modification tacked on by Admiral Sharp: that the closest point of approach be eleven rather than eight miles. Sending *two* ships back into the gulf appealed to the President so well that he made it sound like his own idea when he announced it personally to the White House press corps.

And was that all? Nothing more? Nothing implicit in Moorer's insistence that the patrol, reinforced, keep poking the very center of the hornet's nest, where the Swift boats had attacked and Hanoi's boats had stung back and the tension now could be readily imagined? No thought that the sight of two destroyers running at the land at daylight after disappearing at night would heighten the dramatic effect still further, until some climax was reached?

Restricting the patrol to intrusions of only one mile into North Vietnamese territorial waters, instead of four, may have indicated an intent to lessen the risk of another clash. But the Navy's state of mind at that moment was perhaps better reflected in another message, sent by Rear Admiral Moore aboard the *Ticonderoga:*

> It is apparent that DRV has thrown down the gauntlet and now considers itself at war with the United States. It is felt that they will attack U.S. forces on sight with no regard for cost. U.S. ships in the Gulf of Tonkin can no longer assume that they will be considered neutrals exercising the right of free transit. They will be treated as belligerents from first detection and must consider themselves as such.

A navy ship had been attacked and the President had decided not to retaliate but merely to warn. Wherever navy men gathered, there was a felt need to do something, put the chip on the shoulder, show that the Navy could not be pushed around. The admirals had not expected the August

2 incident. After that, they decided to let time, God and the Navy take their course.

*

* *

One executor of the DeSoto mission who emphatically did not share this suppressed mood of combativeness was John Jerome Herrick. He had been given a job to do, and he had planned to do it as unobtrusively as possible. The job, as he understood it, was a "data-collection program," part visual observation, part electronic intelligence (a vital phase of the Free World's defenses against the forces of expansionist Communism, the same technique the Russians used against us), part oceanography: "We didn't know where the priority lay." No one had told him that this job was a little special, and that the priority, though the formal instructions could not say so, lay in throwing a scare into Hanoi. No one had listened when, startled by what he heard in the gulf, he had worried his way to the decision —doubly hard for a man who did not inquire into what he did not have to know—that the whole thing had been a mistake and they had better get his ship out of there before something happened. And something did happen and, flung from complacency to alarm, he had opened fire (where a more knowing operator might have waited), thus perhaps provoking the torpedo attack that otherwise might not have taken place. Captain Herrick, devoted husband and father, amateur carpenter, connoisseur of navy routine, his first and last brush with danger twenty years behind him, went back into the gulf a deeply worried man.

Sitting at his desk in 1970, Captain Herrick is not about to admit to undue nervousness or doubts about his superiors' judgment at that or any point of the mission.

"The adrenalin was going down. I don't think anyone thought it would happen again. Admiral Moorer's order would make it [the *Maddox*] more palatable to the North Vietnamese. We'd go way out to sea at night. Also, we were more confident because we had air cover." The aircraft had arrived as fast as they did August 2 because they happened to be aloft, making practice runs at a small rock sticking out of the sea; the agreement now was for the *Ticonderoga*'s aircraft to remain airborne at all times. "And I was happy to have another destroyer along, and a more modern one." The *Turner Joy* was sister to the *Edson*, Herrick's old command. "I knew her gunnery capabilities." He smiles wryly. "We were pretty apprehensive, I'll admit that."

Rear Admiral Moore's message about Hanoi throwing down the gauntlet had something else to say:

DRV PTs have advantages, especially at night, of being able to hide in junk concentrations all across the Gulf of Tonkin. This would allow attack from short range with little or no early warning.

He added that the *Maddox* was really "too short-legged" for a mission requiring high speed against PT boats, and her armament was "not too well-fitted for anti-PT operations even in daylight," but there was no other available ship in the West Pacific area with the special communications equipment that was on board the *Maddox*, so the *Maddox* it had to be.

In the predawn darkness of August 3 the *Maddox* blinked a signal to the *Turner Joy:*

Consider the situation not unlike war patrol and demanding of maximum alertness and readiness. If we are attacked, follow our general movements at 1,000 to 2,000 yards. Take your own action as required to unmask batteries or to avoid torpedoes.[2]

There was no sunbathing on deck that morning as the *Maddox* orbited along that same strip of coast between Hon Me and Hon Ngu. The CTs were as busy and as exclusive as ever, but sixteen men on a destroyer will not remain privy forever to information affecting the others' lives, and word had escaped that the ship was attacked and could be attacked again because of some coastal action by the South Vietnamese. "We thought it was kind of a shady deal to be pulling on us, setting us up as ducks," says Stankevitz. "The crew was very resentful of it."[3]

Were Herrick and Ogier beginning to have a morale problem?

"No. It was strictly scuttlebutt," Herrick added, not too relevantly. "There's always a lot of talk going on among the crew. They certainly had no background knowledge that was factual."

* * *

The old sea dog on board the *Oklahoma City* was having second thoughts about his brisk dismissal of Herrick's fears of being connected with the coastal raiders. Admiral Roy L. Johnson was on his way to the Tonkin Gulf. Casting off from Yokosuka as soon as the August 2 incident occurred, the Seventh Fleet commander fired off messages informing all and sundry that he proposed terminating the patrol on the evening of August 4, about twelve hours ahead of the original schedule, so as to avoid any possibility of entanglement with the 34-A operations, and asking General Westmoreland's headquarters in Saigon (MAC/V) for information on whatever other 34-A action was planned, so that interference with the DeSoto itinerary could be avoided.

The response from MAC/V was a request that all Seventh Fleet units remain clear on August 3–4 of a certain designated area in the Tonkin Gulf. Sometime later MAC/V sent a second message, requesting that the northern boundary of this area be moved still farther north. At the time this message was received in Washington it was the morning of August 3 in the gulf and the destroyers were patrolling south of that line in accordance with the new Moorer itinerary, and more messages on avoiding mutual interference passed back and forth. Whatever extra psychological value might have been ascribed in some quarters to having the two operations going on at the same time, it was never planned to have them run into each other: that would have discredited the cover of both. Admiral Sharp had obviously meant it when he ordered Admiral Johnson on July 10 to arrange with MAC/V to keep the two separate.

Johnson's other initiative, however—the proposal to terminate the patrol a little ahead of the original schedule—was knocked down by Moorer, who had just ordered the schedule lengthened by two days. Since the Johnson and Moorer messages appear to have been sent at approximately the same time, they may have crossed each other, with Johnson unaware that he was acting against his immediate superior's wishes. At any rate, Moorer was not slow to make his views clear:

1. Termination of DeSoto patrol after two days of patrol ops subsequent to Maddox incident as planned in Ref. A does not in my view adequately demonstrate United States resolve to assert our legitimate rights in these international waters.

2. Accordingly, recommend following adjustments in remainder of patrol schedule. . . . In order to accommodate COMUSMACV [Commander, U.S. Military Assistance Command, Vietnam] request that patrol ships remain north of LAT. 19–10 North until 060600H [6 A.M. August 6] to avoid interference with 34-A ops. . . .

The above patrol will:

A. Clearly demonstrate our determination to continue these operations.

B. Possibly draw NVN PGMs to northward away from area of 34-A ops.

C. Eliminate DeSoto patrol interference with 34-A ops.

"This cable," Morse observed when he read it into the Congressional Record, "says one thing quite clearly and suggests another. It says clearly that CINCPACFLT was disappointed with the results of the mission thus far—that is, the United States had not yet 'demonstrated' its resolve to assert its legitimate rights in international waters. This seems to mean that we had not as yet had the opportunity to demonstrate this forcibly." And Moorer's suggestion that moving the patrol north could draw the North Vietnamese patrol boats away from the area of 34-A operations fortified Morse's charge that the American destroyers were being used as decoys. The Defense Department hastened to explain that this was Moorer's own personal notion, and that "no action was taken on the recommendation" when Sharp forwarded it to the Joint Chiefs. But there was no denying that at least Moorer thought the North Vietnamese could regard the destroyers as part of the offensive coastal operations.

*

* *

The afternoon of August 3 was tense but uneventful. Herrick had a radar contact over the horizon and asked for air support. Two aircraft arrived and looked around a bit and didn't see anything. At 7 P.M. or so, following Moorer's new schedule, Herrick went out to sea, to the center of the gulf, to cruise in a "squared circle," ten miles to each side, for the remainder of the night.

At about 1 A.M. August 4 he received instructions from Admiral Johnson: Do not go below 19 degrees 10 minutes north.

What did the order signify to him?

"We deduced that some activity must have been going on down there," Herrick says, "but we didn't know what. They purposely kept us in the dark about these activities. They told us only what we absolutely had to know."

The North Vietnamese were quick to enlighten him. As the destroyers steamed back toward shore at sunrise, the coastal radio network was in a frenzy; 34-A had carried out another midnight raid. Two Swift boats bombarded a radar installation on Cape Vinh Son, south of the Hon Me—Hon Ngu area, while two others attacked a neighboring security post in the Rhon River estuary. The boats laid down a half-hour barrage; one of them was pursued for an hour by a North Vietnamese patrol craft on the way back to South Vietnam. It was the first naval bombardment of the North Vietnamese mainland.

Admiral Johnson's order to Herrick would have kept the destroyers a good eighty miles away from the scene of action. But the order arrived a good hour after the action began.

Herrick has no explanation for this delay, so out of keeping with the Roy L. Johnson trademark of efficiency, but he says it did not matter because he had not been anywhere near Cape Vinh Son the previous afternoon before putting out to sea. (The ships' logs would show how far south of latitude 19 degrees 10 minutes the patrol went that afternoon, but there is a gap in information on the log entries at this point. It should also be noted that the *Times'* paraphrase of the classified Pentagon history says, "This time [on August 3] the Maddox and the Turner Joy were definitely warned that the clandestine [34-A] assaults were going to take place, the documents show.")

At any rate, the North Vietnamese were making no more of a distinction between the patrol and the new 34-A raid than they did after the first 34-A attack. Some of the messages picked up by the comvan identified the American ships by name—their names now being headline grist around the world.

By midmorning, having approached the coast in the Hon Me area, orbited north to the Red River delta and come down again, never shaking free of the electronic signals that told him he was being tracked by coastal radar, Herrick had heard enough to convince him of the need for another message to his Pacific commanders. Careful even in coded message not to refer to the intelligence team on board, he said:

Evaluation of info from various sources indicates DRV considers patrol directly involved with 34-A ops. DRV considers U.S. ships present as enemies because of these ops and have already indicated readiness to treat us in that category.

Having failed to get the patrol broken off, Herrick wanted at least to make sure his superiors knew how the North Vietnamese were reacting. He confesses puzzlement over McNamara's description of his warning as "unfounded speculation." "It was founded on what I knew," he says. "It was appearing in those messages."

His cable continued:

DRV are very sensitive about Hon Me. Believe this is PT operating base, and the cove there presently contains numerous patrol and PT craft which have been repositioned from northerly bases.

Under these conditions 15 min. reaction time for operating air cover is unacceptable. Cover must be overhead and controlled by DDs [destroyers] at all times.

He failed to get that too. At noon, a blip appeared on his radar, a "contact" that appeared to be paralleling the patrol's movement. But the *Ticonderoga*'s response was that its aircraft were ready for "launch and support at short notice."

Wasn't he beginning to feel a little bit unheeded with all his requests being turned down?

"Naturally the man on the spot wants all the protection he can get," says Herrick, the picture of a proper navy captain. "You defer to the judgment of senior officers."

The nice thing about Herrick is that his occasional moments of pompousness yield quickly to the claims of plain speech. "We were beginning to feel the pressure. There's no use pretending we weren't pretty excited and concerned for the safety of the ships and their crews."

＊

＊　　＊

Commander Robert C. Barnhart, Jr., and his crew were there by the merest chance. The *C. Turner Joy* (launched in Seattle, Washington, in 1958; named for the late Admiral Charles Turner Joy, who commanded the UN naval forces in the Korean war and represented the UN during the first year of the armistice talks) was in Subic Bay, the Philippines, along with three other destroyers, when orders came in at 2 A.M. July 23 for one of the ships to proceed "at first light" to relieve a vessel that had broken down in the South China Sea. The *Turner Joy* happened to have tied up outside the other three ships, too far to plug into the electric outlets at the dock, and had to keep up her boilers to generate her own power and, for that reason, could leave at once, and did, abandoning laundry and miscellaneous equipment on shore. On the approaches to the Gulf of Tonkin she relieved the *Edson* (now part of the *Ticonderoga* task force), which, it developed, had two cases of hepatitis on board. And when a companion had to be found for the *Maddox* on August 2, the *Turner Joy* was right there.[4]

Now, on the afternoon of August 4, the *Turner Joy* followed the *Maddox* as the patrol zigzagged down from the Red River delta to Hon Me, taking care to stay above 19 degrees 10 minutes. Like Ogier, Barnhart had been a neighbor of Herrick's at Annapolis—when Herrick returned to the Naval Academy as ordnance instructor after the Korean war—and these old associations among the three of them made for an extra bond, a faith in each other's good judgment, now that they were together in this unfamiliar predicament.

The weather had turned nasty; the worst of the typhoon

season was at hand. Dark clouds had formed over the gulf. Herrick's ECM equipment told him he had been contacted by "skinhead" (surface-search) radar. A 2:30 P.M. message from Barnhart to the Pacific command said:

The commander of Task Force 72.1 reported at [deleted] hours position of vicinity of Point Delta, suspect Red shadow [a vessel shadowing him] 15 miles to west. Skinhead radar detected on same bearing.

Then there had been trouble with the *Maddox*'s sonar. It had been repaired, but apparently not everyone was fully satisfied with it. And at about 5 P.M. Lieutenant Moore, the officer in charge of the comvan, showed him an intercepted North Vietnamese message.

This was the first of the intercepts of August 4 that McNamara was to handle so cagily at the Fulbright committee hearing of February, 1968. For the record, McNamara described this message as "indicating there were two objectives, enemy attack vessels, located at a point at which the *Maddox* and the *Turner Joy* were located or located within 3,000 yards of them."

So by 5:30 P.M. Herrick was more than ready to retire to the open sea.

It was about 7:40 P.M. when the surface-search radar in the Combat Information Center of the *Maddox* picked out the "skunks" (unidentified objects) thirty-six miles ahead of the patrol as the ships moved east into the center of the gulf. CIC is the nerve center of the ship, and Herrick had taken his station there, while Ogier was on the bridge. "They seemed to be strategically placed," Herrick says, just about surrounding the area where the destroyers had spent the previous night and where they were now headed for night steaming. Stankevitz, the CIC radarman, agrees: "There were definitely contacts and moving fast"—four or five of them—but they were also playing tricks. "You'd have beautiful pips for a while and then they'd disappear." That may have been because the radar beams were "ducting"—bouncing off the low clouds and picking up objects beyond the horizon. "It was a pretty poor night for radar," Stankevitz adds.[5]

The *Turner Joy*'s radar wasn't picking up anything.

From the time of his night encounter with the swarm of junks before the day of the first incident, Herrick had been preoccupied with the danger of ambush. He turned southeast—never mind now about keeping above 19 degrees 10 minutes!—to see if the contacts would follow. They did. All his conceptions of the enemy—their fanaticism and intransigence as Communists, their wiliness and perverseness as Asiatics—fell into place for him in a logical pattern: They had found no profit in attacking an American destroyer in daylight; they had tracked the patrol to its night station forty-eight hours before; they would lie in wait for it when it returned, as it probably would, unguardedly, the next night.

Herrick sent a message to the Pacific command evaluating the situation as a "trap." He went to general quarters, ordered maximum boiler power and told Barnhart to stay close enough to the *Maddox* for mutual support but far enough away to enable each destroyer to act independently and fire on any attacker that seemed to be threatening either ship. The *Turner Joy* still wasn't picking up anything, but the *Maddox*'s radar, Herrick reports, showed the contacts "across the north above us and down to the south and east, and as it grew dark they started to close in on us at high speeds." A flash from the *Maddox* reported contact with "three unidentified aircraft."

"It was a very disagreeable night," Herrick recalls. "The wind was blowing and there were numerous thunderstorms in the area, and there was some lightning, no moon, completely dark, an inky black night."[6] He also says, "You could see the ship's wake maybe out to 100 yards, but that was it."[7] Barnhart says, "Usually you could see the silhouette of the other ship. It was so dark that night I couldn't see the *Maddox* in front of me." [8] A sonarman aboard the *Maddox*, Patrick Park, recalls, "It was as black as being three miles back in a cave without a candle. You could see the *Turner Joy*'s running lights, and the phosphorescence of our wake, but only when you looked right down on it." [9]

At 9:08 P.M. the planes from the *Ticonderoga* began arriving overhead—about ninety minutes from the time Herrick reported he was in danger—and he asked them to investigate a contact speeding at 30 knots thirteen miles away. They did but found nothing. The *Maddox* reported that the three "unidentified aircraft" had disappeared from her radar screen. The other surface contacts were remaining at a distance.

*
* *

In Washington it was just past 9 A.M. August 4, and at 9:20 A.M. the National Military Command Center at the Pentagon received an intercept from the Gulf of Tonkin that was interpreted as indicating that the *Maddox* and the *Turner Joy* were in danger of attack. This was the message that McNamara was to describe in his opening statement at the February, 1968, hearing as "information from an intelligence source that North Vietnamese naval forces had been ordered to attack the patrol . . . intelligence reports [that] North Vietnam was making preparations to attack our destroyers with two Swatow boats and with one PT boat if the PT could be made ready in time . . . an intelligence report of a highly classified and unimpeachable nature received shortly before the engagement, stating that North Vietnamese naval forces intended to attack the *Maddox* and *Turner Joy*." This was also the message whose contents were described somewhat differently by Gore after the committee heard all the messages in question in the off-the-record interlude, with Marcy and Bader out of the room. Gore, it will be remembered, objected that the message was one "directing them to make ready for military operations" rather than to "attack," and McNamara had to agree that the order was to "make ready for military operations." The point, of course, was that military operations can be defensive as well as offensive.

Herrick says, "We picked up an order. It told us what types of boats they'd be. The impression you would get was that there was going to be another attack."

It is not clear at what time the message was intercepted, but a well-informed source says it took from two to four hours for the messages intercepted in the Tonkin Gulf area that day to reach the Secretary of Defense, so this order from a North Vietnamese shore command could have been intercepted anywhere from about twenty minutes to upwards of two hours after the 5 P.M. (gulf time) message fixing the destroyers' location.

At 9:30 P.M. the blips on the *Maddox*'s radar screen began closing in again at high speeds, and now the *Turner Joy* got a contact as well. Both destroyers, by prearrangement, opened fire with star shells when the contacts came within 8,000 yards, to try to pierce the blackness. But the star shells burst unseen above the overcast and were nearly spent by the time they came below the clouds. At 4,000 yards Barnhart gave the command, "Commence firing." Pitching through rain squalls and choppy swells, the *Turner Joy* blazed away in the general direction of the suspected targets. "Almost simultaneously," Barnhart says, "I got a report from the *Maddox:* 'Torpedo in the water.'" [10]

"We tracked that torpedo boat in from thirty-two miles out," Herrick says. "The contacts on the radar scope were plotted in, they were consistent, didn't appear and disappear as they would if they were ghosts. The boat made a typical firing run at the *Joy*. When it got close enough it made that turn, when you cut away as you fire your torpedo. And just then the *Maddox*'s sonar reported a torpedo in the water."

And, just then, four men aboard the *Turner Joy* say they saw a torpedo wake run up the port side, at a distance estimated variously at 100 feet and 400 feet and along the same course that was indicated by the *Maddox*'s sonar.

Herrick seems to realize the importance of this first torpedo to his whole view of the August 4 incident.

"I've thought all these years about that contact," he says. "The best evidence I have, based on its rate of speed, on the consistent pattern when it was plotted in, proved to me conclusively, on the basis of my experience, that it couldn't have been anything besides a torpedo boat."

And the wake seen from the *Turner Joy* was, he is sure, "an authentic torpedo." "We train with live torpedoes all the time. There are not too many destroyer people who'd be fooled by something that wasn't a real torpedo wake." In fact, he adds, "it could well have been two torpedoes. I'm sure a PT boat coming in would fire both its torpedoes."

Barnhart says there were reports of two torpedo wakes "but I only remember one," reported to him by his gunnery officer. He speculates that "it may have been two stations [aboard the *Turner Joy*] reporting the same torpedo." [11]

Ogier told an interviewer in 1968, while a naval ROTC instructor at Rice University in Houston, that he believed the *Maddox*'s sonar detected two torpedoes at the outset of the action.[12] But in 1967 he said to another interviewer, "I thought they were torpedoes but after three years away from it I have my doubts now. I just don't know." Asked, "Do you think there were targets out there?" he replied, "I don't know. I really don't know." He added that on August 4 he believed there were boats attacking partly "because there was no question about their being there on the second of August, and we know they had torpedo boats, but conclusive evidence of my own knowledge I can't give, which is the bad thing about the incident." [13]

There is also a "bad thing" about the reported sighting of the torpedo wake skimming by the *Turner Joy*. The *Joy*'s sonar did not register any torpedo noise.

Half an hour later at about 10:15 P.M., as the *Turner Joy's* guns found more and more contacts to fire at, Herrick's radar screen in CIC registered what he was sure was an authentic hit.

"I watched the contact come in on the radarscope," Herrick says. "I saw the *Joy's* projectiles going out on the scope and merging with the target pip and the pip disappearing."

The *Turner Joy* claimed one boat sunk.

A little later she claimed a probable. McNamara was to make that one quite definite:

At about 10:24 P.M. one target was taken under fire by *Turner Joy*. Numerous hits were observed on this target and it disappeared from all radars. The commanding officer and other *Turner Joy* personnel observed a thick column of black smoke from this target.[14]

Barnhart himself is less positive, telling one interviewer that he saw "a big black column of smoke" 4,000 yards away (he had told the AP 2,000 to 3,000 yards) by the light of gun flashes in the distance—but that he saw it *just before* the *Joy's* radar picked up the target that was then believed to have been hit.[15]

Herrick says, "I think they hit another one then, because Barnhart says there was a sort of muffled flame. Maybe he hit an oil tank. He was convinced he sank two ships."

The action had assumed a peculiar pattern.

Now that the *Turner Joy* was blasting away at thirty rounds a minute at one radar pip after another, the *Maddox's* radar, which had sounded the original alarm while the *Joy* was still drawing a blank, couldn't find anything to shoot at. Lieutenant Connell, the weapons officer, who was responsible for firing the guns, says:

We could not hold a target long enough in our gun range to do any firing. There were blips on our radar and they were very faint. We'd no sooner get our directors, our fire-control radar, get on the bearing, and the target would then disappear. . . . I

am definitely convinced there were none there. . . . There might
have been some outside of our gun range [18,000 yards, or nine
nautical miles] but there were none around our ship.[16]

The *Maddox* kept firing star shells, and that was all she
fired all night. Yet her sonar was producing one torpedo
warning after another, sending both ships into wild gyra-
tions—while *Joy's* sonar could not detect any torpedo moises
at all. The number of torpedo calls increased to five, then
to ten, then to fifteen—would it never stop? Sonarman Patrick Park, who doubled in gunnery, was manning the main
gun director that night, taking over from a greener man,
but that left an equally inexperienced hand, Sonarman
Third Class David Mallow, manning the sonarscope, and to
Park "it seemed like he [Mallow] was hollering all the time.
I said to myself, Aw, God, if there are that many torpedoes
in the water the whole Seventh Fleet would be blown up
by now."[17] "It got to a ridiculous number after a while,"
Herrick says, "twenty-two or something."

The fault may not have been young Mallow's. Lieutenant
(j.g.) John M. Leeman, who was in charge of the sonar
room, and Lieutenant Connell report that Mallow never
called out "torpedoes" but merely "noise spokes" or "hydrophone effects," and that it was up to the bridge to decide
whether they were probable torpedoes. Herrick agrees that
this is the proper procedure, and concedes that after the
first torpedo, of which he is sure, the bridge may have been
hasty in its evaluation, though he adds, "Of course, you don't
take chances either. You don't say, 'No, that's not a torpedo,'
and then have a torpedo hit you.

"We tried to figure out what was going on," Herrick re-
counts, and decided that the noise effects were the result
of the sharp, rapid turns being made by the *Maddox* as she
dodged nonexistent torpedoes at top speed. As the rudder
was thrown hard over, it provided a surface for reflecting
the sound of the screw beats of the propeller in front of it,
and this sound bounced off the rudder and up toward the

front of the ship, into the sonar's receiver. 'It was an extremely rare situation." Herrick says. "Ordinarily you don't make full-power, full-rudder turns with your sonar turned on. We kept a straight course after that, and things sort of petered out."

But not before almost exploding.

Patrick Park, at the main gun director, has told an interviewer that around midnight he was given a range on a target spotted by the main radar room. Directing his own radar toward the target, he finally found something to shoot at: "About fifteen hundred yards off to the side, a nice fat blip." Park says he requested and received permission to fire, and tells what happened next as he remembers it:

I shouted back, "Where's the *Turner Joy?*" There was a lot of yelling of "Goddam" back and forth with the bridge telling me to "fire before we lost the contact," and me yelling right back at them. . . .

I finally told them, "I'm not opening fire until I know where the *Turner Joy* is." The bridge got on the phone and said, "Turn on your lights, *Turner Joy.*"

Sure enough, there she was, right in the cross-hairs. I had six five-inch guns right at the *Turner Joy,* 1,500 yards away. If I had fired, it would have blown it clear out of the water. . . .[18]

Herrick comments, "I think Park took a little too much credit for that. In any night action, the possibility of shooting up one of your own ships is always uppermost in your mind. The men at the guns were forewarned to keep track of where the *Joy* was. This is part of the job.

"I was in combat. Ogier was on the bridge. Park got a good radar pip on his fire-control radar and locked onto it. Combat was watching a scope identical to Park's radarscope. Combat also has the DRT, the Dead-Reckoning Tracer, which shows you where your ship is and where the other ship is at all times. Combat suspected that this might be the *Turner Joy* and asked *Joy* to turn on her light. That is the common way to tell where your people are. Just for a second, of course."

Then it wasn't one man's presence of mind that prevented disaster?

"A second after Park said it, if he said it first, the gunnery liaison officer in CIC would have said it. Our checks and balances worked."

Whichever version one accepts, a cable sent by the *Turner Joy* minutes after this episode makes ironic reading. "We think," reported the *Joy*, "a PT boat sunk one of its own boats."

It is at this point that McNamara's account of the night's events is adorned by two vivid cameos. Testifying before the Senate Foreign Relations and Armed Services committees on August 6, 1964, he said:

By midnight local time, the destroyers reported . . . that the defensive aircraft from the *Ticonderoga* were illuminating the area and attacking the enemy surface craft.[19]

Commander Wesley L. McDonald, one of the pilots of the eight single-seater Skyhawks launched by the *Ticonderoga*, says, "It was dark as hell. We saw the destroyers clearly several times by flare light and by their wakes. I never saw any other wakes. I never saw any PT boats." The *Turner Joy* tried to mark some targets for him with her shells and he fired "two rocket pods" at the general area but has "no way of knowing if we hit anything."[20]

The AP, it will be recalled, quoted McDonald as reporting that he and the other flyers, unable to see any attacking ships, concentrated on what they thought were wakes and once almost shot at the *Maddox*.

Two pilots, Commander G. H. Edmondson and Lieutenant J. A. Burton, his wingman, told Defense Department interviewers right after the incident that they saw gun flashes on the surface of the water; whether these came from the destroyers or from patrol boats they did not know. They also said they saw a "snaky" wake ahead of the *Maddox* and "light antiaircraft bursts" at their approximate altitude of 700 to 1,500 feet.[21]

The other five flyers did not see anything.

After searching the area for forty minutes the planes ran out of fuel and returned to the *Ticonderoga*.

The other vignette in McNamara's August 6, 1964, testimony was:

The *Turner Joy* reported that during the engagement, in addition to the torpedo attack, she was fired upon by automatic weapons while being illuminated by searchlights.[22]

McNamara supplied details under questioning: "These were probably three-inch or something of that size on the Swatow and/or PT-4 boats."

This adventure-magazine picture of Asian marauders blazing away at a Yankee patrol in the glare of their searchlights was, as Herrick puts it dryly, "imaginative of someone." Barnhart recalls no such report and says his ship was not fired on that night, by machine guns or shells or guns of any kind. Herrick says there was no gunfire against either destroyer.

McNamara's tale may indeed have been the product of enlivened imagination and honest confusion among communications officials in the Pentagon. Yet fiction, once part of the official record, lives on as official fact. McNamara, in his February 20, 1968, testimony, again claimed that "gunfire against the patrol had been observed" from the destroyers. And an official Navy Department account of the August 4 incident declares:

Maddox lit up the night with starshells and the two destroyers nimbly maneuvered to avoid wakes of torpedoes as *Turner Joy* opened on the oncoming enemy with well directed gunfire. For two and one-half hours, the two destroyers fought off pass after pass of the enemy motor torpedo boats which closed within

2,000 yards to attack with automatic weapons and torpedoes. There were at least six motor torpedo boats involved in the attack. Two were believed to have sunk after receiving direct hits and two badly damaged. The remaining PTs, the fight gone out of them, sped north through the black night and out of range.[23]

The Defense Department's *Annual Report for Fiscal Year 1965* does even better than the official history. It says, "At least four of the attacking craft were sunk and others damaged."

Barnhart does remember seeing a searchlight.

McNamara testified in 1968 that Barnhart and five of his crew saw it at 10:47 P.M.; McNamara described it as a beam that "was seen to swing in an arc toward *Turner Joy* and was immediately extinguished when aircraft from the combat air patrol orbiting above the ships approached the vicinity of the searchlight." [24]

Barnhart says it was "more like a Hollywood light" that went straight "up into the sky," lasting "for five to ten seconds." [25]

Herrick says it was seen by "*Turner Joy* observers" (no one on the *Maddox* saw it) at "midnight or shortly thereafter . . . a recall signal apparently." [26]

Barnhart told one of the Defense Department interviewers sent to Subic Bay after the incident that he saw the searchlight at the end of the engagement. He told the AP, "I can't remember when during the attack this occurred."

*

* *

The messages from the Tonkin Gulf that tumbled into the War Room of the Pentagon on the morning of August 4 threw the national-security managers into a tremor of astonishment, semifeigned outrage and barely suppressed glee. They had felt a little *too* restrained after August 2, and here it was actually, incredibly, happening again, and it was

287

even better than anything they could have dreamed of. Who could accuse Lyndon Johnson of recklessness now, after the North Vietnamese replied to his warning with a second and far more serious attack, a night ambush sixty miles from shore, waves of torpedoes? August 2 could have been belittled by the antiwar camp as an isolated incident had Johnson chosen to retaliate then, but this showed a *pattern* of attacks (provided the 34-A aspect was kept dark); this could really mean that the North Vietnamese themselves wanted to escalate the struggle. At any rate, here was opportunity asking to be seized, and this time the civilians and the Commander in Chief were ready.

Among the targets selected by the Joint Chiefs when they worked out their bombing plan in detail in May were the bases used by the North Vietnamese patrol boats and the petroleum storage area at Vinh. It was just a question now of picking the bases to be hit: the aircraft could be off that afternoon. Johnson would be seen by the American voter as resistant to the notion of sending American boys into Asia's battles but determined to protect the boys already there—a strong President goaded too far and telling the North Vietnamese, "Leave our vessels alone." It should take the Vietnam issue out of the political campaign.

But for Hanoi the underlying message would be, "Leave South Vietnam alone. This is the first time we hit you. We'll hit you again, and much more painfully, unless you call off the Vietcong in the South."

As for Congress, here was the answer to all those nasty questions that would have to be faced—after November— when the President asked for a blank-check resolution. Hung as it probably would have to be on an asserted need to respond to some provocation by the Vietcong, the request would stir considerable dispute over the need to be embroiled so deeply in South Vietnam. The request might even be turned down. But a North Vietnamese offensive aimed at testing America's mettle and America's will—ah, that was different. Let the President go to the people and tell them that their navy was coming under repeated, deliberate and unprovoked attack on the high seas, let him ask for a Congressional resolution aimed at deterring the enemy from going any further, and he would release a surge of atavistic emotions precluding discussion with Congress on how the country had gotten into this involvement and how it should now proceed. The simplest answer to all those questions lay in heading off the questions. The resolution was written; all that remained to be done was to take out Bill Bundy's May draft and recast the preamble, making the statute a response to "repeated attacks on U.S. naval vessels in international waters"—much better than a response to difficult-to-prove "aggression against South Vietnam"—and rush it to a vote.

Johnson called Bill Bundy's brother Mac. "We want that resolution," he said. Bill was holidaying on Martha's Vineyard, so George Ball asked Abram Chayes, who had resigned as the State Department's chief legal adviser only that June and was still in Washington, to come into his office. Chayes wrote the final draft—with Ball working with him on some of the revision—in a couple of hours.*

Never mind that the evidence from the Gulf of Tonkin cascading into the Pentagon and spilling over into the White House and the State Department was confused and in places contradictory, the fact of the August 2 incident made a second attack easy to believe. The circumstances were so ripe that the decision to retaliate was automatic, the civilians and the military practically reading each other's mind. On the scrambler telephone line between the War Room and

---

* The official who was to tell Tom Wicker in 1965 that Johnson had carried the resolution in his pocket for weeks before the Tonkin Gulf incidents explained to Wicker later that he had meant it figuratively. Actually, the resolution found lodging in Johnson's pocket only after it was passed.

Sharp's headquarters in Hawaii the admiral's recommendation for strikes by carrier-based aircraft against the patrol-boat bases and any such boats found in bays or at sea coincided with the drawing up of several options along those lines at a meeting of McNamara, Vance, Burchinal (Director of the Joint Staff) and various subordinates in the Secretary's office.

Can the carriers do the job? McNamara asked.

"Hell, yes!" said Sharp.

The huge, modern assault carrier *Constellation* had left Hong Kong hurriedly on the night of August 3, local time, to join the *Ticonderoga*—"a normal precaution," says the Pentagon history. Aboard the *Ticonderoga*, according to its flight surgeon, preparations for a strike began as soon as the planes returned from their bootless search for the North Vietnamese aggressors—a good four hours before formal alert orders were sent to both carriers at 3:00 P.M. EDT. The elation of the moment is captured by a remark said to have been made by Rostow a few days later in the intimacy of his White House circle: "Isn't it interesting how the facts have fitted into our needs?"

*

*   *

The blips disappeared from the *Turner Joy's* radar screen. Her guns stopped firing. The *Maddox* was about out of star shells. The engagement, Herrick decided, was over.

While it was in progress, he reports, "We had no radio contact" with the attackers and "heard no radio communications going on between the PT boats." [27] The boats, he thinks, were maintaining radio silence as part of their ambush strategy. But right after the engagement, Herrick recalls, the comvan team showed him another message. This is how he deals with this subject in the prepared speech he has been giving before Rotary and Kiwanis club audiences:

On the afternoon and evening of August 4th we heard the boats being stationed around our area, intercepted their attack orders and . . . heard their damage report confirming our assessment that two of the boats had been sunk.

McNamara's February, 1968, on-the-record testimony on the post-incident intercept was:

Immediately after the attack ended, the [intelligence] source reported that the North Vietnamese lost two ships in the engagement . . . [the] message later reporting that they had shot down two planes and sacrificed two ships, and adding further details of the engagement.[28]

But, you ask Herrick, isn't there something improbable about all of this? Why would little patrol boats take on the U.S. Navy in the middle of the gulf?

"A torpedo boat is designed to take on big ships. PT boats have been used against battleships—one destroyer is duck soup. It takes one fish to sink a destroyer."

But the so-called attack order spoke of sending out two Swatows and only one PT boat—*if* the PT boat could be made ready in time. *And Swatows don't have torpedoes.*

"The attack message could have been supplemented by another message. We didn't have hundred percent coverage. We thought there were more PT boats than one. Swatows won't make forty-five to fifty knots. I assumed the faster ones on the radarscope were PTs and the slower ones were Swatows hanging on the periphery, directing the PTs."

Where, in that case, would the boats have been when they got the attack order?

"It would have taken them one hour to get there, so they must have been on station, waiting for us. The orders to attack went to them at sea."

Herrick warms to his theory.

"They were there before dark. They felt they had a better chance to hit us if they lay in ambush. They thought we'd just assume they were fishing boats, and it would let them get in close. And use of aircraft would be limited at night."

But the attack order paraphrased by McNamara appears to be directed to boats in port—not at sea.

Yes, Herrick concedes, but, he repeats, there could have been more than one attack message.

Would they be so pugnacious?

"I don't think they expected us to retaliate. They believed this paper tiger thing. Also, there were some of those raids—the 34-A ops. They got mad, and they were going to retaliate. Then when they saw us coming around, that really stirred them up. The North Koreans attacked the *Pueblo*, didn't they? They have the same mentality. Asiatics. They don't think of consequences the way we do. We've been softened in some ways."

Would he still be sure there had been an attack without the intercepts?

"I'd still be sure. The intercepts to me were the clincher, the frosting on the cake."

Yet, as Herrick sat down with his staff after midnight to reconstruct the situation, he also knew that the destroyers' cables had given the Pentagon a picture of an attack of far greater magnitude than the one that Herrick thought had taken place. Ogier proved they had been getting the sound of their own propellers; he put the *Maddox* through a full-rudder turn at full speed and, sure enough, the "noise spokes" appeared on young Mallow's sonar screen again and the "hydrophone effects" were reproduced in his headset.

"I was convinced that something had happened," Herrick says, "but I didn't want them to get the idea that twenty-two torpedoes had been fired when maybe only two were fired. I gave it a lot of thought."

He must have realized that somebody could be doing something drastic—escalating the war, maybe—as a result of his error of judgment. And he made the most difficult decision of his career.

"I sent that message."

Review of action makes many reported contacts and torpedoes fired appear doubtful. Freak weather effects and overeager sonarman may have accounted for many reports. No actual visual sightings by *Maddox*. Suggest complete evaluation before any further action.[29]

"I had to squeeze that one out," Herrick says. "It's hard to back down and admit you made a mistake. I knew I couldn't keep quiet with an incident of that importance.

"I wrote it up and sent it off with some trepidation, thinking I'd get back a sizzler: 'What the hell's the idea, making a stupid mistake like that?' I was getting pretty pooped. We all were. We hadn't had much sleep."

There are three top priorities for navy messages from ships engaged in naval action—Operational (dealing with a tactical situation), Operational Immediate (same as the first but applying to a highly important development and seldom used) and Flash (having to do with contact with the enemy and rarely used). Violating priority regulations, Herrick sent his message as a flash.

The Opportunity 15

McNamara had already had his second morning conference (with the Joint Chiefs, Rusk and Bundy) and obtained the Chiefs' final target list for the reprisal (code-named Pierce Arrow), he and Rusk and Bundy had already gone over the list with the President and obtained his approval for an air strike at daylight in the Tonkin Gulf (about five hours away), when, shortly after 1:30 P.M. EDT, Herrick's flash casting doubt on his previous wires dropped like a sackful of mud into the churning gears of the national security apparatus. An official who was duty officer in the State Department's Operation Room that day remembers seeing the message come over the teletype machine. "Right away," he recalls, "I thought, Oh-oh, there's something wrong about this."

Herrick says, "My only doubt was as to the magnitude of the attack. The *number* of torpedoes was the only thing in doubt as far as I was concerned. There was no doubt in my mind that it happened. . . . That first torpedo was authentic. That first sonar report was credible. We were not maneuvering violently at that time, so we were not getting our propeller beat back as yet."

But given the tenuous and often contradictory nature of the evidence, Herrick couldn't cast doubt on some of it without casting doubt on all of it, and if the Washington managers and the Pacific command could have told him at that moment what they felt, their reply, stripped of profanity, might have read, *Good God, Herrick, what are you saying? Who needs that?*

If the commander of the patrol was backing away from his own reports of the attack, the whole long-range plan being set into motion in Washington and Hawaii and the carriers at sea was endangered. At that moment, John Jerome Herrick became the most important man in the whole operation. The key to the successful launching of this new improvised version of the "pressures program" was Herrick's willingness to confirm that an attack had occurred. McNamara went back to the Pentagon to telephone Sharp.

*

* *

Admiral Ulysses S. Grant Sharp, Jr., was a slender, silver-haired, compact little man who prided himself on his imperturbable manner, seldom raised his high-pitched voice, was sensitive about his resounding name (his father, who used to run a general store in tiny Fort Benton, Montana, had been named after his aunt's husband, the Civil War hero, and had passed the glory on to his son), worked long hours and liked to read history and current affairs. His reading honed the precision of his political-military views. "The point is that we must stop Communist-supported aggression," he said in one of his infrequent interviews. "And if we don't stop it in Vietnam, where are we going to stop it?" [1] Though he had made his mark in the Pacific war commanding destroyers, he had become a champion of naval air power and was convinced that the advance of Asian Communism could be stopped at that juncture only by all-out bombing of North Vietnam. Once the enemy in the North "gave up," the Vietcong in the South would have "no choice but to follow suit." [2]

From his headquarters in the hills overlooking Pearl Harbor, "Oley" Sharp—the nickname was his hometown's appellation for boys with blond, blue-eyed "Swedish" looks —commanded an armada of ships, planes and men that could blow a good-sized piece of Vietnam off the map. It was heady power, at fifty-eight, for someone who never saw the sea until he managed to be appointed to Annapolis, and he was known to be somewhat impatient in private with the slowness of the civilian Vietnam-policy planners to make up their minds to do what he felt had to be done. Of all the military men, he was perhaps the most active in trying to get the bombing started.

McNamara had found him a shade too messianic for his taste when he was Deputy Chief of Naval Operations during the Cuban missile crisis in 1962, and he appointed him Commander in Chief, Pacific, in June, 1964, because it was either that or making him Chief of Naval Operations and McNamara decided Sharp would be safer as CINCPAC. The antipathy between the two men was to blaze into hatred on Sharp's part when the bombing of North Vietnam began in 1965 on the "medium level" favored by McNamara and Taylor, and when McNamara stood fast against the Joint Chiefs' pressure to make the bombing all-out. As Sharp was to write in 1969, he regarded the "tragic failure" of the United States to use its air power to full advantage

perhaps the most serious error we have made in all of American military history.... For this failure, Robert S. McNamara, former Secretary of Defense, must take a large share of responsibility. ... His insistence that we pursue the campaign on a gradualistic basis gave the enemy plenty of time to cope with our every move. ...

When I was Commander in Chief Pacific, I submitted repeated requests to my superiors to bomb additional military targets in order to make the air war really effective. I made these requests about once every two weeks. I have been given to understand that the Joint Chiefs of Staff supported my position 100 per cent. But most of my requests were denied when they reached the office of the Secretary of Defense.[3]

In 1966 and 1967, Sharp was to become McNamara's bitterest enemy, Washington's foremost lobbyist for dropping the bombing restraints, a conduit for information to the Stennis committee on the rebelliousness of the Joint Chiefs, an agent in the downfall of Robert S. McNamara. His demands for all-out bombing became "fulminations" by 1968, according to the Pentagon's history of the war. But all that came later; on August 4, 1964, Sharp and McNamara were on good terms.

Now McNamara was on the phone again, about the Herrick message. They discussed the possibility that there might not have been an attack.

Damn it, Oley, McNamara said, you've got to be certain about this. "Execute time" for the air strike had been set for 7:00 P.M. EDT (7:00 A.M. the next morning in the Gulf of Tonkin), and Sharp, having been informed of the substance of the strike plan, was to get the "execute order" from the Joint Chiefs momentarily. He now recommended that the execute order be held up while he tried to get a more definite report from Herrick.

But McNamara had another problem. An essential part of the political strategy was for President Johnson to announce the North Vietnamese attack and the American retaliation on television at an hour when he would be seen by the biggest possible audience. The plan was for the President to speak at the time the bombs were exploding—about 9:30 P.M. EDT. Any delay now would eat into precious prime time. McNamara didn't put the problem to Sharp that way. He said they didn't want to release the news of the PT-boat attack until they could say that retaliation was under way, and "We obviously don't want to carry out the retaliatory strike unless we are damned sure what happened." The implication was, We want to be damned sure before the President goes on the air. We want confirmation. We want you, Commander in Chief, Pacific, to certify it.

Let the execute order continue in effect, McNamara said, but between now and the execution time he wanted Sharp to obtain a definite report and phone it in.

*

* *

"Things got hot and heavy. They kept hollering at us. 'Why haven't you answered our so-and-so?' 'Verify, verify!' It was almost impossible."

In Herrick's voice there is a hint of the distress into which he was plunged. It must have been hell, you say.

"It was."

Poor Herrick. It really doesn't seem to have occurred to him that "they" would never have rested content with his turning out a disturbing flash like that. One can almost visualize "them" wanting to scream at him, *Herrick, you're screwing up the whole operation! We're not asking you to lie, but are you sure or not?*

Did he feel under pressure to verify an attack?

Captain John J. Herrick, USN, stares at you across his desk. His voice is even. "I felt that the pressure was as much one way as the other. Verify if it happened, and verify if it didn't happen."

With the concentrated attention of three of the Navy's most formidable taskmasters bearing down on them, Herrick and his staff were immersed in a new crisis before the old one had ended. The wardroom was cleared for sorting out the frantic tracks, the times that didn't jibe, the jumble of reports from station to station and ship to ship.

The transmission problems didn't help.

"We kept getting what we call jigs," Herrick says. "That is, they asked us to send messages we had already sent. They asked for answers to questions we had already answered."

This added burden may have been created, he believes, by a "dead spot" around the relay station at San Miguel, the Philippines.

"Maybe it was the electromagnetic field, or the ionosphere. That whole Southeast Asia is generally a poor propagation area. Maybe it was the temperature, the heat, I don't know. But I knew there was some delay along the line."

Beyond that, "It was the sheer mass of the messages. We were swamped."

Herrick won't elaborate on this—his abrupt reticence is a sign that he sees another "classified area" ahead—but the *Maddox* had what today would be considered a rather antiquated encrypting and decrypting system. Newer ships are equipped with machines that take a message typed out in ordinary English and transmit it in code, and receive and decode incoming messages. The machines aboard the *Maddox* would take an outgoing message and put it into code, but the encrypted product had to be sent manually in Morse. With incoming messages, a coding officer would have to look up his code books, set the machine differently in each case, type the message into the machine, and hope to get ungarbled English at the end of the process.

"There was human error," Herrick says. "We'd make mistakes looking up the books and checking it. The men were excited and sleepy. It was slow. We got behind with the coding and decoding. They were getting madder and madder."

(Herrick, surely you must be getting the drift? Surely you must realize that an attack is essential?)

At about 2:30 A.M. Herrick sent a "sitrep" (situation report). The *Turner Joy*, he said, claimed to have sunk three vessels; however,

Joy also reports no actual visual sightings or wake. Have no recaps of aircraft sighting but seem to be few. . . . Entire action leaves many doubts except for apparent attempt to ambush at beginning. Suggest thorough reconnaissance by aircraft at daylight.[4]

About twenty minutes later, under the hammering of the demands for more definite evidence, he cabled that "details of action present a confusing picture although certain that original ambush was bona fide."[5] He added that the *Turner Joy* reported two torpedoes passing near her; also that there had been "visual sightings" of cockpit lights or similar lights passing near the *Maddox*.

Herrick says he had "some reservations" even then about those cockpit lights; they had been reported by two marines attached to the communications van, and "a marine aboard ship can see almost anything." But he threw them in.

Then he sat in the big high-backed chair in the captain's cabin and dozed off for a while.

❋

❋   ❋

At the Pentagon, at about this time, more high-level deliberation was under way.

"The President was greatly concerned about being sure that the second attack had happened, or, if not, to know that," says a former official who was part of the McGeorge Bundy White House set-up. "We satisfied ourselves by turning to the guy we trusted most, namely Bob McNamara."

Bob McNamara was meeting with the Chiefs and Vance in the Gold Room, otherwise known as the Tank, the Chiefs' yellow-walled conference room just off the War Room. He had called the meeting to "review all the evidence." General Wheeler had been caught off base in New York but would be joining them shortly.

All they had before them were fragments of evidence sent at white heat by men who were not sure what was happening. To say, as McNamara was to say in 1968 before the Foreign Relations Committee, that "the apparent ambiguities and contradictions in the reports were examined at this meeting and reconciled to our satisfaction" is to claim the impossible, unless they were satisfied to pick what they wanted out of the cables and fit it into a coherent pattern, rationalizing away or ignoring the rest.

No one acquainted with the vagaries of radar could have concluded that there was an attack on the basis of messages from the destroyers reporting on being shadowed, approached and attacked by high-speed craft and on sinking at least two of them—all this as observed by radar, with no report of any sighting of the boats by human eye. The idiosyncracies of radar beams bouncing off crests of waves or ionized clouds or even a full moon coming above the horizon are legend in the military services. The Tonkin Gulf, with its sampans, fish stakes and flocks of birds, is notorious as an electronic jungle. (An example of what overreliance on radar can produce was to be provided in June, 1968: Four naval vessels, three American and one Australian, were shot up by American aircraft off Vietnam and seven of the crew were killed when radar operators thought they spotted "enemy helicopters" hovering over the surface of the water.) [6] The "freak weather effects" cited by Herrick in his hold-everything message should have been enough to rule the radar evidence out of court.

The most direct piece of evidence in the whole muddle of August 4 is the claim by four of the *Turner Joy's* topside personnel that they saw a torpedo wake (which Barnhart thinks might have been two wakes) passing abeam at the very outset of the action.[7] But the testimony of these men became available in Washington only days later, when the two Defense officials, Jack Stempler and Alvin Friedman, flew to Subic Bay to interview eyewitnesses and brought back written statements gathered by Herrick's officers in response to the broadsides from Admirals Johnson, Moorer and Sharp. When McNamara and the Joint Chiefs met on the afternoon of August 4, their only available evidence on that first torpedo took the form of snatches of cables in which the *Maddox* reported sonar detection of a torpedo and the *Turner Joy* claimed sighting a torpedo wake, with no corroborative detail. It would have taken recklessness of a high order to go to war on the basis of evidence like that.

The other twenty-one torpedo reports, which depended solely on sonar, no sighting of wakes being claimed, would be regarded by any competent analyst as impressive only because of their high number. Sonar is known to be at least as deceitful as radar. Admiral True says his experience with sonar as a destroyer commander in the Second World War was that "at high speed on a maneuvering ship, sonar is practically worthless."[8] And in this case all the torpedo reports after the first one were destroyed by Herrick's flash, with its disclosure that "overeager sonarman may have accounted for many reports."

The only other piece of material evidence that the conference had before them when they met was that pastiche of confusion and fantasy within the Pentagon that had the *Turner Joy* being "fired on by automatic weapons while being illuminated by searchlights." In the fever of August 4, the Pentagon may have mistaken reports about antiaircraft fire by patrol boats against aircraft for machine-gun fire against destroyers; two of the American flyers, it will be remembered, thought they saw light antiaircraft shell bursts, and the *Ticonderoga* doubtless passed this information on to Washington.

But now there came some additional evidence: with the meeting still in progress, Sharp called back.

McNamara had left the meeting to confer with the President again, and the discussion had shifted to another facet of the "pressures program" ready for implementation as a result of the preparatory work of the previous spring and now being put into effect: alerting of certain army and marine forces, transfer of certain naval and air units to the western Pacific, and movement of fighter bombers into Thailand and South Vietnam.

Burchinal took the call. Sharp had received Herrick's latest "sitrep" and was bringing it to McNamara's attention. Burchinal said he'd pass it on. He asked Sharp if the aircraft could still be launched by 7:00 P.M. EDT. Sharp said he thought they could, but it would be tight. Burchinal then called McNamara at the White House, getting him in the Cabinet Room, and relayed Sharp's message; according to McNamara, "the commander of the task group [Herrick] was certain the original ambush was bona fide and had made positive visual sightings of cockpit lights or similar lights passing near the *Maddox*."

There is a certain reversal of emphasis in this. Herrick once again had laid stress on the "confusing picture;" Sharp was emphasizing the "bona fide ambush." In the sitrep immediately preceding this one, Herrick had reiterated that "entire action leaves many doubts;" Sharp slid over that to concentrate on "positive visual sightings of cockpit lights." Herrick concedes that Sharp and McNamara may have drawn more out of his answers than he had put into them. He grumbles, "I don't remember saying *positive* visual identification. . . ."

The more Herrick thought about the two marines[9] in the aftermath of the incident, the more skeptical he became. The men had claimed seeing lights like those of one or more small high-speed boats slipping up the destroyer's port side and down the starboard side as they manned machine guns on deck during the engagement, but to Herrick "they weren't real seagoing types and might have been slightly confused. They weren't sailors, who are acquainted with the sights and sounds of the sea. I didn't buy that." But he had sent it, and it became part of McNamara's arsenal before the Foreign Relations Committee, even though most of the *Maddox* staff thought the marines might have seen phosphorescence from breaking waves, a well-known phenomenon in those waters.

By now the meeting in the Tank was in possession of

all the physical evidence it was to get. All the other evidence—the intercepts aside—was to become available in Washington only after the final order to execute the air strike was released. This additional evidence took the following form:

The searchlight beam.[10] Herrick contends that this "falls in the category of the best evidence. A beam of light would have shown very vividly on such a dark night. If the boats were observing radio silence they'd use a light like that."

Deliberate radio silence and a light signal conform neatly with Herrick's belief that the boats sprang from ambush. Anyone less wedded to this theory could be forgiven for remaining skeptical, particularly in view of the presence of sheet lightning, the enormous power of autosuggestion in moments of mass tension, the descrepancies in regard to the time of night the searchlight was seen and the absence of more than five eyewitnesses—all five, incidentally, aboard the *Turner Joy*. It is difficult to imagine such a display from a patrol boat passing unnoticed by personnel aboard the *Maddox*.

The column of smoke. McNamara told the Foreign Relations Committee the smoke was seen by "other *Turner Joy* personnel" as well as by Barnhart, but he did not give their names or say whether they had supplied affidavits. It is difficult to believe that anyone could have been sure of seeing "black smoke" 4,000 yards away on a night so dark that the wake of the *Turner Joy*, according to Herrick, was visible for no more than 100 yards. Not even the Defense Department's December 22, 1967, list of "conclusive evidence" made any mention of the smoke.

The sighting of the boats. One man aboard the *Maddox* claimed he saw the outline of a boat silhouetted by a shell burst.[11] Four men aboard the *Turner Joy* claimed seeing the silhouette of an attacking boat lit up by flares. One of them, Seaman Kenneth E. Garrison,[12] told the AP he glimpsed the boat a mile away. Admiral True seems to put the matter conservatively enough when he comments, "The . . . reports of sighting 'cockpit lights,' silhouettes, etc., are not convincing. In cases of this sort, it is always possible to find some member of the crew who 'saw' something." [13]

Sightings from the air. As recounted earlier, two of the eight pilots who provided air cover claimed seeing a "snaky" wake "ahead" of the *Maddox.* The destroyers' jagged turns during the incident often placed the *Maddox* behind the *Turner Joy.* An informant who had a hand in assessing this evidence admits that he "didn't put too much credence" in it. The two flyers' claims that they also saw gun flashes on the water and light antiaircraft shell bursts in the air are characterized by him as "vague." "I didn't think they knew what they were talking about," he says. "In that overcast, in single-seater planes, they would have real trouble seeing anything like that." Whatever they said in their written statements, the message that Rear Admiral Moore sent when the planes returned to the Ticonderoga was that the pilots reported no visual sighting of any patrol boats.

But all this additional evidence—whatever its worth—was to arrive, as we have seen, only after the final order to retaliate was released. Prior to retaliation, the only available physical evidence—ruling out radar contacts as unreliable and the sonar reports as discredited—was made up of a few messages about a torpedo wake, the barest inkling of an ostensible machine-gun attack, and a report on the sighting of cockpit lights.

"Everybody was skeptical about that," says an official who was near the center of the action. "But then on top of that came the intercepts. It was the clincher."

The intercepts. The Administration's invisible proof. The factor that made the difference, Rusk is supposed to have said, between August 4 and the illusory "attack" on the September patrol.

Why couldn't McNamara in 1968 reveal the texts of messages to and from North Vietnamese patrol boats that were three and a half years old, when the Administration had made public the texts of intercepted messages to and from North Korean patrol boats in the *Pueblo* incident four days after the event? The intercepts in the *Pueblo* case were read out before the Security Council by Ambassador Goldberg to prove his assertion that the ship was seized well outside the twelve-mile limit. Why couldn't McNamara make public the Tonkin Gulf incidents and prove *his* case in the open? The transcript of the 1968 hearings shows how adamantly he resisted urgings along that line.

GORE: Ambassador Goldberg discussed the intercepts at the UN on television.

McNAMARA: But the problem here involves an intercept *with the particular traffic involved* [italics added]. Our intelligence analysts have gone over this and have stated the area is a danger to us in certain kinds of intercept material and disclosure of it. [Deleted.]

PELL: [The] fact we have publicly stated that intercept information confirmed the location outside North Korean territorial waters of the Pueblo . . . has this not thrown into the public domain quite a portion of the fact that we have access to this kind of intelligence?

McNAMARA: The intelligence analysts believe not. Well, I do not want to get into a further discussion until the rocm is cleared of those not authorized to handle it. We would run the risk of compromising intelligence sources if disclosed.

SYMINGTON: I noticed you mentioned in your statement . . . intelligence reports of a highly classified and unimpeachable nature. If that has been released, does that release us from being more specific [sic] about what the information was?

McNAMARA: No, sir. While you were at the other committee hearing I read a report from General Carroll [head of the Defense Intelligence Agency] that emphasizes the very serious penalties that we faced were the source of the information disclosed.

SYMINGTON: From the standpoint of future military operations?

McNAMARA: From the standpoint of current military operations.

FULBRIGHT: Mr. Secretary, I do not like to take issue with you, but it is awfully hard for me to believe that three and one-half years after that, this is of any significance to current security. It is just incredible. [Deleted.]

McNAMARA: Mr. Chairman, I am quite prepared to have this issue presented to the Foreign Intelligence Board and rely on their decision. I simply tell you that the intelligence, senior intelligence, directors of our Government, CIA, DIA and NSA, state categorically that it would be a serious compromise of intelligence sources.

*   *   *

Sharp called Burchinal again at 5:23 P.M. The meeting in the Tank was still in progress. McNamara was back from the White House. Sharp told Burchinal he was calling to confirm that the attack had taken place—or, as McNamara recounted it, "that he was convinced that the attack had occurred and that all were satisfied that it had." Burchinal told Sharp that McNamara was there and that McNamara and the others there were also satisfied that the attack had occurred.

The execute order had gone out to Sharp at about 4:50 P.M., to be held for release upon final authorization by the President. Sharp told Burchinal the time of launch would now be 8 P.M. EDT because of a slight mix-up: Admirals Moorer and Johnson had been using a different time zone from the one used by him and the Chiefs.

The meeting broke up. McNamara left for a final conference with the President. At 6:00 P.M. the President authorized him to release the execute order. He sped back to the Pentagon. Sharp had called again and was speaking to Burchinal in the Tank. McNamara asked Burchinal to make sure once more that Sharp had confirmed the attack. As he reported the conversation to the Foreign Relations Committee:

"I spoke to the Director of the Joint Staff and asked him

to make certain that the Commander in Chief, Pacific, was willing to state that the attack had taken place. . . .

"He confirmed that he believed the attack had taken place. I stated that after my further discussions with the Chiefs and re-examination of all the evidence, particularly the communications intelligence, that I was convinced it had taken place and therefore he was free to release the execute order."

He then hurried back to the White House for the second National Security Council meeting of the day.

And that's how they reached their decision—not, essentially, on the basis of the physical evidence and the intercepts, although they apparently were satisfied that there was enough there to indicate the *probability* of an attack, particularly since there *had* been an engagement two days previously, but on the basis of an unspoken willingness to share the responsibility—the blame, if anything later went wrong—in a chain of solidarity in which each subordinate was willing to stick his neck out and confirm the desired belief of his superior, until assurance reinforced at each level produced conviction at the top that the thing was firm enough—or firm enough, anyhow, to go into court with. What satisfied Sharp was Herrick's "bona fide ambush" message, imperfect though it was, and the critical piece of information for McNamara was Sharp's willingness to state that he was sure, "damned sure," and McGeorge Bundy and his White House staff satisfied themselves by "turning to the guy we trusted most, namely Bob McNamara," so that the "complete evaluation" urged by Herrick in his attempt to retrieve his mistake took the form, ultimately, of a brief telephone conversation across five thousand miles of continent and sea, not even directly but through a third party, yet good enough for McNamara to tell Johnson, Yes, Mr. President, we are sure, and for the President to believe what he wanted to believe, what they all wanted to believe, though not, of course, in the face of definite evidence to the contrary. For despite their great desire to interpret the ambiguous evidence in a way that would serve their purpose, they did not decide to retaliate knowing there was no attack—it is clear from the testimony of those around them and the unmistakable sincerity of their own later statements that they believed there probably was an attack, though they could not have been positive, and if there was deception of Congress and the public as to the certainty of an attack, as there was, it began with their deception of themselves. If someone among them or around them had said, No, I am not at all convinced, he might have slowed, perhaps stopped, the process, but no one with doubts about it felt strongly enough to speak up, though one junior participant of the drama was later to characterize the main actors as harassed and imprudent men who had gone too far down the road to reverse their course of action.

Herrick's message had arrived too late. The machinery was moving. They didn't want to stop it. They could have postponed the whole action by twenty-four hours to let more evidence come in. But it would be twenty-four hours in which they could not justifiably keep the incident a secret. It would be harder to explain not consulting Congress on retaliation. And would Congress let them retaliate on the basis of that evidence? And in twenty-four hours the evidence might look even weaker. Johnson would lose his Congressional resolution, his message to the American voters, his message to Hanoi. He had to announce retaliation himself, and he had to do it fast. The fundamental purpose of it all was to maintain and strengthen a Democratic Administration capable of preserving South Vietnam from Communism, without plunging the world into war, as the Goldwater Republicans were threatening to do, and with an objective like that should one quibble too much about radar and sonar details?

But what of the new 34-A assault on North Vietnam's coastal installations, the shelling of the night of August 3–4,

——didn't that complicate matters? Didn't that make American "retaliation" harder to justify?

McNamara told the Foreign Relations Committee in 1968 that he had not known that another 34-A attack was scheduled for August 3–4 and still didn't know when he testified before the committee on August 6, 1964, just as he had not known of the July 30–31 bombardment before it occurred. If McNamara did not know, it follows that the White House did not know either. That would not have been too surprising. Under the procedures followed, covert programs like DeSoto and 34-A would have been approved by the Secretary of Defense and the President, but permission to go ahead would be left to monthly meetings of the 303 Committee, and the timing of individual missions, dependent on conditions of weather, moon and wave, would be up to the military. A McNamara or Bundy would not be able to keep track of all the dates of all the covert missions under way during any particular time period.

Would McNamara have recommended retaliation if he had been aware of the second 34-A operation? Was Sharp aware of it? If so, why didn't he bring it to McNamara's attention during their telephone conversations on August 4?

All one can say is that if there was traffic among the Defense Department, MAC/V and naval authorities in the Pacific right after the August 2 incident on avoiding interference between DeSoto and 34-A, someone fairly high up in Washington and the Pacific command must have known that a second 34-A operation was scheduled for the night of August 3–4. And Hanoi's August 2 broadcast disclosing the July 30–31 bombardment should have alerted McNamara to the possibility of another 34-A foray coming up, even if his Pentagon aides did not.

*

* *

Leapfrogging intermediary commands, the questions generated by McNamara four hours earlier kept bearing down on Herrick.

Moorer to *Maddox,* 5:30 A.M. August 5, Tonkin Gulf time:

1. Can you confirm absolutely that you were attacked?
2. Can you confirm sinking of PT boats?
3. Desire reply directly supporting evidence.[14]

Maddox to Moorer, 6:00 A.M.:

Maddox scored no known hits and never positively identified a boat as such. Furthermore, weather was overcast with limited visibility . . . air support was not successful in locating targets. There were no stars or moon, resulting in almost total darkness throughout action. . . . No known damage or personnel casualties to either ship. Turner Joy claims sinking one craft and damaging another. . . . The first boat to close the Maddox probably fired a torpedo at the Maddox which was heard but not seen. All subsequent Maddox torpedo reports are doubtful in that it is suspected that sonarman was hearing ship's own propeller beat.[15]

Moorer to *Maddox,* 7:06 A.M. August 5, Tonkin Gulf time, with request that reply be routed through *Ticonderoga* for faster delivery:

Can you confirm that you were attacked by PT or Swatow? [16]

There was no answer from Herrick ("I think we figured we had already answered that and our answer would be there shortly"), but Barnhart replied at 7:15 A.M., confirming an attack on the *Turner Joy* by two PT craft on the basis of the following evidence: Gun director and director crew sighted torpedo, as did one lookout. Target burned when hit. Black smoke seen by many. Target silhouette sighted by "some topside personnel." On the other hand, sinking of patrol craft "only highly probable" because target tracked on radar; "shell bursts observed on radar all over contact;" hits reported visually; targets disappeared.[17]

Vice Admiral Johnson to *Turner Joy,* 9:00 A.M. Tonkin Gulf time, requesting Barnhart "urgently" to amplify his reports:

Who were witnesses, what is witness reliability? Most important that present evidence substantiating type and number of attacking forces be gathered and disseminated.[18]

At about 9:30 A.M., having reached Yankee Station, transferred the statements of eyewitnesses to the *Ticonderoga* and prepared to resume the patrol, Herrick was ordered to "locate debris to substantiate."[19] He spent an hour or two searching for debris. Finding none, he headed back for Hon Ngu.

Barnhart to Vice Admiral Johnson, 1:15 P.M. August 5, Tonkin Gulf time:

[Officers with] good reliability [saw torpedo wake.] Estimate two PT's attack originally. However, must admit two factors defer. No ECM from PT boats. However, tactics seem to be to bore-sight on wake, thus accounting for lack of radar signals. No sonar indications of torpedo noises, even that which passed down side. Self noise was very high.[20]

Set into motion by Sharp when the question of confirmation was still critical, the Pacific command was proceeding on its own momentum long after Washington's interest in the replies had cooled, long after the focus of the operation had swung from Herrick and his doubts and his semiconfirmations to the President of the United States, ready with his television speech, chafing to go on the air, waiting for his advisers to tell him it was safe enough to do so.

The launch time for the aircraft had been delayed again. The *Ticonderoga* could not perform the whole mission by herself, and the *Constellation* was behind schedule in getting into position or in briefing her pilots, and that was the reason the speech for which the TV networks had been alerted kept getting postponed. McNamara, in tense command in his office, called Sharp at 8:40 P.M., asking if he had heard anything about the launch; Sharp said he hadn't. McNamara asked him to obtain an immediate report as to whether the planes had been launched, and, if not, when they would be, and when the first aircraft would be over their targets.

If the President spoke too soon he would be tipping off Hanoi. But if he delayed much longer he would lose his audience on the whole eastern seaboard. McNamara called Sharp again at 9 P.M. to be told that the *Ticonderoga* expected to launch in an hour. McNamara asked how serious it would be militarily if the President spoke at the time of launch, announcing that air action was at that moment in progress against the gunboats and their bases and support facilities in or near four North Vietnamese ports. Sharp agreed that the enemy would be alerted by radar as soon as the planes were airborne, but advised against mentioning the number and nature of the targets.

Eleven-thirty was the latest the President could speak and still reach the whole country, and he was determined to speak by then. So, having taken the speech out of the teleprompter and struck out the reference to the targets, they decided to risk it and let the President go on the air when the first planes were launched and could be assumed to have been picked up by radar. But time grew short and the *Constellation* still had not reached her launching station, and as John McNaughton joined an admiral and his aides in the vigil in the Pentagon, watching the cables on the *Constellation*'s progress and watching the TV screen, waiting for the President to break in, another mix-up in time zones submerged them all in new confusion and led to greater risks being taken than had been planned. The *Constellation* said it would launch at x hours. Suddenly the Washington managers realized that the launching would be an hour later than they had thought. Consternation. People asked each other, What time are we talking about? At some point a rather high admiral sent a message: The planes had gotten off; it was OK to go ahead with the speech. An hour later there was a message saying the planes were just then taking off. There was a scare, more calls to the White House: Can you hold it until we know the planes are on radar?

In fact, they never knew. Sharp informed McNamara at 11:20 P.M. that the *Ticonderoga* had launched her planes at 10:43 P.M., and the stalled enterprise leaped forward. McNamara's subsequent explanation that it had all been calculated with a nice precision, so that the President would go on the air just as the planes came within reach of radar so as to inform Hanoi and Peking that this was only a limited strike, was an improvisation shown up innocently by Rear Admiral Moore aboard the *Ticonderoga* when he said, "I don't believe they were on radar when the President started speaking." [21]

Not that, at the end, it seemed to have mattered. Not too much time was left before the airborne planes would have had to get on Hanoi's radar, and the North Vietnamese were taken by surprise. The Washington managers had done their job. In spite of the day's seizure of doubts, all satisfactorily resolved, and the night's galling postponements, mercifully ended, everything was set, the planes were on their way, the resolution was ready, the Congress was primed; and at 11:37 P.M. Washington time, just two and a half hours after Admiral Johnson's urgent query about "witness reliability," the networks announced the President of the United States, and Lyndon Baines Johnson, standing behind a lectern bearing the President's seal, faced millions of his countrymen across the nation, looking resolute and grim—a master of political timing in command of a political-military operation that promised to untie his hands in Vietnam and bolster Saigon and force Hanoi to call off the war and strip the Goldwater Republicans of their biggest campaign issue and enhance his chances of getting the biggest whopping majority of any President since Roosevelt—beginning now in the quiet tones of a veteran of a thousand stump speeches who knows when to pour on the bombast but also when a simple gravity is more rousing than the eagle's scream:

"My fellow Americans—"

The Result 16

And it worked.

They hit their targets and moved their planes and ships to Thailand and South Vietnam, underscoring the signal to Hanoi with an informal message through the Canadian member of the International Control Commission warning of further "consequences" if the DRV persisted in its course of directing the Southern insurgency. They got Congress to sign the contract, saying the air strike was just an *ad hoc* measure and sneaking in some fine print about authorization for a larger war. They were able, as a result of the Tonkin Gulf incidents, to do most of the things they had decided on earlier in the summer and had postponed until after the election, so that when in February the Vietcong attack on the American military barracks at Pleiku provided them with the "provocation" they needed to start bombing North Vietnam, they could swing into action without having to go to Congress with any more requests or explanations.

On August 5, 1964, the *Maddox* and the *Turner Joy* stood off Vinh, watching the smoke from the oil depot rise fourteen thousand feet into the air. Was this what Herrick had tried to prevent by urging "complete evaluation before any further action"? If any sense of personal failure lingers to mar his recollection of the first American bombing of North Vietnam, you will not coax it out of John Jerome Herrick.

316

"We were happy to see 'em get spanked," he says. "It was sort of like the old days. When someone hits you, you hit them right back."

Two uneventful days later the destroyers were out of the gulf, and both DeSoto and 34-A were suspended for a while to let things simmer down. A patrol scheduled for August 10 was canceled by Lyndon Johnson, and he agreed to the September patrol very reluctantly, as the Navy by then was fully awake to DeSoto's potential for creating incidents and was making explicit recommendations—with the support of the Joint Chiefs of Staff—on ways of provoking the North Vietnamese into more attacks that would permit more American reprisals. Johnson would have none of it. The campaign was on. Unable to convince McNamara's civilian staff of the need for continuing the DeSoto patrols now that their primary purpose had been achieved and jobs like electronic intelligence and radar fingerprinting could be done more efficiently by aircraft, the Navy was reduced to arguing for the preservation of the "freedom of the seas," leading Johnson to say, "Look heah, I have the right to walk in front of the White House when I choose, but that don't mean I have to send Lady Bird and Lynda Bird into Lafayette Park at three o'clock in the morning." The incident of August 4 was re-enacted during the September patrol, and Johnson said the hell with it. There were no more DeSoto patrols after that. The 34-A raids were resumed—a full week after the September patrol, so they wouldn't overlap this time—and then the bombing began and both operations were swallowed up by the wider war.

And in the end it failed, all of it, because of something in the mind of a scrawny Asian peasant in black pajamas or army khaki for whom the struggle was not a calculated operation with limited objectives but his very life, and who could strive and suffer and endure more before he died than the planners in Washington had ever imagined. They had to send American combat troops against him, something

Johnson had prayerfully hoped he could avoid, when they saw that the bombing, at least the medium-level bombing they had settled on, was not going to make Hanoi tell the Vietcong to lay down their arms. And the President's waving of the Gulf of Tonkin Resolution as his authority for employing combat troops, which it was, marked the beginning of the swing of the pendulum to distrust of everything Johnson did and said and the beginning of his political demise.

Why hadn't they realized that their ruse would come back to ruin them? They, the Kennedy men around Johnson, were the savants of power, and he, the unexpected President, was their political adaptor, and the power they venerated could be held pulsatingly in reserve, exerting its pressure on the adversary just being there, or put to overwhelming use, if need be—or, best of all, employed sparingly, surgically, to produce untold dividends through small, brilliant operations. They had proved they could do the latter by their Cuban missile performance, their revenge for the Bay of Pigs and their inspiration for the future, and faced with a new challenge in Vietnam they were ready to wrap Congress and the country in the flag and march them off to the Opium Wars and the quick win through the use of shock therapy. And if the problem proved to be bigger than the amount of power they were willing to allocate to its solution, they at least would have made the attempt.

The bombing of North Vietnam, for instance: they had not thought it would last as long as it did. There would be, they had thought, an outcry at home and abroad and they would be "forced" into negotiations but from a better position than in the black summer of 1964, and after the doors closed on the conference room they would accept the best deal they could get. It would be politically safe. Even the Chiefs thought that was what would happen, seeing that their recommendation for wiping out North Vietnam's economy from the air had been rejected. But the American public did not fulfill that role. There was not that much reaction, until toward the end. The harsh truth was that the American public had become inured to the bombing of civilians as a result of World War II and Korea. And people in the allied nations, even those who had experienced bombing themselves, were also slow to react.

The bombing went on and on and the devastation of South Vietnam from the air and on the ground made the air war in the North seem mild by comparison and neither the North Vietnamese nor the Vietcong would give up or offer a deal the planners could accept as a face-saving compromise. They had never told themselves definitely that they would win, but they had not clearly defined an acceptable compromise either. Intimations to Hanoi that the Vietcong could have a minority role in the Saigon government on a level approximating the ministry of traffic were contemptuously spurned, and the Vietcong's implicit offer of a coalition likely to be dominated by the Communists was rejected by Washington as something that would be recognized by American voters as defeat. Aside from the enemy's staying power and the tenacity of the American public once engaged in a war, the planners had underrated their own unwillingness to cut losses if things didn't work out—the political difficulty of getting out in any given year or before the next election.[1]

The end for Johnson was abrupt. Coming right after Westmoreland's confident assurance that the enemy was on the retreat, the shattering Tet (Lunar New Year) offensive of February, 1968, lit up the political scene with a flash of comprehension that this was a war without end. Already affected by doubt or antagonism to the involvement as a result of the shape it had taken and the censure it had earned from the Senate liberals led by Fulbright, public opinion shifted dramatically over the course of a few weeks to unmistakable majority opposition to any further escalation of the war. Some of the most important men of the

319

New York–Washington financial-political complex—including McGeorge Bundy—decided that the cost of the war had become too high and that Westmoreland's request for yet another 200,000 men should be rejected. Averell Harriman, dean of the Democratic policy establishment, said, I support the President, but if this is going to result in Nixon's election, ten Vietnams wouldn't be worth it. Nitze produced a paper arguing against "continuing to reinforce weakness" in Vietnam. Clark Clifford, the silky hawkish Washington lawyer who was equaled only by Supreme Court Justice Abe Fortas in entrée to the President, was shaken by the facts and figures produced for him, when he took over as Secretary of Defense, by the civilian antiwar coterie in the Pentagon that was acting more like a State Department in respect to Vietnam than Rusk's demoralized institution at Foggy Bottom. Clifford's counsel to a flabbergasted Johnson was: Deescalate the bombing of North Vietnam. Confine it to the infiltration routes. Hanoi will not yield. It will match us in manpower every time. There is only one thing to do. Negotiate.

If Johnson had worried and fretted over his decision to start the bombing and then to send in combat troops, if he had suffered at the hands of his tormentors when he hunkered down to give his policy of breaking Hanoi's will time to work (his refusal even to hear about stopping the bombing a reflection perhaps of his own secret doubts), all this was nothing compared to the agony of spirit that overwhelmed him in those sullen, sulfurous weeks of February and March. He had wanted to save South Vietnam and, after proving himself in that exemplary struggle, to shower blessings on the Vietnamese, North and South alike, and instead he had led a crusade that had ravaged a country of eighteen million people so horribly that it would take generations for the lesions to heal, enmired his own countrymen in a depth of mass slaughter and mindless atrocity too new to the American experience and too destructive of

the picture Americans had of themselves to be even per-
ceived (except later, when the 1968 My Lai massacre was
revealed in 1969), and sent 50,000 young Americans to an
early grave. He had wanted to build in America a Great
Society of justice and opportunity, going on from where
FDR had left off, and the Vietnam war had smashed everything he had begun so joyously and so well, until now, as
he looked around the country, he saw a dislocated and
embittered society torn by racial strife and starved of the
funds, energy and imagination it required of the Federal
government to head off a political, economic and social
breakdown. He had been dubious of the bombing and
distrustful of the military and unsure of himself on foreign
affairs, and the Yale and Harvard men bequeathed him by
Kennedy had swayed him when he hung back and eased
the process when he was eager to move, dropping away
when things got tough, leaving him only Rusk, "faithful as
a beagle," and Rostow, still cheerfully writing position papers proving that these defeats were leading to victory,
while around the world millions who had always been ready
to forgive America her sins and her excesses because they
had learned to think of her as decent and attractive and
humane stood aghast. What was he to do? To accept a
defeat dressed up as an honorable compromise went against
his strongly felt belief in the need to stop the spread of
aggressive Communism. Yet to accept at length the Joint
Chiefs' recommendation and bomb North Vietnam back to
the stone age was more than he was prepared to do, and
besides he could not go against the advice of his new Secretary of Defense. He could not go forward, and he would not
go back.

Only Johnson himself can know when he decided not to
run for re-election. The professional politicians are convinced that he decided not to seek the party's nomination
for President because he had been humbled by McCarthy in
the New Hampshire primary and seemed likely to be de-

feated by him in a direct contest in Wisconsin, and had decided that with McCarthy exposing such a wellspring of antiwar and anti-Johnson feeling and with Bobby Kennedy evoking the Kennedy legend on *his* campaign trail, the two candidates between them might well succeed in denying him the nomination, or that at least he'd have to get down to a rough-and-tumble fight for which he had no relish. Johnson himself says he had been thinking of bowing out for a long time. The evidence of his being an active candidate right up to the eve of the Wisconsin primary is so well chronicled that there is hardly an impartial political observer who believes that Johnson made a firm decision except at the last minute, although he obviously had been brooding about it and talking about it to intimates for months. One day he was calling up Lawrence O'Brien and Orville Freeman, both of them powers in the Democratic party, and asking them to campaign for him in Wisconsin, and the next day he was on television, a far more haggard President than the one who had savored his moment of mastery on the TV screen on a night of naval action four years before—Johnson announcing a stop to the bombing and an offer of negotiations to Hanoi, and then, at the very end, raising his right hand to his temple and saying matter-of-factly, taking the country's breath away, what no one except his family sitting with him in the Oval Office knew he had added to his speech writer's text:

"There is a division in the American house. . . . What we won when all our people were united must not now be lost in suspicion and selfishness. . . . Accordingly, I shall not seek and will not accept the nomination of my party for another term as your President. . . ."

There were tears in his eyes when the camera lights were switched off. Mrs. Johnson moved quickly across the room and put her arms around him. With his wife and his two daughters and his son-in-law he walked out of the White House into the seclusion of the Rose Garden at night, a

President with a capacity for greatness undone by his guile, his advisers and his true belief.

*

* *

And what of the Congress he had hornswoggled in his days of Presidential apprenticeship and hope? Would Congress—would Fulbright—have raised the issue two years later if the purpose had been accomplished and the intervention in Vietnam had succeeded within reasonable time and with, say, 40,000 men? Johnson, after all, had been able to trick Congress only because Congress had submitted to his will, as it had submitted to Eisenhower's will when he asked for the Formosa and Middle East resolutions and to Kennedy's will when it gave him a resolution in the early stages of the Cuban missile imbroglio without his even asking for it, authority to use armed force proffered both out of patriotic fervor and out of an unwillingness to share with the Executive in an assessment of the situation and to decide after independent thought whether the grant should be made.

Inert and hidebound, the House seemed to have learned little from the Tonkin Gulf affair, content to go on the old way, its right to be consulted processed into a right to ratify, its right to know debased into a right to be briefed; but in the Senate the hearings of the Foreign Relations Committee that were so churned up by Katzenbach's testimony in August, 1967, produced a resolution passed by the Senate in June, 1968, which declared that

it is the sense of the Senate that a national commitment by the United States results only from affirmative action taken by the executive and legislative branches of the United States Government by means of a treaty, statute, or concurrent resolution of both Houses of Congress specifically providing for such commitment.[2]

Affirmative action on a national commitment was, of

course, precisely what President Johnson got from Congress when it passed the Gulf of Tonkin Resolution, but that was done manipulatively, and the Senate was now saying it would not be manipulated again, or rushed into voting except in a grave national emergency, but would insist on knowing why there should be

use of the armed forces of the United States on foreign territory, or a promise to assist a foreign country, government, or people by the use of the armed forces or financial resources of the United States, either immediately or upon the happening of certain events.

As an expression of the "sense of the Senate," the resolution did not have force of law, but it was a political weapon in the struggle that was now begun by the Senate to regain its historic and constitutional role as a partner—though necessarily the less active partner—in the formulation of the broad aims of the nation's foreign policy and as the sole keeper of the power to commit the armed forces to war, whether "limited" or not.

For in going back to the beginnings of constitutional government in the United States of America, the committee had discerned the speciousness of the State Department position as expounded by Katzenbach that the President did not need Congressional authorization to initiate hostilities such as those in Vietnam that fell short of full-fledged general war. With the exception of the declarations of general war against Britain in 1812 and Mexico in 1846, the authorizations of Congress in the early years of the republic were all for specified forms of *limited* war. The concept of limited war was recognized under American law even before the adoption of the Constitution, and all three branches of government agreed that Congress had the sole power to authorize both general ("perfect") and limited ("imperfect") wars, as well as the power to set the limits within which limited warfare was to be waged by the Commander in Chief.[3]

How quaint of President Jefferson—so it seemed to Senators brought up on the hazy latter-day doctrine of the President's "inherent" or "implied" or "plenary" or "incidental" powers to use the armed forces as he sees fit—to report to Congress in 1801 that an American squadron, after capturing a Barbary pirate ship that attacked an American merchantman, had rightly let the vessel go because it was "Unauthorized by the Constitution, without the sanction of Congress, to go beyond the line of defense"; Jefferson requested and received authority to proceed to limited offensive operations.[4] How bold of the House to find the war with Mexico "unnecessarily and unconstitutionally begun by the President of the United States."[5] How redolent of a recent performance of President Johnson's the dissimulation practiced by President Roosevelt before America's entry into World War II when in an indignant radio broadcast he pretended that the American destroyer *Greer*, attacked by a German submarine in the Atlantic, had been on an innocent mail run to Iceland, when actually it had tracked the U boat and radioed its position to a British plane which dropped depth charges—a decision by Roosevelt to exploit the incident so as to enable him to issue shoot-on-sight orders against Axis vessels without going to Congress, since he feared that a request for authority for limited war measures would be rebuffed.[6]

Roosevelt resorted to these means under a desperate compulsion to stave off British defeat, but even he did not claim an inherent Presidential right to commit the armed forces to military action. That claim was first made in a State Department memorandum when Truman sent troops to fight in Korea without seeking Congressional authorization,[7] a claim based on alleged precedent whose audacity went unchallenged at the time, save by a few conservatives like Taft, because Truman was seen to be acting to repel aggression by "Sino-Soviet Communism" against the Western position in Asia, and against so fateful a backdrop constitutional niceties counted for little.

But they had begun to count for a lot in 1967, and if, as the late Professor Edward S. Corwin wrote, the Constitution is "an invitation [to Congress and the Executive] to struggle for the privilege of directing American foreign policy." [8] Fulbright's national-commitments resolution was an acceptance of that invitation after decades of irresponsible absenteeism. What the Senate was telling the President and his successors was:

We can't impinge on your predominance in the conduct of foreign affairs, nor should we, nor do we want to. We can't prevent you from making public declarations of policy such as the Truman Doctrine, or making promises to other governments or entering into informal commitments, or even waging an unauthorized war if you are determined to do so. But we can hamper and block your policies by denying you funds and refusing to ratify your treaties, and we can raise the country against you. We have a will of our own now. We are no longer overawed by the cult of Executive expertise in foreign policy—not after Vietnam. As one of our witnesses, Professor Bartlett, stated, "There are no experts in wisdom concerning human affairs or in determining the national interest, and there is nothing in the realm of foreign policy that cannot be understood by the average American citizen." If you are a wise President you will have to take us into account in determining the bounds within which our foreign policy may operate.

So far so good. But the Senate's bold advance into the forgotten geography of actual instead of supposed overseeing of foreign policy ran into immediate opposition from a new President, a warhawk of the 1950s determined to implement a new Vietnam plan, a plan for neutralizing antiwar sentiment at home by withdrawing most of the American combat troops while escalating the air war to even more murderous heights to keep the enemy at bay and break up his preparations for offensives; a plan that placed baffling reliance on the ability of Saigon's army to

"Vietnamize" the war by coping with whatever numbers of enemy troops managed to get past the shield of American air power; a plan with endless potential for keeping the war going, if not bringing it to a new and even more dangerous flash point—and a plan he claimed the right to pursue on his sole authority as Commander in Chief, without involving Congress in his decisions in any meaningful way.

Rattled by an assertion of unchecked Presidential power going beyond the most pernicious precedent of recent history, Congress in December, 1969, passed an amendment offered by Cooper and Church forbidding the President to send American ground troops into Laos and Thailand. The effect on Nixon was not all that Congress might have wished. On April 30, 1970, he threw American units in South Vietnam into a powerful in-and-out invasion of Cambodia. Congress, this time with protracted balking by the House, passed another Cooper-Church amendment in December, 1970, banning use of American ground troops and advisers in Cambodia.

These amendments were the first attempts by the United States Congress to place limitations on a President's deployment of troops during a shooting war. On the other hand, they left Nixon free to expand the war into Cambodia— and, early in 1971, to stage an incursion of Laos—through the use of South Vietnamese troops under an umbrella of American air power, and to intensify American air action in general in both neighboring countries. And they placed no bars to his implied threat to resume the air war against North Vietnam—even invade the North, perhaps—if the enemy stepped up military pressure in the South as the reduction of American ground troops proceeded.

Discredited and corrupt, the Gulf of Tonkin Resolution was still the only authorization the President—any President—had for waging the war in Indochina, and Congress now proceeded to repeal it with the same haste and confusion of purpose that characterized its adoption six years before. The State Department whose former chief had warned so gravely against the dismay that repeal of the resolution would create among America's allies now shifted to a neutral position, saying it neither advocated nor opposed repeal.[9] On May 11, 1970, the Foreign Relations Committee voted on Senate Concurrent Resolution 64, reading:

Resolved by the Senate (the House of Representatives concurring), That under the authority of section 3 of the joint resolution commonly known as the Gulf of Tonkin Resolution and entitled "Joint Resolution to Promote the Maintenance of International Peace and Security in southeast Asia," approved August 10, 1964 (78 Stat. 384; Public Law 88–4–8), such joint resolution is terminated effective upon the day that the second session of the Ninety-first Congress is adjourned.

The resolution was approved by a vote of 13 to 1; Lausche, defeated for re-election, had been succeeded by Gale McGee of Wyoming as the committee's residual hawk. It remained only for both houses to pass it—no Presidential signature being necessary—and the Gulf of Tonkin Resolution would be repealed in the manner prescribed in its text.

But Nixon's strategists moved in. If the Gulf of Tonkin Resolution was going to be repealed, he didn't want it done resonantly by the very Democratic leadership that had sponsored it in 1964, since the message conveyed to the country would be that the people who had granted the President's request for a free hand in Indochina were now withdrawing that grant. Nixon had a Republican loyalist, Robert Dole of Kansas, beat Fulbright to the draw by attaching the committee's repealer to a military sales bill that was coming up for a vote. Thus Nixon would muffle the repeal procedure and underscore his contention that he did not need the Gulf of Tonkin Resolution to carry on with the war. See, he'd be saying in effect, I don't want this old Johnsonian what's-it. Why, one of my own people is taking it to the scrap heap.

And so the resolution that had seemed so untouchable only three short years before was repealed twice in the Senate—once by a vote of 81 to 10, as part of a routine bill, with Fulbright angrily voting against it, and the second time, by a vote of 57 to 5, as a concurrent resolution of both houses with the clear purport of rectifying, belatedly, a grievous mistake. But the effort to revoke the Gulf of Tonkin Resolution cleanly and with maximum impact remained a half-measure, for the House never did vote directly on the repeal.

The House passed the aid bill with the repealer in it, though, so one way or another the resolution was struck down, leaving the President with the constitutional authority only to take whatever measures were necessary to assure the safe and expeditious withdrawal of American troops from Indochina—though he emphatically did not see it that way. Now was the time, if they were serious about the national-commitments resolution they had passed in June of 1968, for the Senators to join with the President in formulating a national policy for the orderly termination of the war, instead of simply cutting off his war grant and leaving him stranded on an Asian battlefield he did not dare leave: a President convinced that his countrymen preferred to continue with the carnage rather than have the world think them weak, persuaded of the legitimacy of a Presidential-war doctrine based on a misreading of the Constitution and American history yet sufficiently respectable after repeated claims of "precedent" to create deep-seated division on the legalities of the matter; a President, in short, in bad need, if he only knew it, of the involvement of Congress in the painful process of extricating the nation from a lost war and engaging in a fundamental re-evaluation of America's role in the world—most particularly of the question of whether trying to suppress revolution in the underdeveloped countries, even if Communist led, is necessary to or even consonant with American security and well-being.

But not all the Senators who had been willing to vote for Bill Fulbright's resolution in 1968 were prepared to act on it in 1970, and when Mark Hatfield of Oregon and George McGovern of South Dakota wrote an amendment requiring the withdrawal of American armed forces from Vietnam by December 31, 1971, it was too much for the Senate to take, even though in the course of long and thoughtful debate the measure was made flexible enough to allow for generous extensions of the deadline if the need arose. The Hatfield-McGovern amendment was defeated by a vote of 55 to 39—to Nixon's vast relief.

On January 14, 1971, at his "little White House" in San Clemente, California, President Richard M. Nixon signed a bill authorizing easy credit terms for the sale of $200,000,000' worth of United States arms to foreign allies. Tacked onto the bill was the repeal of the Gulf of Tonkin Resolution of August 10, 1964. The signing rated four paragraphs on an inside page of *The New York Times* and three paragraphs in *The Washington Post.*

Thus after all the speeches and all the breast beating and all the bustle and all the stir, the statute that was so central to putting the United States into the Vietnam war died unnoticed and unmourned, its authors shunted into the wings—Lyndon Johnson on his Texas ranch guarding his place in history, with Rostow at his side and an eighteen-million-dollar LBJ Library complex at the University of Texas as a shrine to his forty years in politics. (That Tonkin resolution now, "it was a shame somebody didn't think of calling it the Fulbright Resolution . . . because Senator Fulbright introduced it. . . . Don't tell me a Rhodes scholar didn't understand everything in that resolution. . . . Congress gave us this authority to do 'whatever may be necessary'—that's pretty far-reaching, that's 'the sky's the limit'"); [10] Robert McNamara on the twelfth floor of the World Bank, finding a new sense of mission in the elimination of poverty in the underdeveloped countries and with it, he believes, the roots of violence and revolution and war, bringing to it the same zest with which he had built Fords and produced a dizzying leap in America's nuclear arsenal; Dean Rusk at the University of Georgia, back home amid the accents and rural virtues of his boyhood, regretting nothing, holding no grudges against anyone, telling an old colleague that his great problem was avoiding making every class into a press conference; McGeorge Bundy at the Ford Foundation, doing quiet and massive good with all those grants of money, immersing himself in urban problems of education and race—and, to judge from his occasional articles, viewing Vietnam as a failure not of concept but of expert manipulation of power, a limited operation permitted to get out of hand.

And behind them and their critics—Fulbright, their nemesis, pushing relentlessly and with little success for a fuller consultative role for his committee, using the Bader example to send his professional staff to South Vietnam and Laos and Cambodia and Thailand, and other countries as well, for independent information on which to base the Symington subcommittee hearings, his experience at the hands of the "Pentagon propaganda machine" ripening into concern with the danger of a kind of technocratic Bonapartism in America; Morse, their first and most vociferous denunciator, rejected after twenty-four years by Oregon's voters, partly because he was ahead of his country in his philippics against his President and his party on Vietnam; Mansfield, who disapproved but thought he could work from within; Symington and Mundt, who approved and, each for his own reasons, switched sides; Cooper, Church and the other liberals on Fulbright's committee whose questions, so easily satisfied in August, 1964, became so stubborn by 1968—behind all of them and still with them in memory lay one of the more remarkable events in recent American history: a stratagem by a small number of officials in control of the Executive branch of the government for exploiting an obscure naval incident in order to execute a secret plan for going to war against North Vietnam, even though the reports from the destroyers supposedly under attack were far too fragile to justify the retaliation or the confident affirmation to Congress that the attack took place.

Except, of course, that they had those intercepts.

With the passage of time, the decision makers of 1964 seem readier to admit that the physical evidence on August 4 was not all it was cracked up to be by McNamara in his Congressional testimony, but the conclusiveness of the intercepts seems only to grow in retrospect. Speaking at the Fletcher School of Law and Diplomacy on April 16, 1971, William Bundy, now a senior research associate at the Massachusetts Institute of Technology, had this to say: "Eyewitness reports by the crew of the ship—all of that was extremely muddy and remains muddy to this day. But the evidence that was judged conclusive at the time that the attack had taken place was the existence of plaintext intercepts. That evidence was definitely the crucial factor on the afternoon that the decision was made. It seems to me conclusive today." [11]

But is it?

*

* *

What, to begin with, does Hanoi offer in support of its charge of August 6, 1964, that the reported incident of August 4, 1964, was an American "fabrication"? Hanoi's explanation was contained in its White Paper issued the following month. Declaring that "The alleged 'attack' was deliberately staged by the United States to have a pretext for carrying out its criminal designs against the Democratic Republic of Viet Nam," the White Paper says:

[I]n the day and night of August 4, 1964, no naval craft of the Democratic Republic of Viet Nam was present in the area where the U.S. destroyers were allegedly "attacked for a second time by North Vietnamese PT-boats." [However,] the [U.S. destroyer] *Harry Hubbard* met with the HQ 609 and HQ 11 of the South Viet Nam Navy 60 kilometres off Da Nang. Thereafter, the South Vietnamese ships did not return to their base [at Da Nang] as usual. In the same night, from 20.00 to 22.00, at about the time when "North Vietnamese PT-boats" allegedly "attacked the *Maddox* and the *Turner Joy*," gun shelling was heard, flares and planes were seen off the shores of the Democratic Republic of Viet Nam on international waters.[12]

The apparent belief of this document's authors that the United States Navy could have teamed up with the South Vietnamese to stage a fake battle, and that such glaring chicanery would remain a secret with the American crew, suggests that American ignorance of things Vietnamese is reciprocated by "the other side." Hanoi's explanation is incredible.

So is any suspicion that the intercepts might have been manufactured by someone down the line on August 4 to still the doubts that began coming from Washington as the day wore on. These doubts, as we have seen, were raised only after receipt of Herrick's own confession of uncertainty shortly after 1:30 P.M. Washington time, and all the intercepts, one learns, were in Washington before then. The whole idea of a conspiracy to trick the President and Secretary of Defense into retaliating is dismissed by persons who are knowledgeable in the field of electronic intelligence. "It's just not feasible," one of them says. "Too many people would have had to be cut in. It would have fouled up somewhere along the line."

With theories of simulated battle or forged intercepts ruled out, the messages themselves need closer examination. There were four of them, according to McNamara's testimony of February 20, 1968.

The first message, giving the location of the *Maddox* and the *Turner Joy*, adds nothing of any consequence to the Administration's case.

The message was transmitted by a shore command in the Haiphong area to a Swatow-class patrol boat at about 5:00 P.M. August 4, Tonkin Gulf time, as the two destroyers hovered in the Hon Me–Hon Ngu area, the scene of the first coastal bombardment of the night of July 30–31.

Just the previous night the Swift boats had struck a second time. The North Vietnamese would have been justified in regarding these unmarked craft with their powerful armament and demolition equipment as, possibly, an American force—which, essentially, it was. They may also have learned that some of the crews were Caucasian, either in the course of battle or through the suspected security leak. At any rate, they clearly regarded the two American destroyers off their coast as connected with the coastal raids. It would have been natural for them to keep close watch on the destroyers as the evening of August 4 approached. A message alerting a Swatow unit to their location could be construed more logically as reflecting fear of yet another coastal assault that night than an intention to attack the destroyers.

The second message can also be discarded as evidence of an attack—thanks to Gore's quickness in making McNamara concede that it was not an "attack order," as he had previously characterized it, but an order to "make ready for military operations."

Transmitted just as the destroyers headed for the middle of the gulf for night steaming, or not too long thereafter, this order could well have been part of the North Vietnamese navy's defensive preparations: instructions to patrol boats to follow the destroyers some distance out from shore and see what they were up to. The likelihood that observation was the most the North Vietnamese had in mind is strengthened by McNamara's own disclosure that this order, like the first message, went to *Swatow boats*—two Swatows, he said, with instructions that a PT boat join them "if it could be made ready in time." It is highly unlikely that two Swatows, a class of coastal patrol vessel that has machine guns but no torpedoes, would have been sent out to attack two destroyers. To call this message an attack order is to jump to a conclusion unsupported by the message itself.

The Administration's case, then, really rests on the remaining two messages, the ones in which the North Vietnamese, according to McNamara's testimony, provided details of the August 4 engagement. Actually, these critical transmissions appear to involve two *groups* of messages, referred to here as Intercept 3 and Intercept 4.

What is remarkable about these two intercepts is how badly they fit the incident of August 4 and how well they tally with the events of August 2. Let us go over them again, in terms of the factors involved.

The comvan's role. The North Vietnamese shore commands and patrol boats were almost certainly communicating by voice or international Morse code, as was the case during the *Pueblo* incident. If any cryptology was involved —and Nitze and McNamara, it will be remembered, referred to coded messages—it must have been such a "low-level," primitive code as to lend itself to easy deciphering. Only thus can one explain the comvan's ability to intercept, translate and show the radio traffic to Herrick. Neither patrol boats nor mobile vans are big enough to be equipped with the kind of sophisticated computers required for code-breaking, as that term is normally understood. Nor would it have made sense for the North Vietnamese to lose time and be impeded by garbles and malfunctions in a tactical situation in which speed was so important.

This has a direct bearing on the origin of Intercept 3. McNamara testified that Intercept 3, reporting "that North Vietnamese vessels stated they had our ships under attack," was received in the Pentagon while the *Maddox* and the *Turner Joy* "were actually under attack" on August 4. Yet Herrick in his prepared speech states that "we had no radio contact" with patrol boats during the August 4 incident and "heard no radio communications going on between the PT boats."

Who, then, intercepted this message? It could have been some American listening post on land; there is reason to believe that the comvan aboard the *Maddox* was not the only eavesdropping unit in the general area. But if such a message were transmitted during the August 4 incident, why did the comvan fail to intercept it, especially since the team had performed so well during the previous five days?

"Damage" to the destroyers. Intercept 3, according to McNamara, said the attacking North Vietnamese reported an "enemy vessel wounded." North Vietnam, of course, denied there was an attack on August 4, and neither American destroyer reported sustaining any damage.

But on August 2 the three PT boats that pursued the *Maddox* did open fire: witness the clear and consistent testimony of the destroyer's crew, whose observations were made in broad daylight, and North Vietnam's own account, the domestic broadcast of August 12, 1964, quoted earlier.* The PTs may well have claimed to have inflicted more serious damage on the "enemy vessel" than the one bullet hole discovered aboard the *Maddox*.

"Downing" of aircraft. Intercept 3, according to McNamara, said the North Vietnamese reported "an enemy aircraft falling," and Intercept 4 said they claimed to have "shot down two planes." No American aircraft, of course, was shot down in either incident. The pilots who provided air cover on the night of August 4 reported no visual sightings of any patrol boats when they returned to the *Ticonderoga*, according to a message from Rear Admiral Moore. Though two of the flyers appear to have amended their stories a few days later, talking to officials rushed over from Washington to gather eyewitness evidence, their claims to

* See p. 262.

The Result

have seen a few gun flashes on the water and some light antiaircraft shell bursts in the air seem to have been unconvincing even to their interviewers.

But on August 2 the PT boats did use their 25-mm. antiaircraft guns against the American planes, and one of the American pilots thought for a while that his aircraft was seriously damaged. And the same North Vietnamese domestic broadcast claimed that two planes were shot down and one was damaged during that encounter. The important consideration here is not that the claim was false—false or exaggerated or mistaken claims are nothing new in military annals—but that it was *made* and hence was almost certain to have appeared in the North Vietnamese naval messages of August 2.

Loss of patrol boats. Intercept 4—relayed, according to McNamara, "immediately after the attack ended" on August 4—also said, he testified, "that North Vietnamese naval forces had reported losing two ships in the engagement." This was described by Nitze to Fulbright as the most conclusive evidence of all, since the destroyers had just claimed sinking two attacking boats. And McNamara, after reading the gist of this intercept into the February, 1968, hearing transcript, added, "I submit that any reasonable explanation of these messages leads one to the conclusion that the attack was under way."

Considering that the destroyers' claims to have sunk two boats on August 4 were made on the basis of radar images alone, on a night when radar was particularly apt to play tricks and by men who were strongly predisposed to believe they were under attack, this portion of the intercept seems a good deal less conclusive than Nitze and McNamara tried to make out.

But on August 2, after the engagement, Herrick was shown a message by the comvan team in which, he says, the North Vietnamese did admit that their boats had sustained damage and that one of them had been sunk. Later,

337

in the early evening, reconnaissance planes from the *Ticonderoga* reported seeing two of the boats in a damaged condition and the third one burning and about to sink. The North Vietnamese naval officer who was captured in 1967 informed his American interrogators that he had been told in secret by the North Vietnamese naval high command that all three PTs that took part in the August 2 engagement had been lost.

True, Herrick claims in his prepared speech that the comvan picked up a damage report not only after the August 2 engagement but after the August 4 incident as well: "On the afternoon and evening of August 4 we heard their boats being stationed around our area, intercepted their attack orders and again heard their damage report confirming our assessment that two of the boats had been sunk." This statement, however, invites skepticism on several counts.

Nowhere in Herrick's or McNamara's accounts of the August 4 incident is there any suggestion of intercepted messages indicating that North Vietnamese patrol boats were "being stationed" in the area toward which the destroyers were proceeding for night steaming. Herrick's belief that this in fact is what happened seems to derive from his own earlier fears of ambush and his interpretation of the blips that began spotting his radar screen after 9 P.M. on August 4. If Herrick is talking about Intercept 1, giving the location of the destroyers, that message, it will be recalled, was sent at 5 P.M. while the vessels were still patrolling the coast. It could hardly be said to point to the stationing of patrol boats in an area 50 or 55 miles distant.

As for the "attack orders" he cites, we have seen how McNamara was forced to back away from this tendentious interpretation of Intercept 2, which could just as easily have been an order for defensive or scouting action.

Herrick, however, also speaks in his prepared address of intercepting a damage report after the August 4 incident. Asked in 1971 what the message said, he replied, "That 'we had suffered damage to so and so and did such and such to them.'"

Q: Are you certain they said that on August 4 and not on August 2?

HERRICK: It's so long ago I couldn't be certain.

Q: Could the message have been vaguer than that, merely showing there were boats in the vicinity without mentioning damage?

HERRICK: Yes. It was something to bolster my feeling that something had happened. It helped me in my feeling that there had been an attack.

Q: So it didn't necessarily say they had downed planes and damaged a vessel and lost boats?

HERRICK: Not necessarily.[13]

The PT boat commander. Intercept 4, according to Mc-Namara, gave the name of one of the participants of the attack of August 4. What made that significant, he said, was that this participant was identified by the North Vietnamese naval officer captured in 1967 as the PT-boat squadron commander who had also led the attack of August 2. Moreover, the intercept identified the commander's boat by number, and it was the same number as the one given by the 1967 prisoner; hence, he concluded, in addition to the two Swatows ordered into action on August 4, a PT boat or PT-boat unit had taken part in the attack that night.

This by itself, McNamara implied at the February, 1968, hearing, was proof enough of the actuality of the August 4 attack. If this "comprehensive" and "illuminating" information—which "came to light only within the past few days"—had come to light earlier, he said, "We would have avoided some of the controversy."

Bader looked into McNamara's assertions after the hearing and found them empty. The 1967 prisoner, according to the Defense Department's own report on his interrogation, was not an operational officer but a "political cadre" in the Hanoi naval headquarters and, as such, "had no knowledge of navigation methods and/or naval tactics." He never said there was an attack on August 4. All he did was give his interrogators the name of the Senior Captain of the North Vietnamese navy who commanded the PT boats in the August 2 action.

The Americans already knew the captain's name; a prisoner captured a year earlier, when three North Vietnamese patrol boats were sunk in the Gulf of Tonkin in July, 1966, had told them. This 1966 prisoner was an operational officer —the Senior Captain's second in command, in fact—and he denied that this PT-boat commander or any PT-boat personnel or unit took part in any attack on August 4.

Challenged by Fulbright, the Defense Department in effect admitted that the 1967 prisoner's testimony was nowhere near as illuminating as McNamara had claimed. The reason for the overstatement, according to a letter from Assistant Secretary of Defense Paul C. Warnke, lay in a slip-up within the Pentagon. When Fulbright began his Tonkin Gulf investigation in the fall of 1967, the record of the 1966 prisoner interrogation was brought out of the files by "personnel who had no close familiarity with" its contents, and the significance of the PT-boat commander's name in the report was missed. They became aware of the significance of the name only when they saw it in the 1967 prisoner interrogation report—and then not until early in January, 1968. Apparently it was only when Fulbright pointed it out to them that they realized that the name appeared in the 1966 interrogation report as well.[14]

The point of all this can be briefly stated. Intercept 4 quoted the North Vietnamese as saying that "K——— had met the enemy." Both the 1966 and the 1967 prisoners confirmed that Senior Captain K———, commander of PT-boat Squadron No.———, had indeed "met the enemy"—on August 2.

How is it, then, that the messages that have been cited by the government as the two most critical intercepts of

August 4 describe what happened or what the North Vietnamese claimed on August 2 and bear no resemblance to what can be said with any assurance to have happened two days later?

The answer may be that contrary to all reports and official statements hitherto—even the account of the Tonkin Gulf incidents given in the "Pentagon Papers"—these two crucial intercepts came in on August 2. McNamara's testimony that they were received on August 4 may have been the result of a bureaucratic muddle. The author draws these conclusions from new and reliable evidence. To the best of his belief, the following is what happened:

There was an important procedural difference between Washington's careful handling of the first incident and its precipitate reaction to the second one. On August 2, members of the capital's intelligence community—the DIA (Defense Intelligence Agency), the CIA, the NSA and the intelligence analysts of the Joint Staff and the State Department—participated in the normal fashion in the evaluation of the evidence, including the radio communications from the *Maddox* and the intercepted North Vietnamese messages reporting on attacking and damaging an enemy vessel, downing two planes and losing two of their own boats (Intercepts 3 and 4).

On August 4 the intelligence community was not brought in on the evaluation of the evidence. The usual interdepartmental consultation among experts on the middle level of officialdom was dispensed with. The evaluation was done by the Pentagon alone. When McNamara, Rusk and McGeorge Bundy met with the Joint Chiefs in McNamara's conference room, the emphasis was not on examination of evidence but on selection of targets. They were persuaded that an attack had occurred, largely because they were sure one had occurred two days previously. They were ready to go. The forum for Presidential approval was the "Tuesday Cabinet."

The North Vietnamese messages that came in on August 4 were Intercepts 1 and 2—giving the location of the destroyers and instructing the Swatows to prepare for military action—and, apparently, one or two subsequent messages that were not cited in McNamara's testimony but that indicated the presence of patrol boats somewhere between the shore and the destroyers. These intercepts were not regarded on that day as any weightier than Herrick's reports of radar contacts, sonar soundings and the sighting of a torpedo wake (and that curious fictional item about machine-gun fire)—nor could they have been, since they did not say anything about attacking. What clinched the decision to retaliate after the flurry caused by Herrick's avowal of doubts was the confirmation of an attack that was obtained from Admiral Sharp, a hawk of hawks whose desire to get the bombing started that day must have been as intense as anyone else's in the military establishment, and what apparently was enough to get Sharp to sign on was Herrick's willingness to state that he was at least sure of the "apparent attempt to ambush at beginning."

And so Lyndon Johnson went on the air and the bombs fell.

Some weeks later, with the Tonkin Gulf incidents consigned to history, the contents of the intercepted North Vietnamese messages were put together in a wrap-up for inclusion in the government records. Whoever wrote the summary made a clerical error, confusing the sequence of some of the messages, with the result that the August 2 messages that spoke of damaging an enemy vessel, downing planes and sacrificing two boats (the messages we have called Intercepts 3 and 4) were recorded mistakenly as having been intercepted on August 4.

Three years passed. Fulbright suddenly began questioning the official account of the Tonkin Gulf incidents, expressing doubts that the North Vietnamese attacks had been entirely unprovoked—if indeed the second attack that triggered American entry into war against North Vietnam had occurred at all. Johnson was incensed. The order went out to look through the records for evidence that would convince the perverse Senator that the August 4 attack had actually taken place.

Then it was February 20, 1968, and McNamara was testifying before the Fulbright committee and wrongly citing the intercepts of August 2 as the "unimpeachable" proof of the attack of August 4.

The author does not know what process led to the error in McNamara's testimony on this point. But the records of at least one government agency contained a jumbled wrap-up of the messages of those two days. Therein may lie the explanation.

But would not other—ungarbled—summations in other government agencies, to say nothing of the records of the original intercepts, provide a safeguard against a mix-up of this kind? Would not McNamara himself remember which intercepts came in when?

In considering these questions, one should perhaps take account of McNamara's state of mind at the time. With the fiasco of the TFX, the emerging disaster of Vietnam, the losing struggle to prevent the rebellious Chiefs from enlarging the air war, the draining effort to slow down the missile race, the silent withdrawal of Presidential backing and the final personal defeat dressed up as a Presidential appointment to loftier duties, the end of 1967 and the beginning of 1968 must have been among the cruelest periods in McNamara's life. Now, on top of all this, the past was rising before Washington's eyes to accuse him of deceiving Congress and the people on the facts of an episode superseded in his memory by all that came after—Pleiku and the launching of sustained aerial warfare against North Vietnam, the commitment of an expeditionary force of half a million men, the surge of confidence, the slow sickening ebb of hope. Occupied as he was with preparing for his final annual reports to the armed forces committees of Congress, he would not have had much time to go over the Tonkin record himself. His recollection of the intercepts of August 4 may have been dim, particularly since they were not of such a nature as to etch themselves on anyone's mind. The Defense Department personnel who put the record together for him may have been as unfamiliar with the intercepts as they were with Senior Captain K———'s name.

In short, is it possible that McNamara's subordinates found in the faulty wrap-up the proof they were seeking without being aware of the mistake that had occurred, and that McNamara, not remembering enough about those two days of the summer of 1964 to spot the mistake—and not being in a frame of mind to question official evidence that promised to get his accusers off his back—accepted the evidence and let his lawyers build his case around it?

If the government wishes to dispute these conclusions, it can release the intercepts or at least permit the staff of the Senate Foreign Relations Committee to examine them. It is difficult to believe that the security of the United States would be endangered by the disclosure of a few plaintext messages seven years after the event. But if in fact it was a case of a blend of two different events being used in 1967 and 1968 by men who believed it gave them what they needed to refute their critics, then what the decision makers of August 4, 1964, had to go on was even less than has been generally supposed by the critics themselves. Then the North Vietnamese messages are knocked out as consequential evidence—except that the testimony of the 1966 prisoner that there was no PT boat attack on August 4 is confirmed by the very passage—"K——— had met the enemy"—that McNamara referred to in an attempt to prove the opposite. The evidence that is left, even including the eyewitness reports gathered days after the incidents, is of no greater value than the similar evidence of the illusory September affair.

Then the official story—that though knowing that the United States was predisposed to strike and that President Johnson had ordered the *Maddox* and the *Turner Joy* to pursue and destroy any attacker, the North Vietnamese, after avoiding the destroyers during two days of inshore patrol, went to the sudden extreme of seeking them out sixty miles from land, finding them on a pitch-black stormy night without use of radar, and attacked them with torpedoes and machine guns while revealing to a few men on board the destroyers nothing more than a glimpse of silhouettes and a flicker of light (though losing two of their boats in the battle), only at the end of it all to be caught napping in their bases and to deny doing anything—the illogic of this account becomes overwhelming and one is compelled to agree with Fulbright when he says, "The fact is there was no attack at all."

What remains, then, is a picture of policy formulation in Washington in which the managers of the national security establishment did not provoke an attack on an American patrol, or retaliate knowing there was no attack, or manufacture intelligence intercepts out of whole cloth but, exploiting an unexpected opportunity, deliberately misled Congress and the American people on the nature of the patrol and the evidence of an attack and through that deception were able to obtain Congressional authorization for a war they had secretly decided on months before, while promising the voters peace.

What remains, also, is the irony that all this was done by intelligent, highly gifted and normally honest and honorable men for the usual domestic political reasons and in the belief that preventing the spread of Communism justified the means employed, an outlook that would have been shared at the time by millions of their countrymen—with the result that, betrayed by the opportunity they had seized, they fell into their own trap and, along with themselves, entrapped the country in an involvement whose dimensions at the beginning they had not understood and whose liquidation at the end was beyond their capacity.

What remains, finally, is a warning: With so much power of decision on issues of war and peace concentrated in the hands of so few, the war-bred tyranny of kings that was banished by the war-power clauses of the Constitution returns in democratic disguise and the American republic is in peril.

Notes

Chapter 1
A CONSTITUTIONAL CRISIS

1. Professor Bartlett's testimony, as well as other statements made at the hearing that are quoted in this chapter, may be found in *U.S. Commitments to Foreign Powers: Hearings Before the Committee on Foreign Relations, United States Senate, 90th Congress, First Session* (Washington, D.C.: U.S. Government Printing Office, 1967).

2. *The Records of the Federal Convention of 1787*, Max Farrand, editor (New Haven, Conn.: Yale University Press, 1966), Vol. 2, p. 318.

3. *The Papers of Thomas Jefferson*, Julian P. Boyd, editor (Princeton, N.J.: Princeton University Press, 1958), Vol. 15, p. 397.

4. President Johnson at Omaha, June 30, 1966. Quoted by Arthur M. Schlesinger, Jr., in *Saturday Review*, May 3, 1969, p. 17.

5. The full text of the Gulf of Tonkin Resolution appears in *Southeast Asia Resolution: Joint Hearing Before the Committee on Foreign Relations and the Committee on Armed Services, United States Senate, 88th Congress, Second Session*, (Washington, D.C.: U.S. Government Printing Office, 1966), p. 1.

6. *Public Papers of the Presidents of the United States: Dwight D. Eisenhower, 1954* (Washington, D.C.: U.S. Government Printing Office, 1956), p. 306.

7. Quoted in "The Vietnam War: The President versus the Constitution" by Francis D. Wormuth, a paper published by the Center for the Study of Democratic Institutions, Santa Barbara, Calif., April, 1968, p. 53.

8. *Cornell Law Quarterly*, Vol. 47, No. 1 (Fall, 1961), pp. 1, 2.

9. "Lyndon Johnson vs. the Ghost of Jack Kennedy," by Tom Wicker, *Esquire*, November, 1965.

Chapter 2
AUGUST 4, 1964

1. For the geographic description and historical allusions at the beginning of this chapter the author is indebted to *Vietnam Yesterday*

and Today by Ellen J. Hammer (New York: Holt, Rinehart and Winston, 1966); *Southeast Asia* by E. H. G. Dobby (London: University of London Press, Ltd., 1950); *Monsoon Asia: A Geographical Survey* by Harry Robinson (New York: Frederick A. Praeger, 1967); *Asia East by South* by J. E. Spencer (New York: John Wiley and Sons, 1954); *Here Is Your Enemy* by James Cameron (New York: Holt, Rinehart and Winston, 1965); *Last Reflections on a War* by Bernard B. Fall (Garden City, N.Y.: Doubleday & Company, 1967); *Vietnam: A Dragon Embattled* (Vol. 1) by Joseph Buttinger (New York: Frederick A. Praeger, 1967); and *Customs and Culture of Vietnam* by Ann Caddell Crawford (Rutland, Vt.: Charles E. Tuttle Co., 1966).

2. Crawford, *op. cit.*, pp. 17–19.

3. Fall, *op. cit.*, pp. 44, 45.

4. Eric Widmer, assistant professor of Asian History at Brown University, on the editorial page of *The New York Times* (hereinafter cited as *NYT*), May 2, 1970.

5. *NYT*, August 3, 1964, p. 1.

6. *State Department Bulletin* (hereinafter designated as *DOS Bulletin*), Vol. LI, No. 1313 (August 24, 1964), p. 259.

7. *NYT*, August 5, 1964.

8. *Congressional Record* (hereinafter cited as *CR*), June 23, 1970, p. S-9609.

9. Two outstanding books that approach this subject from somewhat different vantage points, but agree in rejecting the conventional postwar view of the origins of the Cold War, are *The Politics of War* by Gabriel Kolko (New York: Random House, 1968) and *The Cold War as History* by Louis J. Halle (New York: Harper and Row, 1967). A condensed presentation of the "revisionist" viewpoint may be found in *Cold War Essays* by Gar Alperovitz (Garden City, N.Y.: Doubleday & Company [Anchor Books], 1970).

10. A well-informed account of the ideological roots of the Vietminh movement may be found in *Ho Chi Minh: A Political Biography* by Jean Lacouture (New York: Random House, 1968).

11. Kennedy made one statement in a CBS interview September 2, 1963, and the other in an NBC interview September 9. O'Donnell's memoir appears in *Life*, August 7, 1970, pp. 51, 52.

12. Rusk made the statement in a China Institute dinner in May, 1951. Manchukuo, of course, is what the Japanese called the puppet regime they established in Manchuria in the 1930s.

Chapter 3

THE PRESIDENT

1. Material on this public account of the day's events will be

found in *NYT* and *The Washington Post* (hereinafter cited as *WP*) of August 5, 1964, and in *Time*, August 14, 1964.

2. *A White House Diary* by Lady Bird Johnson (New York: Holt, Rinehart and Winston, 1970), pp. 187, 188.

3. *NYT*, August 5, 1964.

4. *NYT* and *WP*, August 5, 1964.

5. *CR*, August 7, 1964, p. S-18461.

6. *JFK and LBJ* by Tom Wicker (New York: William Morrow and Co., 1968), p. 205.

7. *A Thousand Days* by Arthur M. Schlesinger, Jr. (Boston: Houghton Mifflin Co., 1965), p. 542.

8. *DOS Bulletin*, June 22, 1964, p. 953.

9. *DOS Bulletin*, August 24, 1964; *NYT*, August 5, 1964, p. 1.

10. *A Very Personal Presidency* by Hugh Sidey (New York: Atheneum Publishers, 1968), p. 219.

11. Wicker, *op. cit.*, p. 196.

12. Sidey, *op. cit.*, pp. 65, 66.

Chapter 4
THE MANAGER

1. Text of Public Law 88-408 (H.J. Res. 1145), 78 Stat. 384, approved August 10, 1964. In *Joint Hearing Before the Committee on Foreign Relations and the Committee on Armed Services, United States Senate, 88th Congress, Second Session, August 6, 1964* (Washington, D.C.: U.S. Government Printing Office, 1966), p. 1.

2. *Ibid.*, pp. 2–6.

3. "McNamara and His Enemies" by Joseph Kraft, *Harper's Magazine*, August, 1961.

4. Statement in *Hearings before the Senate Committee on Armed Services, 87th Congress, First Session, September 6 and 7, 1961*, p. 3.

5. Schlesinger, *op. cit.*, p. 549.

6. *To Move a Nation* by Roger Hilsman (Garden City, N.Y.: Doubleday & Company, 1964); also in Delta Book edition (New York: Dell Publishing Company, 1964, 1967), p. 510.

Chapter 5
THE HEARING

1. The statements made at the hearing that are cited in this chapter may be found in *Joint Hearing . . . August 6, 1964, op. cit.*, except in cases where the statement was deleted by State Department censors when the transcript was made public in November, 1966. In that case the statement may be found in *Hearing Before the Committee*

on *Foreign Relations, United States Senate, 90th Congress, Second Session, February 20, 1968* (Washington, D.C.: U.S. Government Printing Office, 1968), pp. 29, 30, 37 and 83. The questioning at the hearing tended to jump back and forth, as such informal questioning does. To clarify the discussion, therefore, the sequence of the hearing has been somewhat rearranged.

2. The pilots were identified by the Defense Department as Lieutenant (j.g.) Richard C. Sather, 26, of Pomona, California, who perished, and Lieutenant (j.g.) Everett Alvarez, Jr., 26, of San Jose, California. Alvarez, the Hanoi radio announced, was made prisoner. (*NYT*, August 6 and 8, 1964.) He has by now been a prisoner longer than any other American in any war.

3. For the text of Morse's speech, see *CR*, August 5, 1964, pp. S-18133–S-18139.

4. Murray Marder in *WP*, August 6, 1964, p. 1.

5. Text of news conference in *NYT*, August 6, 1964.

6. *NYT*, August 4, 1964.

7. *WP*, August 6, 1964; Reuters and Associated Press in *NYT*, August 6, 1964.

8. For reactions cited see news stories in *NYT*, August 6, 7 and 9, 1964, including p. 1-E, Section 4, August 9; and *WP*, August 6, 1964, including p. A-15.

9. Rusk interviewed by NBC correspondent Elie Abel; text in *DOS Bulletin*, August 24, 1964, p. 268.

10. David Wise in *New York Herald-Tribune* (hereinafter designated as *NYHT*), August 20, 1964.

11. *The Washington Star* (hereinafter designated as *WS*), August 6, 1964; *WP*, August 6, 1964; James Reston and Henry Tanner, *NYT*, August 6, 1964.

12. *Promoting the Maintenance of International Peace and Security in Southeast Asia, August 6, 1964,* Senate Foreign Relations Committee Report No. 1329, 88th Congress, Second Session.

13. The House Foreign Affairs Committee did not release a transcript of the hearing.

Chapter 6
THE SENATE

1. The quotation is from *Promoting the Maintenance of International Peace and Security in Southeast Asia,* August 6, 1964, *op. cit.* The statements made during the Senate debate on the Tonkin Gulf Resolution are excerpted from *CR*, August 6, 1964, pp. 18398–18430,

and August 7, 1964, pp. 18441–18471. Some description of the debate may be found in *NYT*, *WP* and *WS*, August 7 and 8, 1964. Additional material was obtained in interviews with some of the participants and observers at the time.

2. *News* editorial August 6, 1964, *WP* editorial August 6, 1964.

3. The editorials appear in full in *CR*, August 6, 1964, pp. 18400–18402.

4. In a syndicated column published May 28, 1964, in *NYHT* and other papers.

5. *NYT* editorial, May 21, 1964.

6. "Defense of Vietnam," editorial in *Commonweal*, Vol. LXXV (October 20, 1961), p. 85. The magazine's editorial position on Vietnam did not change between 1961 and 1964. It was only after escalation began in 1965 that doubts about making a stand in Vietnam began to show, and it was not until December 23, 1966, that the magazine came out flatly for getting out.

7. *NYT*, July 24 and 25, 1964.

8. *NYT*, August 9, 1964; DOS Bulletin, August 24, 1964.

9. For a sensitive account of this last phase of Stevenson's career, see *The Remnants of Power: The Last Years of Adlai Stevenson* by Richard J. Walton (New York: Coward-McCann, 1968).

10. "International Law and the Tonkin Bay Incidents," *I. F. Stone's Weekly*, August 24, 1964, reprinted in *The Viet-Nam Reader*, Marcus G. Raskin and Bernard B. Fall, editors (New York: Random House [Vintage Books], 1965); *WP*, August 6, 1964, p. A-14.

11. For two of the best discussions of the international law aspects of the Tonkin Gulf retaliation see *Vietnam and International Law* by the Consultative Council of the Lawyers' Committee on American Policy Toward Vietnam, (Flanders, N.J.: O'Hare Books, 1967) and the legal brief of the Lawyers' Committee on American Policy Toward Vietnam, printed in *CR*, March 1, 1966, pp. 4396–4403. For the Johnson Administration's formal position on the issue, see *The Legality of United Participation in the Defense of Viet-Nam*, Memorandum of Law, Office of the Legal Adviser, State Department (54 *DOS Bulletin* 474 [1966]; *CR*, March 10, 1966, p. 5274 *et seq.*).

12. *CR*, February 28, 1967, S-4720.

13. See transcript of news conference, *NYT*, August 7, 1964.

14. The statements made in the House debate are excerpted from *CR*, August 7, 1964, pp. 18538–18556. Some description of the debate may be found in *NYT*, *WP* and *WS*, August 8, 1964, and *The Washington Evening Star*, August 7, 1964, p. A-4.

15. See text in *NYT*, August 8, 1964.

16. Jack Raymond, *NYT*, August 8, 1964.

Chapter 7
THE CHAIRMAN

1. For some of the material on Fulbright I am indebted to *Fulbright: The Dissenter* by Haynes Johnson and Bernard M. Gwertzman (Garden City, N.Y.: Doubleday & Company, 1968; *Senator Fulbright: Portrait of a Public Philosopher* by Tristram Coffin (New York: E. P. Dutton & Co., 1966); *In a Time of Torment* by I. F. Stone (New York: Random House, 1967), pp. 328–354; "The Fulbright Idea of Foreign Policy" by E. W. Kenworthy (*NYT Magazine*, May 10, 1959); "Egghead from the Ozarks" by Beverly Smith, Jr. (*The Saturday Evening Post*, May 2, 1959); "The Roots of the Arkansas Questioner" by Brock Brower (*Life*, May 13, 1966); and "Mourning Becomes Senator Fulbright" by Charles McCarry (*Esquire*, June, 1970).

2. Speech on April 7, 1965.

3. President's Message to Congress, May 4, 1965; text in *Congressional Quarterly Almanac*, 1965, p. 1372.

4. *CR*, May 5, 1965, p. 9533.

5. *Congressional Quarterly Almanac*, 1965, pp. 180, 181.

6. *Report on the War in Vietnam* by Admiral U. S. G. Sharp and General W. C. Westmoreland (Washington, D.C.: U.S. Government Printing Office, 1968), p. 98.

7. Nixon speaking before the American Society of Newspaper Editors, April 16, 1954, cited in *The New Isolationism* by Norman A. Graebner (New York: Ronald Press Company, 1956), and Nixon in a statement in Washington, September 12, 1965, quoted by Effros, *op. cit.*, p. 80.

8. Interviewed on CBS television network August 1, 1965; text in *CR*, August 6, 1965, pp. 18942–18944.

9. Addressing the Georgia Association of Broadcasters; text in *CR*, June 15, 1965, p. 13193.

10. *NYT*, July 14, 1965.

11. "The Final Troubled Hours of Adlai Stevenson" by Eric Sevareid, *Look*, November 30, 1965.

12. *NYT*, November 16, 1965, and DOS Bulletin, December 13, 1965, pp. 931–933.

13. *Hearings Before the Committee on Foreign Relations, United States Senate, 89th Congress, Second Session, on S-2793* (Washington, D.C.: U.S. Government Printing Office, 1966), pp. 1–89; Lodge's telegram is on p. 82.

Chapter 8
COLLISION

1. The statements made at the hearing that are quoted or paraphrased in this chapter are from *Hearings . . . on S-2793, op. cit.*

Chapter 9
DEADLOCK

1. *Hearings . . . on S-2793, op. cit.,* p. 567.

2. *Joint Hearing . . . August 6, 1964, op. cit.,* p. 23.

3. For a discussion of both sides of the question see *The Vietnam War and International Law,* edited by Richard A. Falk (Princeton, N.J.: Princeton University Press, 1968).

4. *NYT,* January 29, 1966.

5. *NYT,* August 19, 1967, in text of news conference.

6. The Johnson–Ho correspondence of February, 1967, was not made public until March 21, 1967. *NYT,* March 22, 1967.

7. *NYT,* November 27, 1967.

8. *NYT,* February 19, 1962, p. 1.

9. *NYT,* September 28, 1967.

10. At Long Beach, California, April 1, 1967. Quoted in Effros, *op. cit.,* p. 111.

11. Max Frankel in *NYT,* February 13, 1967.

12. Speech in Chicago, May 17, 1966. See *NYT,* May 18, 1966.

13. *Weekly Compilation of Presidential Documents,* Vol. 3, No. 40 (October 9, 1967), p. 1372.

14. Sidey, *A Very Personal Presidency,* p. 212.

15. *Ibid.,* p. 150; *The Lost Crusade* by Chester Cooper (New York: Dodd, Mead & Company, 1970), pp. 310–319.

16. *NYT,* April 29, 1967.

17. *NYT,* December 22, 23, 24, 1967; Sidey, *op. cit.,* pp. 193–195; Cooper, *op. cit.,* p. 513.

18. *NYT,* July 29, 1965.

19. Max Frankel in *NYT,* May 13, 1967.

20. Text in *NYT,* December 9, 1965.

21. *My Brother Lyndon* by Sam Houston Johnson (New York: Cowles Book Company, 1969, 1970), p. 199.

22. *The United States in Vietnam* by George McTurnan Kahin and John W. Lewis (New York: Dell Publishing Company [Delta Book], 1967), pp. 128–129, 137, 141.

23. Quoted in *Current Biography 1961,* edited by Charles Moritz (New York: H. W. Wilson Co., 1962), p. 397.

24. *NYT,* November 23 and 29, 1967.

25. From a lecture delivered at Johns Hopkins University, April 21, 1966, as part of the Christian A. Herter Lecture Series. See *The Arrogance of Power* by J. William Fulbright (New York: Random House [Vintage Books], 1966), pp. 130 and 138, for quoted portions.

26. Johnson and Gwertzman, *op. cit.*, p. 221.

27. *CR*, February 28, 1967, pp. 4714–4723.

28. *CR*, March 1, 1966, pp. 4365–4404. *NYT*, March 1 and 2, 1966.

29. "Lyndon Johnson vs. the Ghost of Jack Kennedy," by Tom Wicker, *Esquire*, November, 1965.

30. From statement released by Senator Fulbright, December 21, 1967. See *NYT*, December 22, 1967.

31. *Truth Is the First Casualty* by Joseph C. Goulden (Chicago: Rand McNally & Co., 1969), p. 202; AP in *NYT*, November 24, 1966.

Chapter 10
THE INVESTIGATION

1. *New Haven Register*, December 6, 1967.

2. John W. Finney in *NYT*, December 23, 1967.

3. For news reports on DOD statement, see *NYT* and *WP*, December 23, 1967.

4. Finney in *NYT*, January 8, 1968.

5. *Ibid.*, January 10, 1968.

6. *Ibid.*, January 21, 1968.

7. *Ibid.*, February 4, 1968.

8. *NYT*, *WP*, *WS*, *Baltimore Sun*, January 31, 1968.

Chapter 11
RETURN ENGAGEMENT

1. The statements made at the hearing that are excerpted in this chapter (and rearranged somewhat for clarity) may be found in *Hearing Before the Committee on Foreign Relations, United States Senate, 90th Congress, Second Session (The Gulf of Tonkin, The 1964 Incidents), February 20, 1968* (Washington, D.C.: U.S. Government Printing Office, 1968).

2. Goulden, *op. cit.*, p. 227.

3. *The Gulf of Tonkin, The 1964 Incidents, Part II*, released December 16, 1968, by the Senate Foreign Relations Committee as a supplement to the February 20, 1968, hearing (Washington, D.C.: U.S. Government Printing Office, 1968), p. 10.

4. *Ibid.*, p. 9.

5. *Ibid.*, p. 6.

Notes

Chapter 12
BACKSTAGE

1. *CR*, February 21, 1968, pp. S-1589–S-1604; February 28, 1968, pp. S-1885–S-1891; February 29, pp. S-1947–S-1953.
2. *The Gulf of Tonkin . . . Part II, op. cit.*
3. The material in this chapter on the background to the Tonkin Gulf incidents was gathered by the author from reliable sources who prefer to remain anonymous.
4. Professor John K. Fairbank in *NYT*, July 18, 1970, editorial page.

Chapter 13
THE CAPTAIN

1. *History of Ships Named Maddox*, Division of Naval History (OP-09B9), Navy Department, Washington, D.C.
2. "Remember the Maddox!" by David Wise, *Esquire*, April, 1967, p. 123.
3. *Hearing . . . February 20, 1968, op. cit.*, p. 26.
4. This and subsequent messages cited in this chapter may be found in *CR*, February 21, 1968, pp. S-1589–S-1604; February 28, 1968, pp. S-1885–S-1891; and February 29, 1968, pp. S-1947–S-1953.
5. Wise, *op. cit.*, p. 123.
6. *Memorandum regarding the U.S. war acts against the Democratic Republic of Viet Nam in the first days of August 1964*, Ministry of Foreign Affairs, Democratic Republic of Viet Nam, Hanoi, September, 1964.
7. Wise, *op. cit.*, p. 124.
8. "From the Files of Navy Intelligence: Aboard the Maddox," *Life*, August 14, 1964.

Chapter 14
THE EVENT

1. *CR*, September 1, 1970, p. S-14829.
2. Associated Press report on Tonkin Gulf incidents for morning newspapers of July 16, 1967.
3. Goulden, *op. cit.*, p. 139.
4. Wise, *op. cit.*, p. 125.
5. Stankevitz quoted by Wise, *op. cit.*, p. 125, and Goulden, *op. cit.*, pp. 142–147.
6. From Herrick's speech.
7. Herrick in interview with the author.

8. Wise, *op. cit.*, p. 125.
9. Goulden, *op. cit.*, p. 142.
10. Barnhart quoted by Wise, *op. cit.*, p. 126.
11. Quoted in *WS*, February 24, 1968.
12. Quoted in "The Tin Ears of War" by Jack Robertson, *The Nation*, June 10, 1968.
13. Ogier's 1967 comments in Wise, *op. cit.*, pp. 62, 126.
14. *Hearing . . . February 20, 1968, op. cit.*, p. 16.
15. Wise, *op. cit.*, p. 126.
16. *Ibid.*
17. Goulden, *op. cit.*, p. 145.
18. *Ibid.*, p. 147.
19. *Joint Hearing . . . August 6, 1964, op. cit.*, p. 9.
20. Wise, *op. cit.*, p. 127.
21. *Hearing . . . February 20, 1968, op. cit.*, p. 16.
22. *Joint Hearing . . . August 6, 1964, op. cit.*, p. 9.
23. *History of USS Turner Joy (DD-951)*, Division of Naval History (OP-09B9), Navy Department, Washington, D.C.
24. *Hearing . . . February 20, 1968, op. cit.*, p. 16.
25. Wise, *op. cit.*, p. 127.
26. In Herrick's speech.
27. *Ibid.*
28. *Hearing . . . February 20, 1968, op. cit.*, pp. 17, 92.
29. *Ibid.*, p. 54.

Chapter 15
THE OPPORTUNITY

1. *U.S. News and World Report*, March 28, 1966.
2. "We Could Have Won in Vietnam Long Ago" by Admiral U. S. Grant Sharp, *Reader's Digest*, May, 1969, p. 123.
3. *Ibid.*, pp. 118–120.
4. *CR*, February 21, 1968, p. S-1592; February 29, 1968, p. S-1950.
5. *Hearing . . . February 20, 1968, op. cit.*, p. 58.
6. AP in *NYT*, June 22, 1968; *The New Republic*, July 8, 1968.
7. The four men are identified in *Hearing . . . February 20, 1968, op. cit.*, p. 16, as Lieutenant (j.g.) John J. Barry, the forward gun director officer; Seaman Larry O. Litton, who was with Barry; Seaman Edwin R. Sentel, the port lookout; and Seaman Roger N. Bergland, operating the aftergun director.
8. *CR*, March 27, 1968, p. S-3412.
9. The marines were Sergeant Matthew B. Allasre and Lance

Corporal David A. Prouty. Both made written statements (*Hearing . . . February 20, 1968, op. cit.,* p. 17).

10. The affidavits on this reported sighting were provided by Commander Barnhart; Walter L. Shishim, QMCS, USN; Richard B. Johnson, SM1, USN; Richard D. Nooks, QM3, USN; Richard M. Bacino, SM2, USN; and Gary D. Carroll, SM3, USN (*ibid.,* p. 16).

11. This was Gunner's Mate Jose R. San Augustin (*ibid.*).

12. The other three were Donald V. Sharkey, BM3; Delner Jones, GMG, SN; and Arthur B. Anderson, FT SN (*ibid.*).

13. *CR,* March 27, 1968, p. S-3412.

14. *CR,* February 21, 1968, p. S-1592.

15. *Ibid.; CR,* February 29, 1968, p. S-1950.

16. *CR,* February 29, 1968, p. S-1950.

17. *Ibid.,* p. S-1951.

18. *CR,* February 21, 1968, p. S-1593; February 29, 1968, p. S-1951.

19. *CR,* February 29, 1968, p. S-1951.

20. *Hearing . . . February 20, 1968, op. cit.,* p. 69; *CR,* February 29, 1968, p. S-1951.

21. *WP,* August 11, 1964, p. A-10.

Chapter 16
THE RESULT

1. For a discussion of this aspect of the problem see "The Quagmire Myth and the Stalemate Machine" by Daniel Ellsberg in *Public Policy* (Harvard Press), May, 1971.

2. *NYT,* June 26, 1968.

3. For a discussion of this subject see "The Vietnam War: The President versus the Constitution" by Francis D. Wormuth, *op. cit.,* pp. 6–14.

4. *Messages and Papers of the Presidents, 1789–1908,* James D. Richardson, editor (Washington, D.C.: Bureau of National Literature and Art, 1908), Vol. 1, pp. 326–327, quoted in Wormuth, *op. cit.,* p. 10.

5. *Congressional Globe,* 30th Congress, First Session (January 3, 1848), p. 95, quoted in Wormuth, *op. cit.,* p. 11.

6. *Roosevelt and Hopkins* by Robert E. Sherwood (New York: Harper and Brothers, 1948), pp. 367–370. *The Battle of the Atlantic, 1939–1943* by Samuel Eliot Morison (Boston: Little, Brown & Co., 1947), pp. 79–80.

7. *DOS Bulletin,* Vol. 23, No. 578 (July 31, 1960), pp. 173–178.

8. *The President: Office and Powers, 1787–1957*, by Edward S. Corwin (New York: New York University Press, 1957).

9. *NYT*, March 13, 1970.

10. In televised interview with Walter Cronkite of CBS, February 6, 1970.

11. As taped and transcribed by the Tufts University News Bureau.

12. *Memorandum regarding the U.S. war acts . . . August 1964*, *op. cit.*, p. 4.

13. Interview with the author.

14. *The Gulf of Tonkin, The 1964 Incidents, Part II, op. cit.*, pp. 11–14.

Index